HOW TO HACK
A PARTY LINE

HOW TO HACK
A PARTY LINE

the democrats and silicon valley

Sara Miles

FARRAR, STRAUS AND GIROUX   NEW YORK

Farrar, Straus and Giroux
19 Union Square West, New York 10003

Distributed in Canada by Douglas & McIntyre Ltd.
Printed in the United States of America
First edition, 2001

Library of Congress Cataloging-in-Publication Data
Miles, Sarah.
    How to hack a party line : the Democrats and Silicon Valley / Sarah Miles.
        p.   cm.
    Includes bibliographical references and index.
    ISBN 0-374-17714-7 (alk. paper)
    1. Santa Clara County (Calif.) — Politics and government.   2. Business and
politics — California — Santa Clara County.   3. Computer industry — California —
Santa Clara County — Political activity.   4. Democratic Party (Calif.)   I. Title.

JS451.C29 S35   2001
324.2736'09794'73 — dc21
                                                                    00-059301

Portions of this book have appeared in *Wired*, *Wired News*,
San Francisco Focus, and *The New York Times Magazine*.

Designed by Thomas Frank

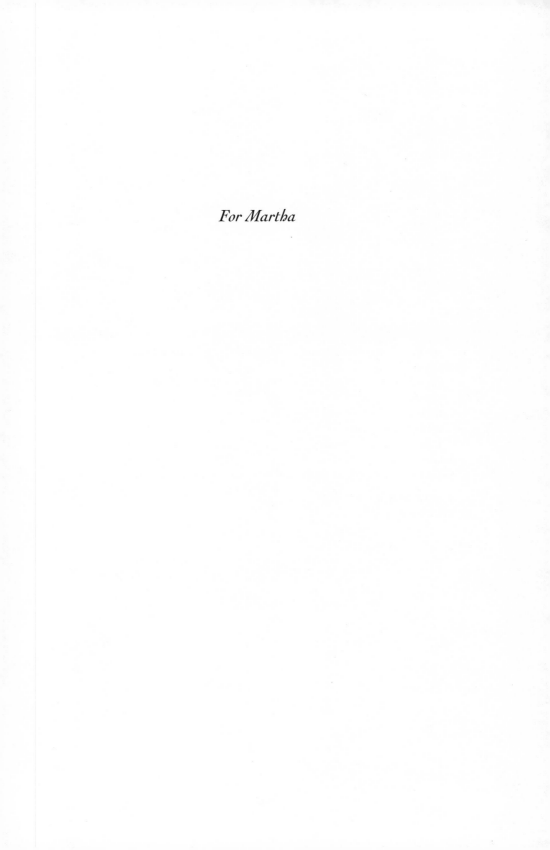

For Martha

contents

PART ONE
    wiring the network   3

PART TWO
    bugs   77

PART THREE
    workarounds   133

PART FOUR
    system crash   193

PART FIVE
    tech politics 3.0   225

PART ONE
wiring the network

CHAPTER one

It was a perfect California morning in the fall of 1996, with the radio reporting a warm front and a hot market, and Wade Randlett was driving fast down Highway 280 toward Silicon Valley, laughing into a cell phone. With his wire-rimmed shades and suspenders, the dark-haired thirty-one-year-old could pass for a successful investment banker, except that he seemed to be having too much fun.

At Sand Hill Road, tires squealing, Randlett turned and raced his black Audi coupe up the landscaped driveway leading to Kleiner Perkins Caufield & Byers, Silicon Valley's most prestigious venture-capital firm.

The car phone rang again. Randlett slowed to forty-five. It was the White House. "I'll call you back," he said, casually.

I'd met Wade Randlett in July 1996, after months of pointless phone calls to various highly paid press secretaries and officials at the Democratic National Committee, the Clinton-Gore election campaign, and the California Democratic campaign headquarters. They were polite when I asked who was in charge of organizing the young entrepreneurs of Silicon Valley for Clinton—"You know, computers, the Internet," I'd say helpfully. "Who's working on that?"—but none of the professional Democrats had a clue. Finally, an embittered union rep I'd met at a party told me about Wade Randlett, a fund-raiser and campaign consultant she thought was connected. "He's one of those right-wing New Democrat boys," she said, her voice dripping with distaste. "Young, arrogant, hates unions, loves rich people. He'll probably know."

Randlett was working out of his home, a small stucco in a pleasantly suburban part of San Francisco, across the street from a parochial school. A Great Dane the size of a sofa got to the door first, but Randlett reached a hand around and greeted me without interrupting his phone conversation. "We've got a twelve-couple that night at fifty a couple," he went on, motioning me in. "Breakfast, no press." A dining-room table was piled high with towers of paper, files, and newspapers, a fax machine in the corner was spewing out documents, and there was a row of Styrofoam coffee cups adorning the mantel. Randlett was typing something into his notebook computer as he talked, and trying to ignore the other ringing phone. The dog lay down. Apart from a suit jacket draped over a chair and a strangely formal glass bookcase holding two framed photos and a dusty bottle of wine, there were no personal effects. The place looked as if someone had just moved in, or out. It looked like the desolate post-divorce wreck of someone who had married too young. It looked like a campaign.

Wade Randlett was a ridiculously handsome man. Tall and deep-voiced, with impeccable public manners and ruthless backroom savvy, he seemed almost physically propelled by ambition. In his early twenties, much as less imaginative members of his generation had taken up extreme sports, Randlett had hurled himself into politics. Now he was playing in the big leagues, building Silicon Valley's first political machine, and years of ferocious intensity and practice were paying off.

I liked Randlett, almost as much as I found him appalling. He had a great laugh grafted over a bottomless capacity for conspiracy. Randlett's personality reflected what I thought of as some of the worst traits of politics and of Silicon Valley combined—aggression, arrogance, and ambition—yet he was neither venal nor dishonest. He was personally generous, professionally cutthroat, and had a wholehearted, contagious enthusiasm for his work. "Hop in," he'd say to me, handing me a cold drink and opening the door to his Audi. "Let's drive down to Palo Alto, and I'll fill you in on the story."

Reared in Danville, one of the whitest, wealthiest, and most Republican strongholds of the San Francisco Bay Area, Randlett had set off for Princeton in the early eighties without any particular signs of political ambition. He carried the usual badges of affluence—good teeth, excellent schooling, and a few perfect navy-blue suits—and an unshakable confidence in his own abilities. The country was in the middle of the Reagan years, and Randlett rejected Reagan Republicanism with a visceral distaste. "First there was their social outlook: Let's all go back to 1952," he said, summing up Reagan's Morning in America vision. "Then there was their idea of economics: screw the environment, don't invest in education, let business do whatever it likes and piss on the rest." And though he had even less patience for "politically correct leftist whiners," Randlett became a vocal pro-choice Democratic activist on campus and a defender of individual liberties.

In 1987, Randlett returned to the Bay Area to earn a law degree, but the life of an upscale lawyer struck him as a fundamental waste of time. "Everyone I knew was a lawyer," he said dismissively. Instead he went to work for George Marcus, a wealthy Greek-American real-estate developer in San Jose and a prominent Northern California fund-raiser for the Democratic Party. Marcus would, in the next decade, become chairman of the largest investment-real-estate broker-age firm in the country, and one of Silicon Valley's top ten political donors. "I was as low as lowly gets, just hanging around and trying to see what I could learn," Randlett said, trying to sound modest. "I made ten thousand cold calls my first year."

Before long, Randlett had set up shop as an independent fund-raiser and political consultant, working out of San Jose and hustling for stalwarts of the California Democratic Party like Dianne Feinstein, John Garamendi, Zoe Lofgren, and Art Torres. For nearly a decade, Randlett practiced the art of campaign fund-raising, developing a remarkable talent for getting complete strangers to write him checks for $50,000. He understood as well as anyone the nuances of the personal check, the corporate check, the check that was in the mail. He knew how to cold-call, how to bid a donor up, how to make one gift the occasion for the next. "I'm talking *money*," he'd say happily as he opened the envelopes. "Money, money, money, money, money."

Randlett's fund-raising style relied heavily on the extraordinarily effective, if contradictory, mélange of class cues he exuded. He could use his prep-school manners and hand-sewn loafers to make his utter lack of embarrassment about asking for money seem clubbily upper-class, then switch in a heartbeat to flawless middle-American male

5

jocularity, pitching as relentlessly as a salesman with a quota to fill.

Randlett had come of political age at a moment when money's rule over politics was a given, a matter of fact—not a trend to be deplored with high-minded whining about the corruption of civic values. Laments about campaign finance were tacky and old-fashioned, Randlett felt, and he affected a blunt, contemporary realism about the way the system worked.

"Money, money, money, money," he repeated. "If you don't understand it, it looks corrupt. But if you like someone, and they like you, there's nothing wrong with giving them money. It gets a conversation started."

Skilled as he was at the task, though, Randlett was too ambitious to spend his life dialing for dollars. Fund-raising occupied an odd position in the hierarchy of political parties: the work was both crass and essential. Good fund-raisers stitched together the networks that would support a campaign, set the candidate's schedule and priorities, learned everyone's secrets, and kept the whole enterprise afloat. In return, they were courted assiduously, rewarded handsomely, and regularly condescended to by snotty twenty-four-year-old political staffers. Like pollsters, fund-raisers earned a lot of money. But they were not supposed to engage in "real" politics themselves: they were considered technicians, rather than thinkers, and were expected to know their place.

Not that Randlett tried to present himself as a thinker; he was way too shrewd for that. Policy guys were even more marginal than fund-raisers when it came to real politics; in a campaign, being tagged as an intellectual was the kiss of death. Unlike a lot of young political operatives, Randlett resisted the urge to craft complicated, subtle arguments in order to show off his intelligence. "That's just dumb," he'd say instead, airily, dismissing an opponent's carefully worked out thesis, or "Everyone knows that's stupid. It's bad. It sucks." As a rule, he tried to sound uninterested in the fine points of policy debates. He usually won them.

What Wade Randlett did want, badly, was power. He wanted to be able to promote his ideas about politics, to make things happen in the Democratic Party, and to affect the country at large. His ideology was centrism, and he argued for it with the intensity of an evangelical. "You're making a big mistake if you think moderates feel moderately about politics," Randlett said. "I am *passionately* centrist. Goddamn it, I *believe* in the center."

Randlett had stayed liberal on social issues like abortion and gun control, while staking out a pro-capitalist, antiunion stand on business and economic issues. Like many of his contemporaries who hailed a moderate "Third Way," eschewing both boomer liberalism and rigid conservatism, Randlett was a devoted Democrat. Like them, he took pains to identify himself, though, as a "New Democrat," which meant that he was intent on steering the Democratic Party away from "failed/socialist experiments," such as the New Deal or the Great Society, that tried to redistribute wealth and regulate business.

Randlett was contemptuous of the angry moralizing of right-wing Republicans whose political agenda centered around such narrow issues as homosexuality, school prayer, and the right to life. Democratic moderates, he felt, were the only hope for the country. "The left lost," he liked to point out. "They're history. The conservatives hate the modern world. I'm a real progressive, because I'm the only one who believes in the future."

Randlett also believed in winning. As a political fund-raiser and consultant to candidates, he wanted to steer Democrats toward the center because it would increase their chances of victory. As he saw it, liberalism was responsible for the Democrats' defeat at the hands of Ronald Reagan; liberalism was what had turned ordinary voters away from Democrats; and liberalism was why businesspeople mistrusted his party. The Democrats had become a minority party, he felt, because they had failed to recognize that the overall sentiment of voters in the mid-1990s was centrist, not liberal or extreme right-wing. In California, his moderate candidates, like Zoe Lofgren, had won. Success for the Democratic Party nationally, Randlett was convinced, lay in electing moderate New Democrats like Bill Clinton and Al Gore — pro-business politicians with mainstream social values and excellent marketing skills.

Like most campaign professionals, Randlett saw little percentage in spending time or money courting partisan true believers. Both Democratic "Jesse Jackson lefties" and Republican "Bible-thumpers," he argued, were a minority within their parties, and, despite their grumbling, the least likely to jump ship in a general election. At the end of the day, labor would always vote Democratic; NRA activists would stick with the Republicans. A winning strategy had to target less ideological, more moderate voters — the great majority of the electorate — even if these swing voters were, by definition, not as interested in politics as the hard-core base. Randlett was determined to push his party in the direction he knew it should go. "Whoever gets to the center faster," he said flatly, "wins."

To party regulars in the mid-1990s, the raw, ugly suburbs of San Jose must have seemed an unlikely launching pad for a young man with political ambitions. "Nobody out here has ever related much to government," explained Larry Stone, a genial real-estate developer and the former Democratic mayor of Sunnyvale. "It's a little hard to care about politics when you're starting up a company and sleeping under your desk."

Randlett hadn't even tried, at first, to look for campaign contributions under those desks: like all the other Valley fund-raisers working on California campaigns, he depended on old Palo Alto families, Atherton's horsey rich, and a handful of real-estate moguls to bring in dollars for his candidates. Yet he watched, closely, studying the rapidly growing high-tech industry from his hole of an office in San Jose. Something was happening here, something that was going to change not only the way America did business but the way it did politics, and Randlett knew that he wanted to be a part of it.

The effects of the Internet explosion hadn't yet rippled out through the country, burnishing the entire economy to a high gloss, but the Valley itself—usually defined as Santa Clara County, though sometimes including parts of San Francisco and Alameda counties—was definitely booming. Years of government investment in R&D and of defense spending, combined with Stanford University's excellent science and engineering programs, had helped create a climate in which engineers could flourish. Earlier breakthroughs in microprocessors and personal computers had given the region a base level of wealth, and established a culture where technical innovation and business daring were valued above all. But now a new phase was under way.

According to Joint Ventures Silicon Valley, a collaborative business-government research institute that tracked indicators of the region's economy and quality of life, the numbers were staggering. From 1992 to 1996 alone, the Valley gained 3,100 new businesses, 230,000 new jobs, and attracted $2.7 billion of venture capital into its businesses. In August 1995, Netscape went public, with an IPO that took its value from nothing to $2.2 billion overnight, and the Internet era was under way. *Newsweek* would crown 1995 "the Year of the Internet," and over the next five years the Web would transform not just computer technology but banking and finance, Wall Street, the media, retail shopping, and, inevitably if more slowly, politics. Randlett watched as hundreds of brand-new software companies, Internet start-ups, and new media enterprises run by people his age joined more established companies—chip, computer, and semiconductor manufacturers, along with a few biotechnology pioneers—in turning the entire high-tech industry into a moneymaking phenomenon of gold-rush proportions.

The boom in Silicon Valley, John Doerr, a venture capitalist, bragged, was "the largest legal creation of wealth in the history of the planet." And it was even more. When the Silicon Valley phenomenon first burst upon the national consciousness, it was packaged not as business but as a "digital revolution"—thanks largely to the efforts of *Wired* magazine, which contributed heavily to the hype.

Wired would wind up, at the turn of the century, being sold to Condé Nast in a deal that celebrated the mainstreaming of Silicon Valley. But when it was first launched, *Wired*'s "revolutionary" worldview owed a lot to the particular and cranky mind of aging hippie Louis Rossetto. His style combined a kind of Whole Earth evangelism and a don't-tread-on-me Ayn Randism with a weakness for futurist big ideas. His message was light on the business realities of the high-tech industry, and heavy on "vision."

Yet Rossetto's prescient view of Silicon Valley as not simply an industry but a driving cultural force made the magazine an instant success with old media. *Wired*'s neon design was immediately copied by every marketer trying to signify digital cool, and its overheated interpretation of the significance of the digital revolution spread.

And its peculiar political stance had a big impact on the way Washington politicians and New York journalists saw the Valley. In its early issues, from 1993 to 1995, *Wired* highlighted the self-conscious radicalism of "cypherphreaks" and "cyberpunks" who worked on the fringes of the programming underground, and embraced the antiregulatory, pro-privacy values of the Electronic Frontiers Foundation. It gave voice to the antigovernment rants of establishment conservatives like George Gilder and to the pro-business manifestos of futurists like Nicholas Negroponte of MIT. And it attempted to brand the politics of the digital revolution as being as defiantly libertarian and proudly capitalist as Rossetto himself. In *Wired*'s pages, Rossetto and his band of "digerati" railed against public education ("the last great bastion of socialism"), mainstream economists ("international economic theory is obsolete"), and the idea of government in general ("a dumb, 18th century dodo").

Few in the Valley subscribed to all of *Wired*'s political convictions. But almost everyone shared the magazine's absolute faith in technology. They believed, without question, its basic assumption that business, rather than government or civic institutions, was the driving force behind all innovation, progress, and social well-being. And most accepted, as well, one of *Wired*'s central myths about the Valley boom — that anybody could be a part of it. "Life in cyberspace," Mitch Kapor, the founder of Lotus, had explained in a *Wired* interview in 1993, "is more egalitarian than elitist . . . [It] shapes up exactly like Thomas Jefferson would have wanted: founded on the primacy of individual liberty and a commitment to pluralism, diversity, and community."

According to industry spin, the people who ran high-tech companies were a new breed of entrepreneur—young, hip, and ethnically diverse. You could be a success in Silicon Valley and be Chinese, the story went, or Pakistani; you could be a socially clueless geek with thick glasses and a bad stutter; you could even be a girl. None of it mattered, because the industry, like the Internet, was a place of unlimited opportunity where only ability and ambition counted.

It was true, up to a point. Yes, the industry ran on youth, meaning that sheer initiative could frequently substitute for painstakingly assembled résumés, and that ambition was valued above orthodoxy. Yes, the explosion of jobs made it essential to knock down hiring barriers, and brought unprecedented numbers of college dropouts, white women, and foreign-born minorities into the high-tech workforce. And though stock options were not ubiquitous enough in the early 1990s to broaden the class of actual owners, the rising status of engineers helped blur traditional distinctions between workers and bosses.

But to say that Silicon Valley had somehow transcended the larger culture's system of social class was to ignore the differences that kept secretaries, coders, marketers, and CEOs firmly in their respective places—not to mention the differences between undocumented Salvadoran gardeners and the venture capitalists whose hedges they groomed. And to brush aside the need for a government that, through defense spending, R&D investments, education, and tax breaks, had created the entire infrastructure for Silicon Valley's success, was not only ungracious but extremely shortsighted. In its breathtaking ahistoricism, this attitude suggested a lack of preparation for navigating the future wisely.

Yet all through the mid-nineties, high-tech entrepreneurs would tell one another how the stalwarts of the old order—the Beltway hacks, the stuffy, clubby Eastern elite, the dinosaur megacorporations, the white-shoe law firms—didn't understand the Silicon Valley ethos. They just didn't get it. What was happening out here was a whole new way of doing business, a new economy, with new values and a new culture.

Someone as canny as Wade Randlett was unlikely to take Utopian manifestos about the wired revolution at face value. But Randlett understood quite well that Silicon Valley's sense of itself as representing the cutting edge of a new culture had potential. The Valley myth, he thought, could be turned to political advantage. The pro-growth, pro-capitalist, antigovernment, countercultural sentiments swirling through Silicon Valley created an environment, Randlett felt, that perfectly illustrated his centrist Democratic principles. "This is what the party should be about," he said. "We believe in lots and lots of equal opportunity. We have to get out the idea that, yes, we are in favor of an economy where a gay fat Korean immigrant engineer can make $100,000 a year. That's the important message: there's just an outrageous amount of money to be made in the New Economy if you educate yourself and work hard."

So Randlett began digging for gold. As he tried to raise money for his centrist candidates, he should have found eager supporters among these new entrepreneurs. But no matter how much money high-tech executives made, their religion apparently forbade them to give any of it away. The geeks, fund-raisers complained, were notorious for their "deep pockets and short arms."

Furthermore, Randlett was forced to concede that most of the entrepreneurs in Silicon Valley were strikingly uninterested in politics of any kind. A dull, default Republicanism prevailed among some of the older businessmen, and a kind of knee-jerk anarcho-libertarianism among the brattier boy wonders, but generally people were too busy making fortunes and rhapsodizing about the future of the digital revolution to bother with anything as dull as government.

To Randlett, though, the high-tech industry was full of exactly the kind of people who should bite at his bait. Young, white, suburban, well educated, they were suspicious of big government, averse to taxes and regulation, fond of the outdoors, and unrattled by homosexuals.

They had no partisan allegiances, no experience with politics. And they were very, very wealthy.

Randlett saw it as the opportunity of his lifetime. "High-tech people didn't understand the political system at all; they considered it inefficient and corrupt," he said. "Political people didn't get the technology or the business model. They thought Silicon Valley was cheap, apathetic, and impossible to organize. But I thought, Here's a group of twenty-eight-year-old CEOs who've created an entirely new economy, and as soon as they understand their political potential they can exert as much power as they choose." Randlett flashed a grin. "And I thought, Whoever cracks Silicon Valley is going to be the cham-peen of the world."

For all the polls and databases and focus groups that purport to chart voters' political mood, nobody can say exactly when a political idea gains currency, or how a realignment of political forces begins. In 1985, Governor Bill Clinton of Arkansas, along with the wonkishly upright Tennessee senator Al Gore, had helped organize the Democratic Leadership Council as a way of "rethinking" the party's values after its humiliating defeat in the 1984 presidential election. Led by moderate and conservative Democrats, and directed by the indefatigably centrist Al From, the DLC worked to purge what it saw as its party's suicidal impulses toward leftism. In public stump speeches and private meetings, the DLC denounced the poisonous influence of "traditional constituencies" such as Jesse Jackson's Rainbow Coalition, public-sector unions, liberal women, New Dealers, and ethnic minorities over the party. With an eye to recapturing Democratic voters who had defected to Reaganism, the centrists attacked liberal "special interests" for maintaining a stranglehold on their platform. Despite counterattacks from liberals who denounced the organization as a group of "Southern white boys," the DLC spurned traditional Democratic stances on race, rejecting affirmative action and government programs aimed at minorities. And, furiously biting the hand that had always fed them, the New Democrats consigned trade unionism, in particular, to the dustbin of history: they urged the country to look, instead, to business as the model for "reinventing" all kinds of public institutions, from schools to government agencies. The DLC philosophy, Al From declared, "offers opportunity to all, demands responsibility from everyone, and fosters a new sense of community in our nation."

High-minded rhetoric aside, the class message of the DLC was about as direct as political statements get, and it wasn't lost on ambitious young centrists like Wade Randlett. "For a while in my party in the late eighties," Randlett told me, recounting the history, "there was this anti-yuppie, fuck-the-yuppies sentiment. It was mostly pink- and blue-collar resentment against young white-collar Democratic yuppies who were making a lot of money. Had that trend persisted, there would have been an enormous chance for Republicans to grab the people we're reaching now, because the traditional Democrats were hostile to them. It was, 'You're rich and powerful? OK, we don't want you in our party.' "

By the nineties, the country's mood had begun to shift. As the influence of organized labor waned, its base diminished by globalization and factory closings to just above 10 percent of the workforce, the Democrats began to reach out to non-union households and middle-class suburban voters. Meanwhile, the culture wars of the Reagan years, largely financed by the direct-mail fund-raising of the right, had given the most militant and uncompromising ideologues of the Republican Party a larger leadership role. Republican candidates kept lurching ever rightward, away from their traditional big-business supporters, replacing the values of the corporate mainstream with the crusades of evangelical Christians and the rants of antigovernment extremists. It made sense for Democrats to begin to craft a centrist Third Way alternative that could capture middle-class swing voters.

In 1992, with help from Al From and the DLC, Bill Clinton and Al Gore ran the first national campaign with a New Democrat message, stressing mainstream social values, questioning welfare, and repeating what would become their winning mantra: "It's the economy, stupid."

In a backhanded way, Clinton's victory illustrated the inadequacy of the old ground rules in a world where the bottom line was fast becoming the only rule. For decades the common wisdom had been that the political system was corrupt and politicians could be bought. But even cynics before Clinton believed that "money" and "politics" were two distinct areas, each with its own set of values and rules. Money talked, but it wasn't a universal language. Political power traded in other currencies as well: violence, patronage, faith, and votes. Money was a tool, a crowbar for influencing politics; politics was a system that used money for its own ends.

Clinton, like many of his fellow New Democrats, tended to be suspicious of ideology in general—an attitude that led, more or less directly, away from principle and toward money. New Democrats said that Old Democrats were tied to sentimental ideas that linked morality with union membership, or saw "principle" at stake in welfare policies. And Republicans, they said, were equally overeager to be loved by the masses; the GOP embraced populist hucksters and fervent evangelicals because they believed these voters could provide a committed, heart-and-soul base like the one the Old Democrats wielded.

In fact, the New Democrats contended, true believers were only a small percentage of the electorate. As the 1992 election showed, the majority were practical, cynical, and disloyal to any party on principle. To reach them you needed, simply, money.

The New Democrats who triumphed with Clinton in 1992 were a perfect match for entrepreneurs whose bedrock conviction was that the rules of the market guided all human endeavor. Silicon Valley business-men acted as if they believed that money was the universal and only ac-curate standard of measurement in the world. They seemed to think that the question Does it maximize shareholder value? meant the same thing as Is it morally right? Efficiency, in their world, had become worth; wealth was proof of rightness. And so the industry whose most influential spokesmen insisted that ideology was dead met the party whose President had no apparent ideology, a party that took their money and hailed them as the future.

Clinton's election in 1992 confirmed the DLC's belief that its New Democratic politics were gaining ground—and that it was attracting a "core" of business support. Simon Rosenberg, a feisty, hyperintelligent young DLC strategist who had worked in Clinton's campaign "war room," expressed the hopefulness that New Democrats were beginning to feel. "Both parties are going through generational and ideological changes," he said. "There are old ways of doing and thinking that won't go away easily. But are we winning? Yes."

Citing a survey by President Clinton's pollster Mark Penn, Rosen-berg's boss at the DLC, Al From, wrote, "Most Democrats today hold decidedly New Democrat views. They believe that government should help people equip themselves to solve their own problems, and not solve problems for them. They believe that government should promote economic growth and opportunity, not protectionism. Their greatest concerns are the weakening of traditional family values, crime and vio-lence, and high government taxes, not income inequality. . . . In short, Penn's analysis . . . shows that the Democratic 'base' has moved solidly and decisively in our direction. Only the interest groups and elements of the permanent party infrastructure still hold out for the old Democratic message that kept Democrats in the political wilderness throughout much of the 1970s and 1980s."

But the Democrats weren't yet out of the wilderness. The DLC, in reality, was a small institution with a staff of forty that was much better at producing polls and policy papers than at organizing voters. Clinton, after his election in 1992, was to disappoint the DLC and many New Democrats by making compromise after compromise with the "Old" wing of the party in Congress, And, despite their pro-business rhetoric, most Washington-based New Democrats had little idea of how to actually attract business supporters. Luckily for them, on the other side of the country something was beginning to stir.

And it had begun before Wade Randlett arrived. The young fundraiser's interest in trolling the Valley for New Democrat recruits was smart, but it wasn't exactly original. Back in the old days of Silicon Valley, before the Internet revolution of 1995, a small but determined number of Democratic executives had kept a political flame lit in the midst of near-universal apathy.

In the early 1990s, a few of the more worldly of the Silicon Valley businessmen had turned to straightforward lobbying, hiring government-affairs representatives and creating some dull trade associations with offices in Washington and Sacramento. The less energetic simply joined the Chamber of Commerce and voted for Republican candidates. And a handful of oddballs, perhaps believing their own myths about creativity and opportunity, became Democrats—though, as a union organizer once pointed out to me, "you couldn't tell them from Republicans without a microscope."

"For years, if you were in business and you were a Democrat," said Larry Stone, talking about the period before the 1992 elections, "you ensconced yourself in the closet. I finally came out because, gosh, I was sick of seeing the Republicans be the only game in town."

I'd met Stone around the same time that I met Randlett, and talking to him made me understand why this "old-timer," as he called himself, had remained quietly at the center of the Valley's political development for so long. Stone was an immensely kind man, with a stutter and a prodigious memory, and his practical civic-mindedness gave him the moral authority to speak about politics to people who professed to hate the very idea. In 1992, he approached Apple's legendary marketing guru, Regis McKenna; the brilliant venture capitalist Brook Byers of Kleiner Perkins; financial wizard Sandy Robertson of Robertson Stephens, a top Democratic fund-raiser; and a few other executives who had inexplicably remained Democrats even as their fortunes grew. He explained that they needed to be heard if they were to free their party from the death grip of special interests and liberals. "A business Democrat without business support is a tough thing," he told them, urging that they form a Silicon Valley group to back centrist Democratic candidates.

Paul Lippe, a forty-year-old lawyer and high-tech executive, was one of the most receptive of the figures Stone ran into. A tall, sardonic Easterner with a well-tuned ear for politics, Lippe had worked for New York senator Daniel Patrick Moynihan, then on Gary Hart's disastrous presidential campaign in 1988. After Hart's fall, Lippe practiced law with him in Denver. The high-tech boom took off, and in 1991 Lippe landed a job with a Silicon Valley software company and resettled his wife and four children in an upscale, picture-perfect suburb in Los Altos.

I would hear the whole story from Lippe years later, in 1996, as we watched one of his daughters play soccer. Lippe had a long face, large brown eyes, and a charming chipped front tooth; he combined the earnestness of a jock with the dark humor of his secret life as a novelist. Lippe told me about his decision to re-enter politics: basically, it was because the pleasant gentile blandness of life in California had begun to wear on his nerves. "I was a Jew surrounded by three thousand WASPs at work each day," he moaned. "And all of them were engineers."

Politics was a way of making things more exciting. Lippe still knew his way around Washington and was connected with centrist figures in the Democratic Party. An outgoing and affable man, he was willing to start scouting around for likely fellow travelers in the high-tech industry. In any case, he shared Stone's centrist politics and was intrigued by the idea of putting together a coalition of high-tech businessmen to challenge the old Democratic labor machine. "It used to be when you talked about the Democratic business constituency all you really had was a handful of Jews," Lippe mused. "You had some in Hollywood, some in real estate, maybe some in a few Wall Street firms. That ain't a serious constituency. I knew we had to pick up some real business guys."

On the phone, at the occasional political fund-raiser, or over lunch at his favorite Indian restaurant in Mountain View, Lippe and his buddies would brainstorm about how to connect high-tech executives with centrist Democrats, and how to build a network of like-minded players. Brook Byers, who had a more Establishment style than Lippe, wanted to bring aboard his colleagues from finance and investment banking, respected Democrats like Sandy Robertson and Bill Hambricht of Hambricht & Quist. Robertson was already a party insider and a well-connected man in the Valley.

Regis McKenna had a different take. A thin, small, silver-haired hipster, McKenna was sharp-minded about media, with an adman's cool. McKenna, who had his own Hart connection, thought that the "unconventional, innovative, rule-breaking" style embraced by high-tech pioneers might make them reject Republican moralism—if Democrats could market themselves better. He saw, in the image of the digital revolution, the possibilities for dragging otherwise conservative businessmen into the Democratic fold. "Regis was really the first guy to intuit the fusion possibilities," Lippe said admiringly. "He saw the cultural aspects of the industry, the same ones he'd used to help define Apple's positioning."

Lippe paused, reflecting on the realization voiced by McKenna—that rich businessmen who enjoyed seeing themselves as countercultural might be persuaded to support Democrats. "In Silicon Valley you had guys like Steve Jobs who wanted to rebel against old business structures," Lippe said. "It was a sort of post-libertarian infantilism. It wasn't the old crank libertarianism of the Hunt brothers; it had a kind of Zen-iness." Lippe laughed. "And Silicon Valley businesspeople, from the beginning, saw themselves as guerrillas—even the venture capitalists got off on calling themselves VCs. Like Vietcong."

More prosaically, though, the task at hand was not purely "image" but figuring out ways to raise money and endorsements for candidates from the executives of high tech. Lippe began to make introductions, and Stone and his friends decided to start the Democratic Forum, a club that would fund-raise, promote "moderate and pro-growth" candidates in the Valley, and simultaneously push the idea that the Democrats were truly identified with the values of the high-tech industry.

In 1992, Larry Stone invited the centrist Governor Bill Clinton of Arkansas to Silicon Valley—"He hit it off with people here right away," Stone said—and, when Clinton became the Democratic nominee, scored "a major coup" by lining up CEO endorsements for him.

"Dave Barram of Apple very patiently put together that first coalition for Clinton," Stone recalled, generously giving credit to a Democratic Forum colleague. It was a warm morning in 1996, and I was interviewing Stone in his office in the Santa Clara County building overlooking the freeways of Silicon Valley. Stone was plucking genially at his suspenders and explaining ancient history to me. "Clinton had no recognizable business support at the time—some wealthy individuals, but no sector of business," he said. I had the sense that I was listening to someone attempting to articulate a creation myth. "Nobody understood back then what was happening."

Stone knew, he told me, that the men they were trying to recruit for Clinton in 1992 were lifelong Republicans, but he hoped he could convince entrepreneurs that Clinton "got it." With help and hustle from Regis McKenna, Stone and Barram succeeded in signing up the famous CEO of Apple, John Sculley, to head their list of endorsers. Twenty-five other CEOs, recognizing the stamp of cool, followed Sculley's lead. "It was a huge deal," Stone said. "Even though our list was only a couple dozen names, it made news. We were the sexiest industry in the world right then, and it gave Clinton instant credibility. A couple weeks later, Dave Packard put together a list of Republican endorsers—hundreds of them—but by then it was old news. The story was, Silicon Valley goes for Clinton."

Al From, who had cultivated a friendship with Sandy Robertson and other Silicon Valley heavies, made a point of trying to stay in touch after the 1992 elections. "I never go to California without sitting down with Sandy and Regis, so I can get a sense of what they're talking about," he said. "It's not a campaign deal where we come in and get their dough—I just think that the Silicon Valley people are very future-oriented, and we should know what's happening there."

Paul Lippe had tried to talk to the DLC about doing even more to tap Silicon Valley's potential. Its leadership made a trip to California in 1994, but there was no real organizational plan. "Al From had a terrible cold," Lippe recalled. "He kept sneezing and talking about the importance of business support, and I kept nodding and passing him Kleenex. It was so frustrating. I was like, 'Al, you don't have to tell me the theory, I'm your acolyte, just tell me what we're going to *do*.' "

After the 1992 elections, and the burst of work by Larry Stone, Lippe, McKenna, and Dave Barram, follow-up organizing languished.

I spent an afternoon once with Lippe at his office, and I saw how far apart the worlds of politics and high tech really were.

It was a sunny fall day, and I had driven to a featureless industrial park to watch Lippe as he tried to introduce the grunts of Silicon Valley to Elementary Civics, in the person of Democratic congresswoman Anna Eshoo of California's fourteenth district. A petite, energetic woman in a smart navy suit and businesslike pumps, Eshoo was known as a strong supporter of the industry, with more high-tech savvy than most. Lippe had scheduled her for an open meeting with employees at his software firm, Synopsys, and he greeted her warmly. The congresswoman got right down to business. "So, what policies get in your way?" she asked. "What needs tweaking?"

Lippe chuckled. "Nothing, we have a parking lot full of Lexuses, we're happy." Then he leaned forward, gazing at her sincerely. "We want the party to understand the future. Fifty years from now Silicon Valley will be more powerful than Washington, but people in Washington don't see that yet."

Lippe rose. "Anna," he said. "We've got a briefing for you on our software, and the new Synopsys approach to automating the process of making chips." Eshoo whispered something to her aide, then smiled up at Lippe as they walked through the carpeted corridors. "This should be fascinating," she said.

"We've replaced RTL code with behavioral compilers," began a twenty-eight-year-old engineer named Tony Dimalanta, launching his show-and-tell in a small cubicle. The congresswoman stared somewhat blankly at a screen full of algorithms. Dimalanta clicked on a flowchart. "Now this is awesome," he continued. Lippe stood above him, smiling.

"Tony," Eshoo interrupted. "Tell me, who is your representative?"

Dimalanta blushed like a ninth-grader caught daydreaming by his social-studies teacher. "Uh, I don't actually know," he said.

Down the hall in the conference room, thirty assorted geeks assembled, curious about this emissary from another planet. "I went to your home page and found a description of the work you do," Eshoo announced, earning a flicker of respect for being the rare politician who knew how to go on-line by herself.

But the employees began to look less sure as Eshoo tried to explain her work. "Representatives serve two-year terms," she started, and a few in the audience nodded, glad to have that information. "The House is very different from the Senate." Then Eshoo described the committee system, seniority, and the norms of congressional politicking. "There are these huge, difficult issues, and the legislative process is very complicated," she said. "You have to be ready to make compromises."

Whatever Eshoo was hoping to communicate about the subtleties of Washington's political process was lost on the crowd: it was as if the engineers just couldn't comprehend such a buggy system. If there's a *problem*, they kept asking, doggedly, why don't you *fix* it? One of the geeks argued that Congress was not "logical." After half an hour of this, Eshoo switched on a bright smile and wrapped up the meeting in campaign mode. "I love representing this district," she said. "Thank you all for your support. And never forget, we have the best country on the face of the earth."

But Randlett was convinced that a match could be made, and he was becoming impatient. He kept proselytizing among his friends in politics for more attention to Silicon Valley. Notably, he kept pestering Holly Page, the smart young DLC organizer who ran political strategy for Al From. Page had a keen eye for trends, and she was interested in getting more business support for the DLC. "You've got a whole generation of entrepreneurs who came of age and made millions on Clinton's watch, and they've invented a new technology and a new way of doing business that is changing everything," Randlett told her one night. "They can be ours."

Page had worked with Randlett before in California, and she had already heard much the same argument from Sandy Robertson, who was a friend of Al From's and a major contributor to the DLC. Page listened carefully. She arranged some meetings in Silicon Valley. She had drinks with a few of Randlett's thirty-something millionaire friends. "They were like little ducklings looking for Mom," Page concluded of the entrepreneurs.

In February 1996, Page hired Randlett to do political organizing for the DLC, giving him the intentionally vague title of "Northern California liaison." She had a hope that Randlett would identify Silicon Valley money and connections for the centrist group, but the DLC had no point-by-point agenda. Page, nonetheless, was excited about the possibilities. Six months after she'd given Randlett the go-ahead, I sat down with Randlett in his dusty living room and scratched his Great Dane behind the ears. Randlett had managed to work himself sideways into a peculiar and unsupervised niche instead of climbing slowly up the conventional ladder of a political machine, and he was extremely pleased with the prospects. Few in Washington knew the difference between Mountain View and Menlo Park, much less the significance of Java programming, fuzzy-logic algorithms, or software IPOs. And nobody in Silicon Valley had a clue what the DLC even *was*.

I saw Wade Randlett as the guy who could be the pivot point for the major political realignment that was under way in the Democratic Party. He wasn't the most important figure in politics or high tech by any means, but he occupied an incredibly interesting position bridging the two. What Randlett represented was nothing as predictable as a political organization or a business entity; he articulated a political sensibility that was new, as yet uninstitutionalized, and utterly of the moment. His intelligence, his shrewdness, and his unfettered ambition made him someone well worth following. If the Democrats were going to be able to claim high tech as their own, and if Silicon Valley was going to choose the Democrats to represent its interests, I was sure Randlett would be there at the center of things. If I kept track of him, I thought, I'd be able to watch the connection happen.

During the last months of the 1996 presidential campaign, Randlett found a way to bring it all together. Flush with cash from his fund-raising days, armed with his enormous Rolodex and some new DLC business cards, Randlett began to make himself ubiquitous, searching out the handful of Silicon Valley insiders who would help him build his machine.

CHAPTER two

I'd head for Silicon Valley in early 1996, going south on Highway 101. The magnificent hills and shifting light disappeared behind a curve as I drove away from San Francisco and toward the twenty-first century. On weekday mornings, it could take me two hours to crawl forty miles to visit some corporate cubicle in Sunnyvale, and the view along the clogged freeway revealed little more than a numbed landscape of power lines, billboards, tract houses, strip malls, and thousands of office buildings ringed by parking lots. And even if I made too much of nostalgia—the light, the hills, those beautiful wooden houses behind me rising out of the fog—still, I often had dread about the future when I crossed the unofficial border of Silicon Valley, and Oracle Software loomed from the landfill like a squat green plastic toilet-paper dispenser.

At the time I started exploring Silicon Valley, the real changes represented by its boom were hard to see. American business in general had been undergoing gigantic shifts in the last fifteen years, but I didn't really understand the process. Various management gurus and CEOs seemed to be constantly popping up, touting their theories with the confidence of evangelists or diet doctors. They'd left assorted cultural artifacts in their wake: the craze for Japanese-style corporations; companywide outdoor bonding experiences; "excellence"; PowerPoint presentations; downsizing; casual Fridays; "teams."

But in fact the entire landscape of the economy really was shifting, driven by forces too big for any single industry to control. Many of the changes were charted in a report called *The New Economy Index: Understanding America's Economic Transformation*, by researchers at the Progressive Policy Institute, a DLC think tank. For thirty years, the study said, America's mass-production manufacturing jobs had been falling steadily, until in 1995 factory workers made up less than 20 percent of the workforce; the service sector, by 1995, represented 75 percent of total employment. By 1996, high-tech manufacturing and services were the fastest-growing sector of the economy.

America's new economy, focused not around mass production but around the flexible production of services and goods, was centered in offices, not factories. Its growth was strongest not in old industries and established businesses but in small, new companies that developed and exploited new technologies. Its businesses were increasingly competitive, constantly "churning" and working at ever-faster speeds. And this new economy was more integrated into the global economy than ever before: from 1970 to 1996, trade increased from 11 percent of GDP to 25 percent.

The changes in the American economy meant huge changes for American workers. In 1960, there were fewer than five thousand computer professionals in the United States, and by 1996 there were more than a million, almost all of them earning well above the median income. Overall unemployment was declining, and would, by 1999, reach its lowest point since 1960. But skilled factory and trade jobs were disappearing, as were many skilled service-sector and office positions. Unskilled, low-wage jobs grew alongside high-wage, skilled jobs, suggesting a trend of social and economic bifurcation that would only intensify as the new economy developed.

There was also, according to the U.S. Census Bureau, a trend of growing income inequality. Between 1980 and 1996, real incomes went up 58 percent for the wealthiest 5 percent of American households, but less than 4 percent for the lowest 60 percent. Since the 1970s, workers who had no college degree had seen their real wages fall; in the 1990s, even as compensation for managerial and professional work increased, the incomes for moderate-skill jobs stayed flat, and the incomes of less skilled jobs declined. In addition, because of the shift away from traditional unionized, skilled blue-collar manufacturing and public-sector jobs, employees' relationships with their employers were changing. A smaller number of Americans than ever before were receiving such benefits as retirement plans and health care, and more were employed as "contingent" workers, in part-time, contract, and temporary jobs.

But in Silicon Valley, as in other high-tech centers around the country, such meta-changes in the American and the global economy were overshadowed by the sheer size and excitement of the high-tech boom. With the demise of the Valley industries associated with the Cold War defense-spending boom, high-tech companies had changed their relationship to government. Despite ongoing government investment in some infrastructure, computing, and biotechnology research, the main source of capital for technology development now came from the private sector—from investment banks and, increasingly, venture-capital firms eager to put money into new ideas. Venture capitalists were looking less for stability and track records than for entrepreneurial energy: they were less interested in what IBM was doing than in what some kid in a garage might dream up.

Some financiers, of course, were worried by the speed with which the Silicon Valley boom had taken off, particularly after the Netscape IPO made everything Internet shine like gold. In April 1996, investment banker Sandy Robertson sounded a note of caution, telling *The New York Times* that "whenever the market is ebullient, like it is now, the filter is very coarse and a lot of junk gets through." By 2000, with the number of IPOs still skyrocketing and the market at a level Robertson could not even have dreamed of four years earlier, his concern would seem old-fashioned.

But a tidal wave was beginning to sweep through the Valley. It's hard, looking back, to see how it happened, now that the entire phenomenon has the weight of inevitability. The fact is that in 1996 even the most hyped-up optimist couldn't imagine how big the boom would get. "E-commerce," as a term, would not even be invented until 1997, and the use of the Web for retail and business-to-business commerce would not really take off until 1998. Old media companies and the biggest high-tech firms had not consolidated their positions in 1996; independent start-ups proliferated, and the control of a number of important markets was still up for grabs. On-line trading and the accumulating wealth produced by the boom had not yet "democratized" the deployment of capital; investment in new technology businesses was still more about plugged-in venture-capital firms and investment banks than about the general stock market. And the American public's view of what was happening in Silicon Valley was still cloudy, at best. For many of those in Washington, it was almost entirely opaque.

But in Silicon Valley itself in 1996, what was clear was the amazing mix of ideas, products, technologies, and companies—many of which would eventually crash and disappear—that made up the landscape. The high-tech industry already encompassed everything, as venture capitalist John Doerr frequently said, "from bits and bytes to bugs and drugs"; from software and hardware to biotechnology. The hot trends in high tech would change constantly, as the speed of computing and the ubiquity of the Internet and other "network effects" grew. Product cycles seemed to shorten dramatically, from three years to two to six months; the time it took to find financing for a start-up seemed to fall from years to months to a couple of meetings.

There was fierce competition, at every level, framing the industry's growth. In 1996, the most notable were the "browser wars" between Netscape and Microsoft, as the giants battled to see whether the Internet could trump Bill Gates's control of personal-computer software. As time went on, high-tech businesses and financiers would pause to consider politics, as they reached for every tool at their disposal to beat back their competitors and came up with the idea of using government. But for now, most companies focused on the immediate challenges of starting up, and then on the next quarter. The big picture took place on another plane. And an astonishing number of successful new businesses just kept coming.

It was crazy to think that any entity as broadly defined as "high-tech" or "Silicon Valley" could ever be accurately represented by a single political group. But Wade Randlett believed that it could be given a political identity, meaning that somewhere between the image and the reality of high tech lay a set of interests that could be addressed through politics. In the months leading up to the 1996 presidential election, what Randlett needed to do, he said, borrowing an industry term, was to "brand" his political project.

"July 2, 1996, at 6:30 p.m., I met John Doerr of Kleiner Perkins," Randlett intoned solemnly. He grinned. "A moment that will live in infamy." Doerr, who was a registered Republican, had agreed that fateful evening to attend a fund-raising event at Sandy Robertson's home for DLC stalwart Senator Joe Lieberman. Randlett, his DLC business cards tucked inside the pocket of his double-breasted suit, seized the chance to talk. Clearly, the calculator in Wade Randlett's head was exquisitely calibrated to nuances of power, because it couldn't have taken him much more than twenty seconds after their first handshake to understand the indispensable importance of John Doerr to his political future. "Of course, John was completely off the radar screen politically," Randlett added. He didn't seem to mind.

Kleiner Perkins Caufield & Byers, the citadel of high-tech venture capital, was nestled in a leafy glade off Sand Hill Road in Menlo Park. Its offices were spacious and graceful, with soaring ceilings and wide windows and bright spills of orchids. Kleiner Perkins had none of the dark panels and claustrophobic corridors that weigh down East Coast banking firms, none of Wall Street's metallic, high-rise masculinity. Calm in the eye of Silicon Valley's stomach-churning storm of growth, the venture capitalists who worked here affected a casual, very Californian self-assurance about their success. No matter how many investors called in hysterically, you couldn't hear the phones ring; no matter how many millions of dollars poured out, you never saw the wires. Walking into Kleiner Perkins's airy lobby on even the busiest day was like entering a particularly tasteful, upscale spa.

Venture capitalist John Doerr, at forty-five, was inevitably described by reporters as "boyish"—a word meant to evoke the fair, archaically Midwestern model of boy, not the surly dreadlocked skateboarder kind found roaming California malls. Bespectacled and slight, with a sandy cowlick, Doerr was arguably the most powerful man in Silicon Valley, and almost certainly the best connected. It was hard to figure out exactly how much he was worth, but by 1996 most estimates had put it at more than a billion dollars.

With degrees in electrical engineering and business, Doerr had moved to Silicon Valley in 1975 to work for Intel. In 1980, he became a partner at Kleiner Perkins, and begun backing an astonishing number of high tech's biggest success stories—among them, Sun Microsystems, Compaq, and Intuit. Doerr took equity in the businesses he backed, and held board seats; he became an adviser to as well as an investor in the industry's most important companies. In the summer of 1986, he took a brief leave from moneymaking to work for Congressman Tim Wirth, the New Democrat from Colorado who served on the Armed Forces Subcommittee; there, Doerr studied the Pentagon's Arpanet, learning about new technologies that he would later build into commercial Internet ventures.

Back in Silicon Valley, Doerr helped set up high-yielding, exclusive investment funds with corporate money from Kleiner Perkins's portfolio companies. By the mid-nineties, Doerr had scooped up hundreds of millions for his work, along with personal friendships with most of Silicon Valley's top executives. An early and aggressive proselytizer for the Internet, Doerr took Netscape public in 1995, then cashed in on the Web boom by jump-starting winners like Amazon.com and @Home, developing a circle of grateful young protégés in the process. Doerr frequently referred to his network as the Kleiner Perkins *keiretsu*—a Japanese term for a network of companies with interlocking directorships and central financing.

Doerr's partners at Kleiner Perkins tended to be calmer men, if equally aggressive once it came to making deals. Most of the fifteen partners—among them, Will Hearst, scion of the publishing family, and Sun alumnus Vinod Khosla—liked to keep a low profile outside the business world. A few, like Floyd Kvamme, a gruff sixty-eight-year-old who was an ardent Republican, or Democrat Brook Byers, who had helped create some of biotechnology's most successful companies and worked with Larry Stone on the Democratic Forum, had become politically active, but most stayed out of the public eye. And after founding partner Tom Perkins scaled back his involvement with the firm, the face identified with Kleiner Perkins Caufield & Byers was, most frequently, John Doerr's.

In the *keiretsu* tradition, Doerr was a full-service venture capitalist: he liked to play chess with the companies in his network, handpicking their CEOs, advising their boards on business strategy, introducing their leaders to one another, and masterminding their mergers, buyouts, and deals. He was known for identifying the most talented people in the industry, both technical and managerial, and recruiting them for his companies. Start-up entrepreneurs chose Kleiner Perkins over other venture-capital firms offering larger investments, in the belief that Doerr's reputation was worth more to them than cash. And even when Doerr turned against people, he was not attacked in return; in fact, I never heard anyone say a single negative word about the man in public. "Why would anyone want to cross John Doerr?" one entrepreneur once said in amazement when I asked if such a powerful figure had enemies. "He's the one who makes everything happen."

John Doerr scared me, and not just because he ran the Valley. This was a man who had no interest in being flattered, but no tolerance for being crossed. He didn't chat. He didn't scream. He didn't have a sense of humor. He led most meetings with the narcissistic impatience of an overly bright child, instantly sweeping away everyone and everything that was irrelevant to his goal. With the arrival of his first daughter, in 1994, Doerr had begun limiting his hours at the office, but his pace, and his intensity, remained near-manic. In action, Doerr gave off tics like a shower of sparks, tugging at his hair, chewing his lips, tapping his feet, rapping his fingers, and destroying pencils by the score—but he was never out of control.

It was the summer of 1996, when Doerr and Randlett met, that an unlikely threat from outside made Doerr lose it. For perhaps the first time, he had to consider the limits of his power.

Securities-litigation reform isn't generally thought of as an especially burning interest—except for the groups to whom it means everything. Unnoticed by most politicians, a storm had been brewing during President Clinton's first term over legislation governing shareholder lawsuits against companies. Trial lawyers who favored making it easier to sue pitted themselves against executives who feared being held personally responsible if their companies' stock lost value. In 1995, Bill Lerach— the slickly flamboyant head of the American Trial Lawyers Association and the nation's second-largest individual donor to federal candidates, almost all of them Democrats—had met with Bill Clinton, and convinced the President to veto a federal-securities-litigation-reform bill that would have restricted shareholder lawsuits. High-tech CEOs, including the few who had supported Clinton in 1992, were livid about the veto; in the exploding market, technology stocks were constantly rising and falling for reasons that had little to do with performance. More than half of the companies in the Valley had already faced shareholder lawsuits when their stocks lost value, and settlements with Lerach and other aggressive trial lawyers had cost the industry at least $600 million. In early 1996, Intuit co-founder Tom Proulx, a man long on outrage and short on common sense, had raised $12 million to sponsor a litigation-reform ballot proposition in California, but his initiative was poorly organized and failed in the March primary.

Lerach counterattacked with his own ballot initiative for November 1996. Called Proposition 211, it was designed to open the door for shareholder lawsuits against executives in California. It would prevent companies from indemnifying officers or directors who were found personally liable in investor-fraud suits—which directly threatened the personal fortunes of venture capitalists sitting on high-tech boards. The proposition would also allow lawyers, for the first time, to seek punitive damages in investor class actions, without any regulation of their fees — which, as Silicon Valley executives saw it, meant that Lerach would be free to shake them down and extort settlements by threatening action.

Proposition 211 meant war to Doerr, who hated trial lawyers on principle and Lerach in particular. "He's an exceptionally smart, shrewd, entrepreneurial, economic terrorist," Doerr said to a reporter from *Wired*. (The magazine, capturing the mood of the Valley accurately, entitled its profile of Lerach "Bloodsucking Scumbag.") Doerr, who knew that the threat of expensive litigation would only make it more difficult to find executives and board members for his high-tech start-ups, vowed to stop Lerach. "He won't get away with this," Doerr told his partner Brook Byers angrily. "We'll crush him."

In Silicon Valley, John Doerr's wishes made things happen. But in the parallel universe of politics, Doerr's discontent about Proposition 211 didn't even seem to register. A tantrum at Kleiner Perkins meant nothing to the California Democratic Party, which endorsed Lerach's initiative. Most state politicians fell in line reflexively behind their long-time trial-lawyer friends, unaware of the Valley's rage. John Dean, the chairman of the Silicon Valley Bank, was called one afternoon by Doerr and asked to take a six-week leave to work against the ballot initiative.

Dean, a soft-spoken, bespectacled banker, was more than willing. "John was passionate about 211, but we were all believers," he said. "This bank had experienced lawsuits, as had many of our clients, and it was a cause we cared very deeply about." Dean began systematically working through the network of influence that ran the Valley, calling potential donors and organizers. "First we focused on the venture firms, and they each selected a representative or two to work on this," he explained. "We went industry by industry: the venture firms, the law firms, the investment banks, the accounting firms, and finally the technology firms themselves. We sized up the market, decided who was dominant, and then picked the individuals who would be most effective at leveraging alliances."

The money began flowing: largely in response to 211, the Valley formed its first political-action committee, the California Technology Alliance, which raised $660,500 for state candidates, giving especially generously to Democrats who opposed their party's stand on 211. Taxpayers Against Frivolous Lawsuits, the umbrella group fighting 211, got donations of $500,000 from companies like Intel, Sun, and Cisco.

Dean's calls pulled in support from places like Wilson Sonsini, Silicon Valley's leading law firm; from investment bankers like Dan Case of Hambrecht & Quist, and from the accounting firms Ernst & Young and PricewaterhouseCoopers.

But further from the fray, in the White House, Clinton's advisers were urging the President to stay "on message" with his national re-election campaign, and to avoid getting entangled in unimportant local issues such as John Doerr's crusade against Proposition 211. Stuck, Doerr realized the need for some basic training in Politics 101. And that was when he met Wade Randlett, who was ready to teach.

The first time Wade Randlett took me up Sand Hill Road in his new convertible, we roared into the Kleiner Perkins parking lot and stopped directly in front of the entrance. I got out, astounded, staring at a huge, unseemly banner draped above the doors like a revolutionary mani-festo. NO ON 211, it read, in scarlet; the thing must have been twelve feet tall. A coiffed businesswoman with an expensive briefcase trotted up the stairs beneath the banner, oblivious. "Welcome to ground zero," said Randlett, looking pleased with himself and trying to sound casual. "John agreed to let me run the campaign out of here."

Later, everyone would agree that the fight against 211 had been "galvanizing" for Silicon Valley. Brook Byers would proclaim that "a sleeping giant has been awakened," and other industry heavyweights would refer to the "wake-up call" represented by 211 with an awe usu-ally reserved for discussions of Paul's experiences on the road to Da-mascus. But when the NO ON 211 campaign was first launched, most high-tech executives joined in with the sense of rallying to overcome a temporary obstacle: few in Silicon Valley realized how profoundly their entire relationship to politics would be transformed.

Wade Randlett, on the other hand, understood that winning the fight against 211 was the single most important thing he could do to es-tablish his credibility with Silicon Valley's elite. Once he'd proved him-self effective and trustworthy, he could start to influence the direction of high tech's political involvement, and lead previously apolitical exec-utives into his New Democratic fold. "I'd known for nine and a half years that there was potential for [Silicon Valley figures] to get in-volved in politics, but nothing was there," Randlett said. "All of a sud-den, with 211, it was there. They took me on faith with what I was saying, and decided to go for it."

First, Randlett decided, he needed to teach the executives a bit about the world of politics, and guide them through the logic of this alien culture. Except for the handful who had already developed their own convictions, Randlett hoped that his interpretations of politics, and his representation of the way things worked, would become the default for the Valley's political outlook. Usually impatient, Randlett was careful to treat his students with respect, and to defer to Doerr on every decision; his restraint, as much as his knowledge, helped establish his role as trusted adviser. "What Wade did for a lot of us was clarify the very confusing world of politics and politicians," said an appreciative Brook Byers. John Dean put it differently. "I used to be an idealist with realistic tendencies," he said. "Now I guess I'm more of a realist, with idealistic tendencies."

While Dean and Doerr worked the phones, raising $40 million from their *keiretsu* for the NO ON 211 war chest, Randlett turned the elegant offices of Kleiner Perkins into a cadre school. On Monday mornings, the "dawn patrol" met to work the phones, plot strategy, and raise funds. Evenings, around the boardroom's vast conference table, CEOs leaned forward in leather chairs as Randlett taught them how to talk to legislators and decode their doublespeak. High-tech whizzes listened as he diagrammed the circuitry of political machines. And the whole class nodded when Randlett summed up the rules of his game: "Politics is just common sense and human nature," he told them. "You help people, and they help you."

Randlett didn't, of course, explain all the tricks of his trade. Nor did he share with anyone but Doerr the political contacts in Washington who made him an indispensable go-between. But most of the executives, impressed by Randlett's skills, seemed eager to let him figure out how to cut the right deal behind the scenes. Much to the dismay of Tom Proulx, a conservative who loathed Democrats on principle—and Randlett in particular for his youthful arrogance—Randlett was hired to run the California Technology Alliance. His ambitions were clearly going to take him beyond California, but a state PAC—the only high-tech one that existed—was a fine place for him to start. "If Silicon Valley spends $2 million a year, it can be the most influential political force in the state," Randlett promised CTA directors when he took the job.

It was an interesting arrangement. Randlett was still working for the DLC, responsible for organizing Silicon Valley around New Democrat principles. He was also still working as a fund-raiser, getting his high-tech executives to write checks for local Democrats and for the

Clinton-Gore campaign. And now, as director of the CTA, he was representing the interests of the industry back to politicians. John Doerr was clearly impressed. "Wade's bright, aggressive, results-oriented, and he's working hard to win," the venture capitalist said. "These are all qualities that fit really well with the ethos of Silicon Valley. Wade's an entrepreneur; this is his start-up."

All through the summer months of 1996, Randlett worked on his "start-up." But it was clear that the relationship between high tech and the Democrats was becoming too complex for any one person to steer.

In August, DLC stalwart Simon Rosenberg and Celia Fischer, who was running the Clinton-Gore campaign in California, watched as John Doerr swept through the Democratic convention, with Randlett always at his side. "Celia and I had done this three-hour dinner, talking about how to organize the Democrats' relationship with Silicon Valley, and Wade pitched us about Doerr and 211," Rosenberg recalled. "So we arranged the first significant meeting with the main players."

Years of working in Democratic politics and on campaigns had given Simon Rosenberg a raspy voice and lasting scrappiness; he was small and smart, with a terrier-like tenacity. With his pink cheeks and unruly hair, Rosenberg looked like a schoolboy, but he had a long résumé. A fervent New Democrat, he was part of a circle of young DLC strategists around Al From who had realized that their political futures were contingent upon the Democratic Party's changing. Rosenberg wanted to see the party identify itself with the future: the old machine of union bosses and ward hacks was an obstacle to his ambitions.

Rosenberg had blossomed in the entrepreneurial atmosphere of Clinton's 1992 campaign, where irreverence and the ability to think independently were rewarded. He admired Clinton's political skills, and he thrived on the energy in the war room. After the election, he went to work for the DLC, building a network of New Democrats in Congress.

By the time Rosenberg got to the convention in August 1996, he was a well-connected man, with an extensive network on Capitol Hill and in the party. I wouldn't meet Rosenberg in person until November 1996, but when I did, I was struck by his insider's knowledge and his outsider's taste for adventure: he wasn't interested in doing things by rote. Speedy and funny, Rosenberg seemed to draw daily enjoyment from the practice of politics.

Fischer, then thirty-four, had a more complicated relationship with the old Democratic Party. A creative strategist with a formidable intelligence, she had worked on Democratic campaigns in New York, Missouri, and Pennsylvania, where she became close with Philadelphia mayor Ed Rendell, a rising star who would later head the Democratic National Committee. When I first started talking with Fischer regularly, in 1997, she struck me as someone who had devoted her time in politics to learning lessons and gaining perspective, rather than to grabbing short-term advantage for herself. Fischer believed in "thinking outside the box," but she had a lot of respect for older politicians. "I was never a screw-the-DLC person," she told me. "I had some doubts about the DLC's attacks on Old Dems, because during the Carter years I had seen how destructive intraparty fights could be."

In 1992, like Rosenberg, Fischer went to work for Bill Clinton. First in the Pennsylvania primary and then in California, she began to get excited about the political potential of the New Democrat message he was offering. "People—citizens, voters—know in their guts that the past is gone," she said. "One of the most appealing things about Bill Clinton is that he told them nobody would be left behind. People knew the world was changing, and Clinton made them feel like they could be part of it." Fischer helped craft Clinton's victory in California, putting together her years of experience in the organization of campaigns with a creative message that responded to voters' gut feelings.

Now, at the 1996 convention, Rosenberg and Fischer were well positioned within the centrist wing of the Democratic Party. They shared the authority that came from proven expertise in Clinton's first campaign; both had a reputation for looking ahead for the party's next big opportunity. It didn't take long for the two young strategists to see how Randlett and Doerr might help them.

Rosenberg and Randlett were longtime ideological comrades, if frequently competitive. Neither man knew how to yield an argument gracefully, and they could make each other bristle. Fischer and Randlett couldn't always agree on politics, but they teased each other easily, and laughed together over beers.

At the convention the three were working as a team. As he introduced Doerr to key Democrats, Rosenberg realized how important the venture capitalist was going to be. Rosenberg was already working with a group of New Democrats in Congress through his PAC, the New Democrat Network, and he understood the importance of developing the right connections between politicians and the high-tech industry. "Before Doerr, there was no there there," Rosenberg said.

"Where did you go when you wanted to talk with Silicon Valley? But everyone could see this was the real thing."

Doerr had a statesmanlike aura: he didn't represent a single company but loomed over the entire Valley with unquestioned authority. As a political neophyte, he carried no partisan baggage; he had been a Republican and had given money to Democrats, but he had no party loyalties and he owed no political favors. Through his position at Kleiner Perkins, his network was huge, his influence unmatched, his credibility golden. *And* he was rich. Fischer saw immediately that Doerr was the figure they needed to forge an alliance between high tech and the Democrats. "I could tell right away this was gonna be the guy," she said. "I mean, John was intense. He was focused like a laser beam. He was listening to each and every word, and to the punctuation."

Randlett teased Fischer for taking an "un-Democratic" interest in a multimillionaire businessman. But Fischer was generally less interested in ideology than in winning, and she badly wanted Doerr on board with her in California. "John Doerr never says he's gonna do something he doesn't do," she explained. "He is *the* guy. I've learned that in politics you cling to rich donors, great spokespeople, and people who get shit done. Doerr is all three."

To get Doerr behind the Clinton campaign in California, however, the Democrats were going to have to give on the only political issue that mattered to Silicon Valley. Fischer began lobbying the White House, and veteran Democrats like Larry Stone stepped up their pressure on Clinton. "I pestered him every time he came out," Stone said. Doerr, meanwhile, kept steamrollering ahead with the NO ON 211 campaign, determined to win with or without Clinton's support—though the venture capitalist made it clear that he wanted an alliance. "Doerr was an organizer," said Fischer, admiringly. "He made things happen. He never overpromised, he did what he said he'd do, and he did it really well."

By the end of the summer, Randlett was forging ahead. He was getting help approaching tech executives from Elizabeth Greer, a former DLC staffer who had been put in charge of serving as a liaison to Silicon Valley for the Clinton-Gore campaign. A thin blond political professional with years of experience working in Washington, most recently for Hillary Clinton, Greer was an unbelievably competent organizer. Businesslike and discreet, she wore pale-pink nail polish and pastel twinsets, and kept her jokes to herself. Greer was as smart as a woman could be in politics without threatening men, who tended to treat her as if she were some kind of executive secretary. This was a persona that Greer herself seemed comfortable with; she was hardworking and conscientious, but not particularly ambitious. She got on well with Randlett, letting him take the lead in organizing, which was easy to do, as few others in the Democratic Party even knew what was happening in the Valley.

By August, Randlett had heard that the President was willing to switch his position and oppose Proposition 211. Investment banker Sandy Robertson, as a major Democratic fund-raiser and Clinton backer, met privately with the President to warn him that the wrong stance on Proposition 211 would lose him Silicon Valley supporters. When the candidate showed up for a fund-raising dinner at the home of fashion designer Suzy Tompkins in San Francisco, Brook Byers, who had paid $50,000 to sit at Clinton's table, said the same, then extracted a promise from the President to oppose 211. A few weeks later, in a meeting with high-tech executives at a Silicon Valley middle school, Clinton made his commitment public. Proposition 211, the President said, "would be highly disruptive to investment in new companies throughout the country. I don't think it's good for the economy."

When Randlett called to tell me the news, he sounded ecstatic. "We flipped him!" he yelled. I could hear Greer, in the background, cheering.

The next major press event was a conference call to the White House on behalf of seventy-five of the Valley's leading executives, who phoned to formally endorse Clinton and Gore. It marked a turning point in Clinton's attempts to identify himself and his party with a pro-business, New Democrat agenda. As the *San Jose Mercury News* put it, "The endorsements said to other industrial leaders: This guy is OK for business. In fact, he's tuned in to the most forward-looking sector of American business."

The list of endorsers included such luminaries as Steve Jobs, then at Pixar; Bill Joy and John Gage of Sun Microsystems; the CEOs of Palm Computing, Xerox, Sybase, E-Loan, and Adobe; and even Republicans like John Young, the former CEO of Hewlett-Packard, and Ed McCracken of Silicon Graphics. John Doerr, who was still identifying himself to journalists, somewhat disingenuously, as a Republican, led the conference call. "This administration really gets it," Doerr told Clinton and Gore. The President returned the compliment, pouring out his appreciation. "You don't even have any idea of the kind of appeal that your voice has to Americans all over this country, who see you as our leaders in the march to the future," Clinton said to the venture capitalist and the assembled CEOs.

Doerr had become, Randlett knew, the key to the next stage of the Valley's political involvement. "We branded him," Randlett concluded. "Now, I didn't make him who he is—that's an important and very sublime distinction. But starting with taking John to the convention, having him be the point person with Clinton, that was a very detailed and methodical process of branding him as *the* leader in Silicon Valley. Somebody had to be the answer to the question Who do we call in Silicon Valley? And John allowed it to be him."

As if to demonstrate a final lesson to his students about win-win back-scratching, Randlett set up a cozy Sunnyvale dinner for Clinton, Doerr, Regis McKenna, Brook Byers, and seven other high-tech leaders—an event that broadcast Silicon Valley's new image as a powerbroker at the same time that it netted a cool half million dollars for the Democrats' campaign.

On November 5, 1996, Proposition 211 was soundly defeated. The $40 million raised by Silicon Valley to fight it broke all the records for money spent on a single ballot-initiative campaign. And Bill Clinton was elected President, winning 56 percent of the vote in Santa Clara County—more than any Democratic presidential candidate ever had.

In the months following the election, Wade Randlett and John Doerr hammered out a strategy for cementing the Valley's new role in Washington. "Very methodically, one person at a time, one office at a time, we built up a network of people supportive of our broad philosophy," Randlett said.

Randlett kept pushing Doerr forward into his new role. The hyperactive financier started popping up at political gatherings, giving interviews to reporters, meeting with legislators, and chatting up committee chairs, usually with Randlett at his side. Doerr's public style was a little brusque at first—he'd rush past politicians with an impatient nod, or tap his fingers anxiously while they spoke—but he soon learned to smile automatically as he shook hands, and to say "That's a very good question" when answering a dumb one for the fortieth time. Doerr described his teacher in phrases that would have sounded curt were they not the highest form of praise in Silicon Valley. "Wade's very efficient," the venture capitalist said approvingly. "He does the job well, he knows everyone. He makes things happen."

Randlett was the kind of man who always had to be making something happen. The election should have been an immense triumph for him, both personally and politically. He'd pushed the formerly apathetic high-tech industry onto the national political stage, he'd won a round for the centrist, New Democrat ideals he cherished, and he'd expanded his own public profile by about a thousand percent. Now Randlett talked daily with the best-known venture capitalist in the world, and he got to drop in on whichever high-tech businesses he felt like chatting with. "Let's see," he said to me once, gleefully, when I stopped by his house in San Francisco to catch a ride down to Palo Alto. "I'm trying to decide who to mooch off—sushi at WebTV or Thai pizza at Kleiner Perkins. I should just get them to fax me the lunch menus before I drive down to the Valley." Randlett was clearly happy: his face glowed, and he looked fit and energetic, with a spring to his step. But he wasn't satisfied: success only made him want to hustle harder.

It was an attitude that John Doerr could respect. Randlett and Doerr kept talking over their vision for helping Silicon Valley to become as powerful politically as it was economically. At the core of their plan was the concept that they referred to as "New Economy." It was a term that had already been floated in the industry press, and among some cutting-edge economists studying the shifts brought about by information technologies, but Randlett and Doerr saw it as a political slogan as well. "New Economy," to them, was a kind of shorthand for a hyper-optimistic, capsule version of the Silicon Valley success story that also neatly illustrated the economic thinking of the New Democrats. "It's not about any one bullet point but about a set of attitudes," Randlett explained.

In a van together, heading for the airport one afternoon, Randlett and Doerr had sketched it out. "We were playing a word game, and we kept tossing out ideas," Randlett said. "Old is wages, new is equity; old is job training, new is lifelong learning; old is job security, new is risk-taking and entrepreneurship. Like that."

The New Economy was a buzzword, Randlett believed, just waiting to take off and lift his entire coalition higher. And all that was needed to turn it into a national phenomenon was some well-developed advertising—an infomercial to explain the political and economic miracle that everyone wanted to hear about. Randlett decided to launch with a splash. A dozen of his brightest Silicon Valley stars, led by John Doerr, would fly to Washington to meet with the vice president, with New Democrats, and with a host of Beltway bigshots on the day before the inauguration. Randlett and Doerr would debut their presentation about the New Economy, appropriately, at the very beginning of a new Clinton-Gore term.

Randlett's dress rehearsal took place the day before he flew his group to Washington, at a DLC conference for California legislators in Sacramento. It felt like a small-town event; the night before, we'd all sat around the gas-jet hearth of an expensive, nominally Italian, restaurant in a strip mall, trading business cards. Doerr and Randlett were off in a corner together, discussing strategy; a gaggle of lobbyists and legislators were mingling and drinking. Ted Roth, a lobbyist representing the pharmaceutical industry, presented me to Tina Nova, the CEO of a start-up biotech firm from San Diego. Nova, a petite, pretty woman, winked at me as her name was formally intoned—"*Dok*-tor No-va"— then bounced across the room to greet the next group of eight white men in suits. One of them, Morley Winograd, a strategist who worked with the DLC and ran the Institute for the New California, came over and introduced himself.

I was always hearing from New Democrats and Valley CEOs how much the digital revolution was changing California. Forty percent of the state's exports, they never tired of saying, now came from the high-tech sector, and tech was changing the way all Californians did business. Winograd and two colleagues had just come out with a study that put a political spin on the economic facts. This study identified "wired workers" as the key to winning California—and eventually the nation—over to New Democrat principles.

Winograd's analysis relied on loose and somewhat questionable categories. He defined "wired workers," for example, by "how often they use computers on the job . . . the extent to which they work with others to decide the best way to solve problems, and the extent to which they prefer to work in unstructured environments and as part of a team." Offhand, I could think of a number of people who fit Winograd's profile and had nothing to do with the "wired workers" he wanted to tap into. The tattooed twenty-year-old employees at my neighborhood pizza place, for example, enjoyed an "unstructured environment" that drove me nuts with its loud thrash rock; they certainly preferred to work as part of a team, probably so that they could keep flirting with one another while sprinkling on extra cheese; and they did use a computer to keep track of their deliveries. I was dubious about their deep interest in the New Democrat trade and tax agenda.

But Winograd's study had attracted attention with its insights about the confluence of demographics and politics in California. "The New Deal coalition that dominated American politics for the past 50 years was based on two principles," Winograd had written. "The first was a principle of government: the large industrial organizations that controlled our economy had to be made to operate in the public interest. The second was a principle of politics: People who worked in factories and whose sole source of income was what they earned in wages were more likely than others to support policies that limited what big business could do. [Thus] blue-collar workers became the largest single faction within the New Deal Coalition. The coalition that will dominate American politics for the next 50 years will be built upon an entirely different set of workers who have radically different ideas about government. These 'wired workers' already make up more than half of California's workforce, and their number grows every day."

After polling eight hundred adults, Winograd had further broken the electorate in California down into "contented" and "disgruntled" workers. Contented wired workers, 38 percent of the state's workforce, made up 23 percent of its electorate, according to Winograd. "Wired workers are highly optimistic," he wrote of them. "This optimism arises at least in part from their work experience. . . . They have little use for people who spend their days blaming others for the problems that exist." Contented traditional workers, by contrast, made up only 19 percent of the workforce and 12 percent of the electorate; they were "classic Industrial Age employees." Thirty percent of the workforce (18 percent of the electorate) were disgruntled traditional workers. "They want to be part of the new economy and feel trapped in the old one," Winograd wrote. "Not to put too fine a point on it, they are mad as hell about being left out." All this added up, he argued, to a major shift in political attitudes.

Winograd was a short, balding, friendly man, and one of the sharpest people at the dinner. "Frankly, wired workers have no great loyalty to any party," he told me. "But they're optimistic about the future, and if we can capitalize on that, we can bring them into the Democratic fold." I nodded. Across the Exposition Highway at the Motel 6 — thirty-six dollars a night, located conveniently next to a chain steakhouse — microchips from Silicon Valley might power the cash register, but that didn't make the high-school graduates at the front desk experts in embedded computing. Nor, I suspected, did it make them wildly optimistic about their personal economic futures. "Education," said Winograd, smiling at me as we took our seats and the waiters arrived with wine. "Lifelong education, that's the key."

The next morning, I strolled through downtown and into a rented auditorium of soul-numbing banality. Tina Nova was seated next to me, whispering asides and riffling through her purse. At the front of the room, Doerr fidgeted on a makeshift dais, flanked by Randlett, sharp in his double-breasted navy suit. In less than twelve hours they'd be in the White House with Al Gore, and they would need to have their presentation polished.

As we waited for the legislators to seat themselves, I tried to determine what was at stake for Doerr. His public persona wasn't about vanity or ego: his entire career had shown him to be an impressively calculating strategic thinker. Doerr had surveyed the future of the exponentially growing high-tech industry, and had realized that at some point very soon it was going to intersect with an entire universe of government policies and regulations—that what Wade Randlett termed the "Wild West" of the Valley would soon meet the law. When that time came, I thought, Doerr wanted to be the person who represented the Valley to the powers that be in Washington; he wanted to ensure that he had the brand recognition to speak to Washington on behalf of the industry's interests. Doerr wanted to establish his authority now—instead of letting Bill Gates, for example, be the spokesman for the entire high-tech industry, or instead of allowing a hundred parochial industry lobbyists to define the issues. This way, he could make sure that the Kleiner Perkins view of the world, with the firm and *keiretsu*'s interests at the heart of it, prevailed.

At warp speed, biting his lips and pulling at his hair, Doerr proclaimed the end of the industrial age and the dawning of the New Economy. The revolution in technology, Doerr said, pointing to some pie charts projected from his laptop, was creating "incredible opportunity and outrageous prosperity" for those who understood its principles. He rattled off some figures about growth and returns and the number of households that had computers.

This New Economy, Doerr said, was behind the current boom in California and the coming age of global prosperity. It was led by innovators, entrepreneurs, and risk-takers; encouraged by incentives; managed by decentralized teams wired in networks; and regulated best by the market alone. Its advocates believed in education, the work ethic, and strict meritocracy, but they were tolerant and globally aware. With their stock options and sixty-hour weeks, they were too forward-looking for class warfare: the workers of the New Economy didn't need unions. Too practical for partisan politics, these results-oriented young engineers could debug, recode, and miniaturize government until it ran as efficiently as their machines. "The New Economy isn't just about high-tech products," Doerr declared. "It's about the politics of education, constant innovation, job creation, and unlimited growth."

At its fuzziest, Doerr's presentation resembled the sort of grandiose Tofflerian Third Wave cyberbabble promoted by Newt Gingrich. In a less hysterical vein, it seemed disappointingly commonplace: standard business-school ideas about entrepreneurship, incentives, and teamwork presented, complete with dorky graphics, as breakthrough insights of the twenty-first century.

But the speech's effect on the audience was gratifying. As Randlett guided his delegation out to catch their plane, legislators flocked to the prophets of the future. "Mr. Doerr," said a pale, eager woman with a briefcase. "We have an extra $55 million in appropriations for education. How do you think we should use it?" A hearty man with a Mormon haircut clapped Doerr on the back. "I'd vote for you!" he boomed. A few lobbyists from suddenly unfashionable companies like Texaco and Union Pacific stood forlornly by the coffee urn. Randlett was crowing. "OK," he said, checking his watch. "This is it. It's the New Economy, stupid."

As they headed for Washington and the inauguration of Bill Clinton, Doerr and Randlett had reason to feel satisfied with their work. Thanks to Proposition 211, Silicon Valley had been politicized, and now, with the idea of the New Economy, it had a marketable concept that could take that political consciousness to the next stage. "We are fucking *happening*," Randlett said to Doerr, sounding giddy. He closed his eyes for a brief nap.

CHAPTER three

The weather was bitterly cold and the staff hysterical on the day before Clinton's second inauguration. Vice President Al Gore was scheduled to sit down and schmooze for a while with a dozen tech leaders, including Doerr, Tina Nova, Ted Roth, Paul Lippe, Scott Cook of Intuit, Chuck Geschke of Adobe, Kim Polese of Marimba, David Singer of HeartPort, Ken Coleman of Silicon Graphics, venture capitalist and New Democrat fund-raiser Chris Gabrieli, Mark Simon of Robertson Stephens, and Bill Hambrecht, the chairman of Hambrecht & Quist. The combined wattage of this group would have been dazzling in the Valley; in Washington, most of the names drew a polite blank from protocol officers and White House insiders alike. Yet somehow, on the busiest day imaginable, while the chairmen of every state Clinton-Gore committee were wrestling with major party donors and elected officials for tickets to public events, Randlett's technology delegation managed to score more than an hour in private with Gore.

Tim Newell, the senior adviser to the White House chief of staff, remained calm. A husky, thirty-two-year-old Vermonter with an easygoing manner that belied his political shrewdness, Newell had invested heavily in this meeting, and exuded his confidence in it to his partners from the Valley. "All set," he'd told Randlett that morning by phone. "Bring 'em in."

Newell was a well-connected man. While on staff with Congressman Norman Mineta, he had met and married Beth Inadomi, a wry lawyer with a background at NASA who worked on Capitol Hill. (Inadomi soon went to work for Podesta Associates, the high-powered lobbying firm run by Tony and John Podesta, both consummate Democratic insiders with high-tech clients.) Newell had then spent four years at the White House Office of Science and Technology Policy, and become close to Greg Simon and others in the vice president's office. He took time out to work on campaigns, where he thrived. Newell was big and friendly, with a jock's hearty handshake. His friends tended to have fluid career paths, albeit within a very narrow world: they moved easily from staff positions on the Hill to private law firms on K Street; from the Old Executive Office Building to New Hampshire campaign headquarters. "We knew a lot of folks" is how Newell described his life in Washington.

When they first met in 1996, Newell and Randlett had recognized in each other a passion for big-picture politics. Like Randlett, Newell had ambitions that went far beyond the successful execution of others' ideas: "message" was what he cared about. And Newell, like Randlett, was convinced that the political message coming from Silicon Valley was vitally important for the White House to embrace now—as it would be for Al Gore, running for President, in 2000. "Politics is about attaching yourself to symbols," Newell said. "And what you have to understand is the symbolic importance of the [high-tech] industry. It represents the American Dream. When you can walk in and say here's a thirty-year-old CEO worth $50 million, that's what everyone wants their kids to be."

During the 1996 campaign, Newell had spent, according to Randlett, "an extraordinary amount of time and energy pursuing entrepreneurial new politics," stumping, schmoozing, and bonding with a range of important geeks. After the elections, Randlett had brought Newell out to California and introduced him around in a series of meetings at the Kleiner Perkins office. Doerr was immediately impressed by the sharp young White House aide, as was Sandy Robertson of Robertson Stephens. Neither man had an immediate, specific agenda, but both knew that high tech's relationship with politics was only going to become more important as the industry grew. Both Doerr and Robertson saw Newell as one of the individuals who could be a key link in extending their *keiretsu* to Washington.

But, back at the White House, Newell's networking threatened his superiors at the Office of Science and Technology Policy, and he was transferred out abruptly. "Tim was doing politics the way we respected and could identify with," Randlett said. "So when he got fired for it, there was nothing more important for us to do than put a great big footprint on his boss's desk." Randlett, telling Doerr that "no matter how much we need to spend of our political capital to get Newell where he can be useful, it's worth it," had vowed to buttonhole every "power-fucker" he could reach in the White House. "Don't let this happen," Randlett warned his contacts. "There aren't enough people who understand us to make it work, and we need this guy there." Then Doerr, from the ski slopes in Aspen, where he was vacationing, called the vice president directly and asked, respectfully but firmly, that Newell be re-hired and reassigned. Newell was transferred to the Office of the Vice President, where he advocated tirelessly for the importance of Silicon Valley to the new administration.

For a month before the inauguration, Newell had been consulting several times daily with Randlett to get the mix of high-technology figures he thought would be appropriate for this first get-together with the vice president. "Gore was already deeply committed to their issues, intellectually interested in the technology, and he got it that this was a political constituency, not a trade group," Newell said. "He took the executives very seriously. I believed they were natural allies, and once we got them in the room together they'd click."

Newell's confidence in Al Gore's ability to serve as the point person for high tech's involvement with the administration was not misplaced. The vice president was a genuine nerd, with a geek reputation running back to his days as a futurist "Atari Democrat" in the House. Long before computers were comprehensible, let alone sexy, the poker-faced Gore had struggled to explain artificial intelligence and fiber-optic networks to his bow-tied, sleepy colleagues. In the Senate, Gore took time out from his environmental crusading to secure federal support for the Internet. Along the way, he coined (or at least lifted from a speechwriter) the cliché "information superhighway."

As geek veep, Gore had spent his first term poking into every hot issue facing the administration on the cyberfrontier: e-commerce, computers in schools, the next-generation Internet, the Human Genome Project, encryption, the R&D budget, Net "decency," FDA reform, bioethics, intellectual property rights, medical technologies, information-technology training, telecommunications policy, and public-service obligations for digital-TV broadcasters. Ahead of virtually every other national politician, he had succeeded in identifying himself with the information revolution and the New Economy. "Politics is like surfing," Randlett commented to me once, gloating about Gore's far-sightedness. "You don't make the waves, you just look around and see what you can ride to shore. Al Gore has grabbed that wave, ridden it in, and is already on the sand with a pillow getting a tan."

But as he prepared for the inaugural weekend, Randlett admitted to some nervousness. "I remember the first time I brought some CEOs to Washington," he told me anxiously. "We'd sit in these meetings and you could just see the congressmen going, 'My *God*, these guys are green.' " Paul Lippe had tried to reassure him. "We weren't quite as much the babes in the wilderness as we were being presented," Lippe pointed out. "I mean, Sandy Robertson's a huge Democrat, John [Doerr] worked for Wirth, and I know people in Washington."

Lippe knew that the real objective of the trip was to establish rela-tionships early that would bear fruit over the medium and long term; as far as he was concerned, getting Silicon Valley executives conversant with the mores and customs of Washington, and identified with New Democrats, was the most important thing. But he admitted to a tiny bit of anxiety, too. "It was like a trip to another world for most of our group," he told me later. "And we really wanted it to go well."

Randlett had prepared a memo for the group in which he cautioned them to behave, tried to keep them "on message," and laid out his polit-ical objectives. "While we all have *agenda items*, which we will pursue to varying degrees during the next year, the inaugural is not the appropri-ate time to press our agenda," he wrote. "The *reason* for this trip is to put a human face on the known fact that Silicon Valley supported the President and the Vice President during the 1996 campaign. The *mes-sage* for the trip is that this group of Clinton-Gore supporters would like to serve as the key political link between Silicon Valley and the Ad-ministration."

It was well past midnight on January 18 when Tina Nova called me from her hotel in Washington to report on the visit with Gore. She'd told me about her background earlier: the granddaughter of Greek im-migrant farmers, Nova had grown up in a small Central Valley town where she earned a reputation as a troublemaker. "I remember the guidance counselor told me I'd never amount to anything, because I failed home economics and said I didn't care," she recalled. Stubbornly, Nova had persisted through the state university system and medical school, developing a distinguished research career in biochemistry, then a string of biotechnology ventures financed by Brook Byers of Kleiner Perkins. Now the CEO of Nanogen, a San Diego start-up she'd launched to develop diagnostic products combining human genetic material with silicon chips, the woman was a certified success. But Nova, with her unruly hair and seditious grin, retained the look of someone who might snap her gum any moment.

Nova, whose grandparents had kept a shrine to FDR in their kitchen, seemed less than a complete convert to her new class position; she felt uncomfortable identifying entirely with the New Democrats' slide away from liberalism. "Sure, I'm much more conservative now," I remembered her telling me with a shrug in Sacramento. "Making money changes you." She'd laughed, then added, "But I still get considered a screaming radical. I'm a scientist in a male field, a CEO in a male industry, and I have a picture of Hillary Clinton in my office." She'd adjusted her leopard-print silk scarf. "It drives the guys totally crazy."

Despite Nova's relative lack of political experience — limited, essentially, to her friendship with former California governor Jerry Brown, whom she described as "really smart but really out there" — I didn't take her for a naïf. "I used to be idealistic, and I thought politics would be like chemistry, where hard work and brains are what count," Nova explained. "Then you walk into a meeting, and there's Mr. No Ethics up front in the best seat, and gee, how did he get there? I learned that if you don't write checks you can't play the game."

But now Nova was telling me something different. "Al Gore blew me away," she said. "What a day." She launched into her narrative. "OK, so around six I meet the guys and we walk over to the West Wing. We go past security. It is so cool. The place is a little overdone, maybe, from the interior-decorating point of view, but hey" — she laughed — "it's the White House.

"We get ushered into this room, and there's this awesome little fireplace. It's like a little house in there — fireplace, pictures, flowers, a big dining-room table — and when we come in, everyone stands up." She sounded amazed. "We're like, 'Hi, we're the future and we're here to visit you.'

"And then Clinton walks in, and I'm like, OK, I can die happy now. Then the vice president shakes everyone's hand, and before I know it we're talking." Nova, who had clearly spent a lot of time giving presentations to the science-impaired, sounded genuinely impressed. "Gore was on top of everything we talked about," she said. "From Java programming to the use of genetic material for diagnostics." She gave a delighted laugh. "Plus, the guy is a hunk."

I'd hear, later, from other members of the delegation how Gore had "wowed" the techies with his obvious and genuine interest in the details of their businesses. "This was in the days when the only way most politicians could relate to us was to say, 'Oh, computers, my daughter has a computer,' " Paul Lippe said. "But Gore was right there with us, nerding out." And when the vice president turned to Kim Polese and asked her a programming question, John Doerr recalled, "That did it for me." Another member of the delegation summed up the mood: "The mutual-admiration society was so overwhelming it was like 'love-bombing' à la Sun Myung Moon."

But I also knew, from Randlett and Newell, how carefully scripted the meeting had been. As Randlett's memo to the delegation had explained, with fervent capital letters underscoring Randlett's seriousness, "This is NOT the appropriate time to discuss specific policy issues. This is an opportunity to EXPRESS OUR SUPPORT for the White House, and to express our interest in being the conduit for the administration's relations with the technology sector." Or, as Newell put it more mildly, "It takes time and effort to build relationships."

Bill Clinton's inaugural address was at least as gratifying to the geeks as their private White House meetings had been. Using rhetoric as sweeping as anything coming from the Valley, Clinton proclaimed the shift from an industrial to an information economy the most important dynamic affecting American and world society—now and forever. His voice husky and sincere, the President intoned, "At the dawn of the twenty-first century, a free people must choose to shape the forces of the Information Age and the global society to unleash the limitless potential of all our people and form a more perfect union." He hailed the invention of the microchip and the personal computer as politically significant events, claiming that the Internet, personal computers, knowledge of the human genome, and microchips would revolutionize education, unleash unheard-of prosperity, and decentralize knowledge. And, echoing Gore's ideas about "reinventing government," he said that advances in technology would reduce the role of central government and empower people to do more on their own. "Government is not the problem," Clinton declared in his best centrist, Third Way form. "But neither is it the solution." It was an impressive display of what the Valley liked to call "cross-marketing." The speech, the *Los Angeles Times* noted the next day, was "an unparalleled affirmation of [Silicon Valley's] world view," and an attempt to claim the power of the information economy for Clinton's centrist ideological allies in the DLC.

To a satisfied John Doerr, Clinton's address was notable not only for its over-the-top cheerleading for technology; he sounded thrilled that the President had reinforced the Valley's view of government in general. "We want less government, but we want it to be more effective," Doerr explained. To him, Clinton's endorsement of this particular idea about the role of government meant, by extension, that Clinton was rejecting the classic Old Democrat view in favor of aligning himself with New Economy, New Democrat principles.

In the next year, as issues of interest to the high-tech community appeared on the national agenda, it would be striking how many of them—expanding visas for foreign workers, creating more charter schools, deregulating the Internet—would pit Silicon Valley directly against Old Democrat constituencies. Right now, as he surveyed the political landscape, Doerr had reason to be optimistic about the Valley's ability to prevail.

In Washington, the political landscape Randlett was interested in exploring included far more than the White House. His schedule for the delegation extended through a series of meetings that Simon Rosenberg had arranged with his friends in Congress, with the DLC, and in the Washington world of lobbyists and policymakers.

In 1996, Rosenberg had left the DLC to take charge of a new PAC, the New Democrat Network, a political enterprise that self-consciously modeled itself on Newt Gingrich's GOPAC. Before the NDN was born, in 1996, the DLC, as a tax-exempt organization, had been able to generate ideas on policy but not cash. Rosenberg knew it was important to tap supporters of the DLC for contributions that could be used directly to elect pro-business, centrist candidates: he expected to raise $1.5 million for the 1997–1998 election cycle. At the same time, Rosenberg sought to make NDN "a mini-campaign operation, not just a pass-through PAC," by holding conferences for its members, developing talking points and policy papers for them, and helping with campaign publicity.

Rosenberg, who had been involved in both of Clinton's campaigns, was more loyal to New Democrat ideals than to Bill Clinton himself. He was realistic about the progress that any one man—even a leader as charismatic as Clinton—could make in changing an entire party, and he'd seen how Clinton, in his first term, had been forced to compromise with Old Democrats on the Hill. Rosenberg believed that a New Democrat president needed a strong cadre of New Democrats in Congress to keep him from backsliding into the pro-union, pro-liberal policies traditionally favored by the party.

With an eye toward changing the balance of power in Congress, Rosenberg intended to work to create a coherent political grouping and voting bloc among his sixty-three House New Democrats—not just to best Republicans but in order to keep pushing the Democratic Party toward the center. Rosenberg had looked carefully at shifts in the electorate, and had decided that the moment favored his centrist politics. "Under Clinton, there's been a wild economic expansion, and a net loss of union jobs," he said. "Over time this demographic works in our favor, if we can create a party responsive to new constituencies."

Chaired by Senators Joe Lieberman and John Breaux, leaders of the DLC, the New Democrat Network had installed at the head of its board Chris Gabrieli, the Boston-based venture capitalist. (Lieberman, a conservative pro-business senator, would later, as Al Gore's running mate in the 2000 campaign, be a strong supporter of Silicon Valley.) Gabrieli and Rosenberg had decided that the NDN should focus on building relationships with high tech, which represented a new, affluent, relatively unaffiliated and untapped business sector. Rosenberg thought that with a strong enough base in business, he could wrench power in his own party away from the Old Democrats, who voted along the ideological lines of the labor unions, which were their biggest financial supporters.

Silicon Valley, Rosenberg believed, could be key to the NDN's fund-raising efforts and visibility, and he was thrilled to be showing Randlett's delegation around town. Behind the scenes, he had already helped Newell organize the White House meetings, and he was determined to make sure that the delegation got plugged in to Capitol Hill as well. "I put an enormous amount of time into telling the people in Washington about the importance of this sector," Rosenberg said. "I'd say, 'Listen, if we're going to be the majority party of the next century, we need Silicon Valley support.'"

Rosenberg was a tireless go-between: he often had to spell out the basics of Washington life for the high-tech executives. "Note," he wrote in a memo to Randlett's delegation, explaining what would have been obvious to executives from any other industry. "John Kerry is the head of the Democratic Senatorial Campaign Committee (DSCC) and is thus part of the Senate Democratic leadership."

At the inaugural festivities, over dinners and in private meetings, Rosenberg made his matches. New Democrats who'd been cued by Rosenberg to the importance of Silicon Valley—among them, Senate Democratic leader Tom Daschle, Senators Joe Lieberman and Bob Kerry, House Representatives Cal Dooley, Tim Roemer, and Vic Fazio —presented themselves as students of the New Economy. Bob Squier, the venerable Democratic media guru, shook their hands and showed them around his hip, black-walled offices. And Dianne Feinstein, the senator from California, put aside her Old Democrat liberal principles long enough to host an intimate dinner for the group at her Capitol Hill town house.

By the end, Rosenberg was convinced that Silicon Valley was "something that every forward-looking person in D.C. understands they have to learn about." John Doerr was talking about establishing "a new relationship with the political world." And Randlett was pleased enough to proclaim the two-day trip "the beginning of an era."

CHAPTER four

The thrill of courtship and the first kiss were all very well, but as the romance between Silicon Valley and Washington progressed, it became necessary to get closer. In the months following that first, January 1997 visit, Randlett continued to "wire the network" between his executives and Washington. So did Simon Rosenberg of the New Democrat Network, who had begun to bring his own delegations West. Jay Rouse, a partner at Bob Squier's political consulting firm, took one of those early trips out to meet with John Doerr, Brook Byers, Jerry Yang, and other stars of the high-tech world. "You had the sense of being on the edge of something brand-new," Rouse said. A thoughtful man steeped in the nuances of politics, Rouse remembered feeling "as if you were in Detroit at the beginning of the automobile age. Everything Internet hadn't become mainstream yet—it was almost a subculture, yet you knew this was going to take off."

More than almost any other politician, Al Gore was busily mining that subculture for ideas. The vice president, Randlett bragged, had "picked up the idea of the New Economy and started to use it verbatim; now he takes it on the road to people he's gonna need votes from in three years. Last year it wasn't even a term people used, and now it's gone, in Web time, from nonexistent to everywhere. It works, we're ahead of the curve."

Tim Newell agreed. "By talking up the New Economy, Gore's got a chance to own the future," he explained. "Take a mid-level manager who's afraid and threatened by the New Economy. Then ask him what he wants for his kids. It's computers. It's the future. He wants tech because he has a sense that's how his kids can get ahead."

Newell's logic was supported by Ed Kilgore, political director at the DLC's think tank, the Progressive Policy Institute, who had just shown Newell the results of a new poll by presidential pollster Mark Penn indicating that Gore's New Economy speeches were right on target.

"There's a growing segment of the electorate that views technological change as positive, and younger voters see themselves benefiting from it," Kilgore said. Gore, he noted, had seized on images that allowed Democrats, often skeptically viewed as defending entrenched interests, to "appear to welcome and shape rapid change." And though Kilgore acknowledged that an all-new economic future "is obviously a little threatening," he thought Gore could build his image—and win in 2000—by projecting a message of "safe change."

Of course, before Gore even got to the voters, he'd have to convince Silicon Valley that he backed the industry's much more rapid view of change. And to do so few things were more helpful to Gore than establishing his friendship with the Mayor Daley of the Valley, John Doerr. Within the context of the Internet and the Silicon Valley boom, Doerr's friendship with Al Gore did not go unnoticed by the press: effusive stories hailed it as a partnership for the twenty-first century.

Inside the White House, Newell and a small but influential group of staff and advisers plotted together with Wade Randlett and Simon Rosenberg. They set up a series of monthly meetings dubbed the "Gore-Tech" sessions, in which high-profile executives from the hottest new companies—many of them, like Kim Polese of Marimba, Jerry Yang of Yahoo!, and Marc Andreessen of Netscape, young protégés of John Doerr's—would sit down with Gore to discuss policy and talk about the New Economy. "Younger people are more willing to work," Polese had explained to me, discussing the Gore-Tech guest list. "We're not jaded, we have a fresh perspective."

In the first few months of 1997, the Gore-Tech network kept growing—as did the vice president's increasing appropriation of high-tech language and ideology to burnish his own political image. Don Gips, Gore's chief domestic-policy adviser, sounded delighted. "He's been able to kind of take the metaphor of Silicon Valley and extend it across the country," Gips said.

The process had been thought through by key proponents of the New Economy inside the White House, who saw the changes taking place in Silicon Valley as just one piece of the administration's overall economic policy. "Our high-level strategy was to balance the budget, open up foreign markets, invest in things like education, training, and R&D, and provide people with the tools they need to make most of these opportunities," Tom Kalil of the National Economic Council explained. "That's how the revolution in information technologies will pay off." Kalil was a likable, unpretentious advocate of Gore's New Economy approach and one of the White House's most serious tech thinkers. Tall and slightly stooped, with deeply shadowed eyes, Kalil always seemed slightly sleep-deprived—a look that made him blend in equally well among White House staffers and start-up entrepreneurs. "The unique contribution the vice president has made is that he's been thinking about these issues for a long time," Kalil said. "Over twenty years before it was clear to most people in government and industry that, for example, the Internet was going to be a big deal."

John Podesta, President Clinton's deputy chief of staff and a lifelong political dealmaker, pointed as well to Gore's skill in urging "an essentially deregulatory approach" to business, through his work on Food and Drug Administration reform, e-commerce, and other "reinventing government" initiatives. "When he talks to the Gore-Tech people, the message is: this administration gets it," Podesta said. Small and sharp-featured, with a reputation for honesty and ruthlessness, Podesta acknowledged that the vice president's overtures to New Economy businesses still required some work. "I think what we need to do is keep [the message] fresh, broaden it," he said. "And really deal with the young entrepreneurs, the new kids on the block, who in a funny way are slightly distrustful of government but easily engaged by the challenges of public policy, and who can end up being lively partners with us."

Tim Newell summed up the change in White House attitudes. "In the last year, technology issues have moved to the front burner—both in terms of policy and of politics," he said. "Now there's a big competition to see who's going to be in charge of the relationship with high-tech business."

Republicans were less than thrilled about the lively partnership potential of Gore-Tech. "It seems to be a tight-knit group of folks the

White House sees, just about fifteen or twenty people, and Gore spends most of his time with that cadre," grumbled John Doerr's partner at Kleiner Perkins, the conservative Republican Floyd Kvamme. "Gore's positioning himself with a heavy Valley flavor, but not that many people here know what he's actually doing."

Kvamme had a point, but the number of people involved in Gore's network was growing. In Silicon Valley, Gore and an increasing number of New Democrat congressmen kept showing up for meet-and-greets, mastering a few phrases of geekspeak and holding earnest "issue forums" on the New Economy.

Wade Randlett was in the middle of it all. The California Technology Alliance had been quietly put to sleep after Proposition 211 was defeated, a victim of ego struggles among the CEOs who backed it, so he no longer had an institutional home. Yet he was talking, constantly, with key players in Washington and the Valley. He checked in by phone with Simon Rosenberg, keeping current on Hill politics; he schmoozed with Beth Inadomi and Tim Newell; he kept abreast of the White House gossip. Even Celia Fischer, who had moved to Los Angeles to become a screenwriter, was tapped; Randlett called her regularly for advice. I couldn't quite figure out where he was going, but he seemed more than confident.

He was definitely staying busy. Randlett tried to sound humble about his growing role as go-between linking up politicians and executives—a role that, however unofficial, was amassing him more power every day. "Look, these are people who should know each other," Randlett said. "Successful people, successful politicians. It's not about me. I give guidance and do decoding of the political message. I have, on occasion, dragged an executive out of the room to rescue the meeting before it got completely wrecked, but . . ." He shrugged. "In the old politics, I'd be a gatekeeper. This is the new politics, and my job is to create as many relationships as I can."

As the relationships between Silicon Valley and Washington grew, it became necessary to reinvent some of the issues that could bring them together.

Education reform had long been a defining issue for Gore, Clinton, and the New Democrats, whose education initiatives ranged from national testing to charter schools and putting technology in the classroom. In March 1996, Eric Schmidt of Novell and John Gage of Sun

Microsystems had developed a project called NetDay, and had convinced thousands of high-tech volunteers to go to their local elementary schools throughout California and pull wires into old classrooms. It was a dramatic metaphor for business partnership with the schools, however short-term, and it helped publicize some of Silicon Valley's most popular ideas on education.

Those ideas—about accountability, measurable standards, efficiency, and the importance of performance incentives for teachers— were remarkably similar to the ideas articulated by New Democrats. They centered around the notion that unions and government bureaucracy had crippled public schools, and that enlightened entrepreneurs could transform American education.

Kim Polese, at twenty-eight, was one of the entrepreneurs who exemplified, for New Democrats, the values that they wanted to see transferred to the educational system. With her long, curly blond hair and her backpack, Polese looked more like the Berkeley student she used to be than the millionaire businesswoman she had become. A driving force behind the Java programming language, Polese was generally cheerful: she tended to exude a somewhat unfocused enthusiasm for doing good works. "I want to be part of building a stronger country," she said. "Education is absolutely required for the twenty-first century."

John Doerr was of a similar mind, and had used his position to champion education reform, declaring it "the single most important task" for businessmen to undertake. He'd begun a venture fund, the New Schools Fund, to put money into the hands of educators and charter schools he deemed "innovators"; in a few months, he'd raised more than $5 million in $50,000 investments. "The quest for education reform will fail if it's left to the politicians," he said.

Doerr's understanding of education was fairly nuanced. Unlike many Valley executives, he admitted, for example, that "wiring the schools is not enough," that "there is no silver bullet for reforming the system," and that "many teachers are dedicated and caring and energetic." Still, the venture capitalist summed up his critique by asserting that, "while education is complicated, subtle, and demanding, it isn't rocket science." In Doerr's view, the biggest problems of American education were bureaucracy (especially teachers' unions), a lack of national testing and national standards, and a shortage of market-based "incentives" for teachers. "The New Economy's ability to achieve its full potential will be retarded if it doesn't have a continuous and voluminous supply of strong minds to feed off of," Doerr wrote in a manifesto published in the industry journal *The Red Herring*. And that, he argued, required schools that ran on the principles of Silicon Valley businesses. "We need accountability," he explained. "Testing. Choice. Competition. Leadership."

All this rhetoric was hard for me to take. My father, Matthew Miles, had spent his life researching educational change—and, in the process, observing the cycles of superficial, politically motivated "reform" efforts. "Wishful thinking and legislation have poor records as tools for social betterment," he had told the American Educational Research Association in 1992, in an address that summed up forty years of his experience. Offering detailed analysis of what he called the "social architecture" of schools, based on thousands of case studies, he pointed to one of the most common reasons for the failure of reform: "symbols over substance." For my father, as for most other professional educators, understanding "the core technology of schools, teaching and learning," was at the heart of all organizational as well as classroom innovation.

But the appeal of wishful thinking, of symbols, and of the quick fix remained powerful. In April 1997, Kim Polese, John Doerr, and Wade Randlett, for the Gore-Tech group, had come up with something they called Education Dashboard. It was a project that fit in seamlessly with Gore's ambitions to cast himself as the "reinventor" of the failing public schools, and embodied Doerr's faith in technology as a cure for troubled institutions. Using Dashboard, parents would log on to home computers or WebTV sets and automatically receive information about their children: classes, attendance, grades, homework assignments, and comments from teachers, as well as more general reports from the administration. No longer would parents have to talk to teachers to find out how their children were doing; in fact, they wouldn't even have to talk to their children.

The idea hit all the hype buttons of the day: it was "push" media that would deliver information automatically to consumers; it was "empowerment" of parents; it was "interactive." In short, Dashboard was the future.

In June 1997, with a demo of the program on her laptop, Polese flew to Tennessee with Randlett for the unveiling of Dashboard at Gore's annual Family Re-Union Conference. "[Dashboard] comes from a desire we have to improve our country," Polese told the assembled crowd of parents and educators, earnestly. "We realize that we have resources that can be put to good use. It's very exciting to use our programs in schools. It makes us feel good."

The symbolism of Gore's invitation to the techies was interesting, coming as it did at a moment when the overall image of the Internet had been anything but family-friendly. Electronic commerce had not yet leaped to the $40-billion-a-year level it would achieve by 1999; cyberspace still retained a noncommercial and slightly seedy aura, its unexplored dark zones the technological equivalent of the unconscious. Battles in Congress over the Communications Decency Act and alarmist news stories had suggested the potential of the Internet as a haven for pedophiles, pornographers, and terrorists. Gore's high-minded education-reform proposals, and his choice of Polese — a young woman of irreproachable Up with People wholesomeness — to present them, made the Internet seem suddenly less threatening.

A few educators grumbled nonetheless, scoffing at the idea that wiring could replace old-fashioned community involvement. Some sounded impatient with outsiders who had no experience with conditions in real schools, let alone any grasp of more than a century of attempts to reform American education. "I can't imagine a classroom teacher sitting down and every day writing a report on every student," June Million of the National Association of Elementary School Principals had told a local reporter. "Who's going to do the inputting?" Others wondered aloud who was going to pay for the project, and how poor, computer-less families would be able to participate.

But the glamour of Polese and, by association, the Internet, seemed to drown out most doubting voices. "Everyone [in Tennessee] wanted to get close to us," Randlett said. Although no software existed, and there were no plans for anyone in Polese's working group to actually write the code needed to develop it, Dashboard was a huge success. "It isn't important whether Education Dashboard ever lights up — what is important is the innovative thought it demonstrates," a glowing newspaper report said. "Polese's brainstorm is just an inkling of the many creative ways we are going to see technology used in the near future." In the best Silicon Valley style, it was the *concept* that mattered most, not anything as prosaic as a product: Dashboard was classic vaporware.

I heard all about the Family Re-Union Conference from Randlett and Polese when they got back to California. We were hanging out at Kleiner Perkins, waiting for an engineer to bring the software needed to reinstall a demo of Dashboard on Randlett's computer. The program

had a few bugs, Randlett explained sheepishly, or maybe it was something he'd done to the disk. Polese seemed as happy to be helping out
with the tech problem as she had been to boost Gore. "My lifelong view
of politics was always that it was a series of backroom deals that eliminate the chance of having an effect," she told me, as she fiddled with
the machine. Polese's visit to the White House with Randlett six
months ago had been her first contact with national politics. "But, quite
to the contrary, I've found that in fact if you have people who have a
fresh perspective and energy and resources, in terms of time or tech or
energy or —" She paused, apparently shy about mentioning money. "Or
whatever. And you have political leaders who want change, and technology is becoming increasingly important, and you combine all of that
with the philosophies behind entrepreneurism, and with relentless optimism, you can actually get something done." Polese took a breath and
smiled. Randlett smiled back at her. "I've been really pleasantly surprised," she said.

I drove home to San Francisco alone. As I passed through the
South of Market area, I could see markers of the kind of wealth that
would, within a few years, transform even my cruddy immigrant neighborhood into a place where houses started at half a million dollars.
There were the first tasteful, trendy restaurants, one or two stylishly re-
designed offices, a brand-new loft building. But in the spring of 1997,
the New Economy was still not as visible as the Old.

In fact, by the time I got home to the Mission, even the Old Economy—with its factory workers, civil-service employees, and small manufacturers—was less visible than the informal economy that shadowed
it, unofficial and sometimes illegal, but vibrant nonetheless. I passed
the storefront where a seamstress had set up shop; passed the men doing auto-body repair in a parking lot, passed the drug dealers. On my
block, a guy was sitting on a stoop with a pile of fresh *nopales* between
his legs, scraping the thorns off the cactus with a bowie knife. He
wheeled a Styrofoam cooler around on a little luggage cart all day, selling bags of cut-up *nopales* for a dollar. Like the hawkers of homemade
tamales or boiled ears of corn who roamed the neighborhood, he was
an entrepreneur. I wondered if an entrepreneur like Polese would see
him that way.

I bought some *nopales*, and went to pick up my daughter at her best
friend's house three blocks down. Jacinto, the dad, was away at one of
his two grueling, off-the-books, five-dollar-an-hour jobs. Elena, the
seventeen-year-old sister, was propped up on an old couch watching

TV. Her baby was due any day, and she told me she was getting too big to lie down comfortably. The scary thing about Polese's "relentless optimism," I thought, was that it was powerful enough to make me doubt my own resistance to it. For people in Silicon Valley, the future was so shiny, so patently desirable, that any doubt seemed perverse. So why did I still cling to an archaic, nostalgic humanism, seeing people as bent and complex and tragic, when technology promised everyone a straight path to a better future? Why would I get sentimental about the poor and their outmoded, dysfunctional economic behavior, instead of embracing the ways in which the market could make them modern and productive? Why couldn't Elena and her family and the guys on the corner get it together? The girls were shrieking and giggling in the back room, so I went in to see what was so hilarious. When we came out, Elena was still watching TV, and sucking her thumb. We said good night and walked home in the dusk.

Education was one issue, but there were others that were far more explosive. I wondered how Silicon Valley and the New Democrats would deal with race—an issue that had been at the center of the Old Democrat agenda and was still one of the most powerful forces bringing the Old Democrat coalition of liberals and ethnic minorities together. Given Silicon Valley's vision of itself as a kind of post-racial meritocracy, and the New Democrats' insistence on challenging traditional Democratic assumptions about affirmative action, it seemed possible that a high-tech–New Democrat consensus around race might emerge, as it had around education.

The first time I met David Ellington, at a high-tech industry soiree in late 1996, he was, as he put it to me sardonically, "the only Negro in the room." The second time I met him he was "the only Negro in the room." About the twelfth time I met him, he was sitting at a table with two other black men in a room full of white Valley CEOs breakfasting with a U.S. senator. The other African-Americans, he told me, represented not high-tech business but the Golden State Warriors basketball team.

Ellington looked around. "These guys really believe they're creating a tidal wave of wealth that will raise all boats," he said of the Valley businessmen, who were munching happily on Danishes. "They believe the whole system's a meritocracy. They believe technology will fix everything. They live in a vacuum." Ellington's smile was cold. "And they're Californians," he added. "Which is to say they don't have a clue how narrow their world is."

David Ellington would have been the perfect embodiment of W. E. B. DuBois's "double consciousness," were he not more modern, more ironic, in his practice of double, triple, and sextuple consciousness. A solidly built, handsome, bespectacled Georgetown Law graduate, Ellington was fluent in Japanese and experienced in entertainment law. He served as the president of San Francisco's Telecommunications Commission, and was the founder and CEO of NetNoir, the leading black-oriented Internet service provider and presence on the Web. He was still, however, finding it hard to secure the kind of venture-capital funding that his white peers pulled in. "They hem and haw and say they have to think about it some more," he said bitterly. "Plus, at the end of the meeting I still have to try to get a cab." At thirty-one, Ellington exhibited a political worldliness few in the high-tech industry could match.

"Look, I know how it works," Ellington told me one afternoon, leaning back in a lawn chair on the deck of a white friend's four-million-dollar Telegraph Hill home. "There's always one black company in each sector of the corporate world, one business that white people choose to represent the black community. I'm planning to be that business for the Internet. I'm going to be the Percy Sutton for the digital age. I'm going to be anointed by the white guys as the authentic black voice on the Web."

Attempting to be the single authentic representative of a fractious, complex, and wildly unorthodox "community" is an old and basically impossible political game, and Ellington was not unaware of the ironies of his position. If he succeeded in getting more African-Americans involved in high tech, his own value to white people would decrease. But if he stayed the only Negro in the room, he'd remain — except on a symbolic level — powerless. Ellington took off his horn-rims and rubbed his eyes. "As long as I'm by myself, nobody feels threatened," he said. "Silicon Valley can handle Asians. A Chinese-American engineer, that's OK. But I guarantee you if there were five black men sitting around a table at Kleiner Perkins together, it would be freak-out time."

None of Ellington's white peers, though, seemed capable of understanding his clear-eyed view of the sociology of Silicon Valley. Perhaps he was right, and it was the prevalence of the meritocracy myth that made them unable to see the inequities in hiring at their companies: maybe they really believed that success in Silicon Valley was color-blind. But I thought there was also a particularly seductive hope hidden in the white geeks' refusal to see racism at work in their industry, and it had to do with their idea that technology itself was a liberating force for social change. After all, depending on which futurists you spoke to, computers and the Internet were going to make schools, television, retail stores, and print media obsolete, so why wouldn't the digital revolution also do away with inequality? It was an article of American faith that bad things of all kinds could be made better by a combination of information, hard work, and a positive attitude. In their embrace of high tech, maybe white Americans were just hoping, once again, that they themselves wouldn't have to change in order for racial unpleasantness to go away.

On the other hand, even Ellington was a New Democrat. He believed in business, in growth, in capitalism. "My heart is on the left, sort of," he told me, "but everyone's a capitalist now." What he wanted was to be at the table with his white Silicon Valley friends when politicians came calling. And that was the point of the New Democrat–New Economy approach to the issues. Whether it was about education or race or a whole range of policy questions, the men I was talking with believed in conducting their politics in a businesslike way. Whether they were entrepreneurs or politicians, they believed in the bottom line.

CHAPTER five

"It is good to make money," Chairman Mao announced near the end of his long life. It was a statement of faith that had little to do with China's actual economic policies, but it said a lot about the fortunes of the century's most successful anticapitalist revolution. To embrace making money, Mao had come to believe, was to embrace the future: money, the revolutionary leader meant, was *modern*.

China and the world have turned over so many times since then that it seems, sometimes, as if making money were the only value that has endured. By the end of the twentieth century in America, at the height of Silicon Valley's boom, not only was it good to make money but money *was* good. To be rich, everyone knew, was proof of moral worth; to make money was a sign of intelligence and character. Only the stupid, the wicked, and the catastrophically unlucky — Rwandans, for example — were poor.

Without ties to the past, Silicon Valley's money was able to transform the way a generation had allowed itself to understand wealth. The do-gooder, play-poor, small-is-beautiful urges of the baby boomers were long over, as was the nakedly selfish ethos of the junk-bond, cocaine-sniffing eighties. Instead, the earnest mythology of the New Economy combined a medieval belief that wealth was God's gift to his favored ones with the thoroughly American, power-of-positive-thinking conviction that money flowed automatically from hard work.

"The real issue is, are you in favor of folks making some money or not?" Randlett once asked me rhetorically, soon after I'd met him. "That knee-jerk Robert Reich populism has been gotten rid of, and we need some way to view the new compensation world. It's not about if you make money you can't be a good person."

As I looked around the Valley in 1997, I could see a multitude of ways, both vulgar and ethereal, in which the "new compensation world" was being expressed. Money was yachts and jets and grand landscaped mansions in Los Altos Hills; it was whispered gossip about market caps and stock options. It was a sleek little Porsche Boxster, a $700 bottle of red wine, and a venture capitalist in his thirties giving millions to engineers in their twenties. Money was deals. It was meetings. It was the vast, mysterious pit of the Internet, into which sensible businessmen regularly threw tens of millions of dollars, watching cheerfully as the money disappeared and then doing it again.

And money, it began to occur to a few people in the high-tech industry, was an instrument of surprising political usefulness. High tech's involvement in political giving was still tiny, by the standards of mainstream American business. In the 1996 election cycle, for example, Hewlett-Packard would give $66,000; Philip Morris $4.2 million. Federal candidates would receive $7.3 million altogether in combined PAC, soft money, and individual contributions from high-tech companies, which hardly matched the amount forked over by more seasoned industries—telecommunications companies, for example, gave more than seven times as much. But after the defeat of Proposition 211, the idea of money's utility had lodged itself in the minds of a few far-seeing executives.

"These are intelligent businessmen," Randlett would say approvingly of the first CEOs who had begun to write checks. "They understand the relationship between investment and productivity."

Which they were starting to do, in droves. "We're on Internet speed, we're moving at Web time," Randlett liked to boast, as he ferried delegations of congressmen in the summer of 1997 through the ever-expanding landscape of the high-tech industry.

The fog was rolling in over the Marin Headlands and softening the contours of the Golden Gate Bridge when Randlett and Simon Rosenberg of the New Democrat Network arrived at the high-walled Sea Cliff mansion of Halsey Minor for an NDN fund-raiser. It hadn't taken much for them to assemble a posse of New Democrat congressmen eager to fly out from Washington to meet with Minor, the CEO of the booming new media company C/NET, and a dozen of his wealthy peers. "There's such immense growth out here right now," Rosenberg was saying to Randlett, "that Silicon Valley has a disproportionate amount of influence, based not just on money but on mystique. There's this sense of mystery and magic about what's happening."

Inside, the opulence of a different era reigned. Minor's vast living room was empty of computers, decorated with Italian antiques and shimmering bowls of lilies. Heavy, apricot-colored silk drapes framed a sweeping view of the sunset; a brigade of butlers circulated with Chardonnay. I stood by the window, watching Randlett and Rosenberg work the crowd, and thought about style.

Generally speaking, Silicon Valley was a fashion zone that combined the worst excesses of hippie California—Birkenstocks, sweatpants, multipocketed cotton shorts with drawstring waists—with the dismal, drip-dry aesthetic of engineers. Of course, there were still San Francisco's investment bankers, in dark wool and Johnston & Murphy wing tips; they accessorized with sleek cell phones and Palm Pilots but kept their clothing resolutely analog. Still, on casual Fridays in the Valley, it could be hard to tell the mid-level corporate salesmen from the venture capitalists, given the near-ubiquity of polo shirts and khakis in every office.

Halsey Minor was an East Coast preppie by birth, so he invariably appeared as he was tonight, wearing a well-cut navy blazer and a gold Rolex; his wife, Deborah, a former advertising executive at Condé Nast, was a *Town & Country* blonde given to cream-colored silk slacks. But indigenous Internet journalists were more likely to be technopagan Goths with boots and eyebrow piercings; scruffy ex-newsroom guys in corduroys and sports jackets clutching canvas shoulder bags, or pale twenty-two-year-old girls sporting red lipstick and black nerd glasses. When new media got together with hard-core geeks from the Valley and frat boys from the VC firms, as they did each year for *Wired*'s Christmas bash, it wasn't a pretty sight. Once, when the invitation had specified "fancy dress," I'd seen an Internet executive arrive self-consciously decked out in his best orange fleece pullover.

Wade Randlett stood out in this landscape: he'd managed to overcome the standard heterosexual American male shame about dressing well. "Socks and sandals," he said to me once in disgust, describing software engineers. "They go to work in those raggy wool socks." Randlett had the good breeding to seem unaffected while wearing suspenders. And even before he hooked up with his fiancée, Tamsin Smith, a beautiful and savvy government-affairs representative for The Gap, his jeans fit perfectly. "Wade looks like a real slick operator," a software executive once complained to me. "It makes people suspicious. It's those suits."

Tonight, at Minor's party, I found the excellence of Wade Randlett's clothing, and even the vain pleasure he took in it, endearing. The rigidly controlled casualness Randlett normally worked so hard to project, along with the ostentatious modesty demanded of a handsome man, kept getting undercut by his insistence on wearing those Egyptian-cotton shirts with the monogram on the cuff, those custom-tailored double-breasted tropical wool suits.

By the picture window, Randlett was talking shop with half a dozen Gen-X millionaires, including David Ellington and Kim Polese. "It's a very granular business plan that gives you really skinny function for free," said Gilman Louie, the beaming Chinese-American CEO of the game company Spectrum Holobyte, describing some new Dashboard detail to Randlett. Louie, a few years later, would be running a venture-capital firm that "incubated" promising firms for the CIA; now he was just another nerdy rich guy, albeit a well-connected one.

"A data appliance, you called it?" asked Randlett, accepting a canapé from a butler. "I love that term." He turned to face Louie. "Can I talk politics to you for a minute?" he said quietly. Louie, Randlett knew, was one of the rare young industry executives who had a political past. Louie had given money to candidates, worked with Mabel Teng of San Francisco's Democratic machine, and even considered a bid for city supervisor himself; his fiancée was a member of the state party's Central Committee. "We're supposed to raise a million by September," Randlett confided to Louie. "A one, five, ten event and sop up two hundred and fifty thousand, then a high-end dinner with Clinton, fifty a couple, a hundred for the co–pooh-bah hosts. Think you can host the little one?"

Across the room, Minor steered Rosenberg among the guests, greeting John Doerr and nodding at a visiting politician who was grilling a geek about bandwidth. "It's a kind of out-of-the-way neighborhood, but it's a special spot," Minor said, settling Rosenberg in a plush armchair. "We're *so* glad you could come."

Irony, I thought, was almost completely absent from Silicon Valley. It wasn't simply the ubiquitous literal-mindedness of engineers, or the intensity of the drive to make money, that tended to crowd out more subtle states of consciousness. Irony just seemed to be "very New York" to Californians, which was to say perverse, Jewish, and complicated—in brief, a bummer.

Irony belongs to those who suffer from and reflect on the consequences of history. The Valley, where companies spawned and died by the thousands each year, harbored little sentimentality about the past. It cultivated, instead, a blunt, ahistorical pragmatism, and an unselfconscious faith in progress. The myths that sustained Silicon Valley demanded a pure, aggressive belief in technology and capitalism, and a conviction that the future would always be better.

"See you next time," Rosenberg called to me as I thanked Deborah Minor and left the party. I turned and saw his beaming, flushed face. "We're looking forward to more."

"To our future," said John Doerr, grinning. He was standing on a chair, balancing himself against the shoulder of Netscape CEO Jim Barksdale, and waving a glass of champagne at the hundred and fifty high-tech executives packed into the Kleiner Perkins reception area. "We're building a new economy here, and now by working with political leaders we're going to keep growing it." Barksdale, a courtly Mississippian with white hair, lifted his glass happily. A few steps away, at Doerr's right, Wade Randlett was shaking hands and accepting congratulations.

It was a few days after the Fourth of July, 1997, and Doerr and Barksdale were announcing the birth of the Technology Network, or TechNet, a bipartisan membership organization made up of the CEOs of the industry's leading companies. The new group would wield a political-action committee, Silicon Valley's first industrywide federal PAC, distributing at least $2 million to Democratic and Republican candidates in its first year. That was a relatively small amount compared with the $3.5 million the trial lawyers' PAC gave, or the United Auto Workers, whose PAC distributed $3 million, but it was a very respectable start, and would put TechNet among the country's top-twenty PACs. And, given the earnings of the companies involved, it was obvious that more money could easily be forthcoming.

Doerr and Barksdale, as co-chairs, headed the group; Barksdale, whose personal worth would climb to more than a billion dollars by 1998, was supposed to represent the Republican wing of TechNet, and Doerr the Democratic. They had recruited as founding members of TechNet some of the most prominent CEOs in the Valley: John Chambers of Cisco, Scott Cook of Intuit, Scott McNealy of Sun Microsystems, Kim Polese of Marimba, C/NET's Halsey Minor, John Young of Hewlett-Packard, Sandy Robertson of Robertson Stephens, Floyd Kvamme and Brook Byers of Kleiner Perkins, and Brian Halla of National Semiconductor. It was, Barksdale told the assembled guests, "an all-star team." And it represented a new level of maturation for the Valley. "We've observed firsthand how government can help or hinder the technology industry," Barksdale said. "We've learned that working with the government is far more productive than trying to ignore it."

Barksdale and Doerr didn't share the entire history of how TechNet had come to be, but from Randlett and several entrepreneurs I'd heard about the discussions an energized Doerr had been having with Valley executives all summer. After the demise of the California Technology Alliance, Doerr was intent on pushing ahead to cement his and the Valley's newfound influence. He believed that to do its new politics well, the industry needed a vehicle more flexible than a traditional trade association or a few hired government-affairs representatives. Randlett had convinced Doerr that only a group with the capacity for focused political giving could be effective. "If you like a politician," he said, "and he likes you, and everyone knows you're rich as God and you don't give him any money, how do you think he'll feel?"

It was a sentiment that made perfect sense to Doerr. In every way, the model for TechNet was very much a venture capitalist's. Doerr himself dealt with CEOs, not underlings, and he assumed that important politicians would want to do the same. Doerr was used to a world where big investments were required up front before anyone got a seat on the board: he set the minimum fee for a company to join TechNet at $10,000, going up quickly; the first year's operating budget was around $2 million. Doerr knew the business advantages of belonging to an exclusive network, and figured that TechNet would leverage its political strengths in the same way. And, like Randlett, he knew how money talked: unlike conventional trade associations, TechNet would donate directly to candidates. TechNet was set up to bring Silicon Valley business values to bear on the world of politics: it was a high-profile, big-spending, fast-moving association of chief executive officers. It was a group that wouldn't have to piddle around with staffers to work out the tiresome details of legislation but could go straight to the top of the political food chain and demand action, fast.

The first president of TechNet, Gary Fazzino, was standing with a group of well-wishers and chatting. Fazzino was a likable standard-issue government-affairs representative from Hewlett-Packard, and he had an easygoing style. "The technology industry doesn't care if politicians are Republicans or Democrats," Fazzino told me earnestly, echoing the "nonpartisan" line that Randlett had been so careful to promulgate during the campaign against Proposition 211. He smiled at Jeanette Morgan, a government-affairs representative from National Semiconductor, who was the new group's vice president, and she nodded eagerly. "TechNet is going to be about the issues, not about politics," she agreed.

But even at the launch party it was clear that hired hands like Fazzino and Morgan, with their corporate suits and careful, bland pronouncements, weren't going to be the real power running TechNet. Fazzino would be the public face of the organization, someone who could give predictable quotes and deliver conventional opinions. Far more important would be the two experienced political operatives who had been picked to direct the political side of things, raise money, and choose which candidates TechNet supported. I slipped over to find Randlett, who was laughing uproariously in a corner with Dan Schnur, the former communications director for Governor Pete Wilson. A blunt, aggressive spin doctor, Schnur had been hired as the Republican political director of TechNet—"to keep the operation from being an Al Gore 2000 front," as he told me rather bitterly. His counterpart, the Democratic political director, "a very hardworking guy" as Schnur conceded, was Wade Randlett. Lezlee Westine, a Republican fund-raiser, would work with Schnur; Randlett had already snagged Elizabeth Greer, who was used to dealing with him—and who knew both the Silicon Valley scene and the ins and outs of Democratic Party politcs.

Randlett and Schnur grinned at each other, with a mixture of hostility and respect. They were both political professionals, and they both knew the value of appearing to be bipartisan. But both were also aware that they were in an intense competition to steer TechNet toward their own partisan purposes. Randlett would do his best to get Democratic candidates linked up with TechNet executives; Schnur would do the same with Republicans. Each man would raise as much extra money as possible for candidates of his own party, and would try, at all times, to spin his party's programs as the most tech-friendly. Either could arrange, for example, a "TechNet" event on behalf of a candidate; Republicans and Democrats could hold simultaneous "TechNet" fundraisers. It was an open competition, to see whether the TechNet brand would automatically be associated with Democrats or Republicans.

Political bipartisanship was relatively easy for Schnur and Randlett to fake in the world of high tech: the Valley's political inexperience and most executives' lack of strong party loyalties made Republican-Democratic feuds rare. But when it came to business, intrigue swirled around the precise meaning and alignment of TechNet.

Despite the range of companies involved, I noted that Doerr's *keiretsu* predominated; it was easy to see how TechNet could be perceived as a Kleiner Perkins instrument. But it had also been suggested to me that TechNet was a key part of Kleiner Perkins's rumored anti-Microsoft conspiracy, the existence of which was a bedrock of Valley gossip. Doerr was, after all, on the boards of two of Microsoft's main rivals—Sun Microsystems and Netscape—and behind a $100 million Kleiner Perkins fund set up to invest in Internet start-ups using Java, the programming language that was viewed as a direct challenge to Microsoft. He professed nonalignment, but his competitive drive to claim Internet terrain for the companies in his *keiretsu* was obvious. As Netscape's Marc Andreessen told a reporter, "The purpose of the Java Fund isn't to overturn Microsoft. The purpose of the Java Fund is to drive a paradigm shift that, if it plays out, would overturn Microsoft."

Whether or not Doerr saw TechNet as a potential tool to use against Microsoft—and later, when the Justice Department filed its antitrust case, there would be conjecture about the influence Doerr and TechNet companies had exerted on the administration through their political clout—right now, few at the launch party had detailed expectations for TechNet. But they believed Doerr, who believed Randlett, who had asserted convincingly that politics mattered. "It's always been odd to me," Randlett explained, his voice deep and confident, "that you would want to do so many things so well—make money, capture markets, et cetera—and one of your goals would be to do politics shitty." He looked around the room at the executives chatting with one another; Jim Barksdale, his collar open, was laughing and nodding as Sandy Robertson leaned in close with a joke. "These people are successful because they do things well," Randlett observed. "They understand that it just doesn't make sense for them to run a great company and have bad relations with the government."

Randlett, gleaming with champagne and pleasure, couldn't have sounded happier with TechNet. The new group, he said, was going to "change the way people think about politics." A young investment banker came over to us, and Randlett flashed him a high five. "Hey, pal," he said, and then turned back to me. "Yeah," he said. "We're here, and we're going to have a lot to say."

TechNet's offices were in Palo Alto, on the second floor of a neat stucco building near the train station. But most days I could find Randlett working at home in San Francisco, or catch him as he zipped around the Valley from meeting to meeting. We talked a lot during the summer, as Randlett began to direct the organization in the direction in which he thought it should go.

I couldn't always follow what Wade Randlett told me about Tech-Net's political strategy: it seemed both wildly overambitious and strangely shapeless. Randlett definitely kept busy; I couldn't spend more than a minute with him before he took a phone call, and in the latter half of 1997, following TechNet's launch, he was constantly on the move. Yet he always insisted that TechNet was not a traditional industry-lobbying group that weighed in on every bill. "We're not going to be all over the map," he said. "We're just going to focus on two things a year. And we're going to win them both."

Part of the problem I had in keeping track was that Randlett was the Democratic political director for the group—in which capacity he raised money for New Democrat candidates, for the Democratic National Committee, and for Al Gore's Leadership PAC—as well as an unofficial proselytizer for the vice president, in which capacity he flew around the country organizing Gore-Tech sessions and laying the groundwork for a network of tech supporters of the Gore 2000 campaign. Simultaneously, he was busy developing a "nonpartisan" strategy for TechNet, helping to decide which issues the industry as a whole would take on in its first year.

Randlett had outlined his basic agenda for me: just two issues, education and federal-securities-ligitation reform. Lobbying in Washington for federal standards for shareholder lawsuits was a popular idea among the TechNet members, who wanted to preempt other state-by-state fights, and who were fired up by their success in defeating Proposition 211. But Randlett wasn't interested in nitpicking arguments inside committee conferences. He soon handed the task over to a professional—the lobbyist Mark Gittlesplan—for some serious, inside-the-Beltway dealmaking.

Randlett himself would focus on education, both in Sacramento and in Washington—a "big-picture issue," he pointed out. "And nonpartisan, without obvious, naked, self-interest." This work would establish the credentials of the high-tech industry as a civic-minded, socially aware group, rather than a selfish bunch of traditional businessmen. Less explicitly, though, it had a partisan edge. It would further Randlett's New Democrat agenda by putting the Valley's money and prestige behind national standards, stricter testing, "accountability," and charter schools—all issues on which Republicans, who tended to want to leave education to the states, had not been visible. The education focus would likewise benefit Gore, who continued to make the issue a priority, and it would strengthen the hand of California gubernatorial hopeful Gray Davis, a New Democrat who had been speaking out for more charter schools.

As a first foray into politics, John Doerr and Randlett had convinced TechNet to back a California Assembly bill that would double the number of school charters granted by the state. They enlisted the help of Reed Hastings, a software entrepreneur who had studied education at Stanford and was an enthusiastic backer of New Democrat–style school reforms. Hastings, a trim, bearded man with a low-key manner, began lobbying lawmakers in Sacramento.

Randlett complemented Hastings's reasoned appeals for educational excellence with his own tactics. All along, he had seen the fight as a crucial one for TechNet to win. "Get there early on your issue and kick ass," Randlett explained. "It's always the right strategy." To do so, he relied less on the appeal of charter schools than on old-fashioned arm-twisting. He went to the California Teachers Association, whose members bitterly opposed measures to expand charter schools and vouchers, and announced that unless it supported the bill backed by TechNet, Silicon Valley would go on the attack. Pointing to the $40 million raised to fight Proposition 211, Randlett threatened that Reed Hastings was planning to ask high tech to raise money to put its own initiative on the ballot. That initiative, he warned, would allow charter schools without limit in California. "We can spend as much as it takes," Randlett vowed.

Union leaders at the CTA were as aware as anyone that ballot initiatives were an effective way to do end runs around the legislative process, and that money was the determining factor in whether an initiative passed. Prodded by Assemblyman Ted Lempert, whose district included most of Silicon Valley and who was familiar with the industry's power, the CTA agreed to back TechNet's bill.

I saw the outcome at a bill-signing ceremony that Randlett set up at the San Carlos Charter School, in the heart of Silicon Valley. We stood in a light drizzle on the playground, watching Governor Pete Wilson and a group of local officials assemble. "Look, it's the government!" an overexcited kindergartener squealed, as John Doerr and his Kleiner Perkins partner Floyd Kvamme walked in. "Hi, government!"

The five-year-old wasn't the only one who seemed more impressed by the venture capitalists than by the real government. Governor Wilson, citing "bipartisan support for our state's children," nodded to the entrepreneurs when he said that "public schools must be driven by the same values that guide the Silicon Valley success story—excellence, competition, and quality control."

Hastings, standing next to Doerr, sounded delighted. "The initiative tipped the balance and made Sacramento understand it would be quite disadvantageous to oppose us on this issue," he said modestly. Randlett couldn't resist crowing. "For anyone who doesn't believe you can get a good idea made into a good law, check this out," he told me. "From the first conversation I had with Ted Lempert to today, it took us just forty-five days. Forty-five days and $3.5 million—yeah, I think people will pay attention now when we raise other issues. We're going to keep pushing hard."

And he did. As Randlett traversed the Valley, talking to executives about TechNet, he was networking with a purpose. Education and securities-litigation reform were perfectly adequate issues on their own merits, but Randlett wanted to use them—and his position with Tech-Net—to the Democrats' advantage. His efforts were leaving Dan Schnur's Republican outreach in the dust. He'd suggest to one CEO that a visit to the White House might be arranged; to another that Republicans in Congress were blocking a bill favored by TechNet. He'd present the administration as the industry's best friend, and gather intelligence on potential sources of donations to Democratic candidates. Casually, he'd drop Al Gore's name, or Clinton's, and make sure the CEOs understood that he had a direct line to the White House.

Randlett's style bothered Gary Fazzino a bit, though he was clearly trying not to voice any explicit criticisms. "I'm used to the H-P way," Fazzino told me one afternoon a few months after the launch. "At

Hewlett-Packard, things are quieter, bipartisan, always civil, and focused on a long-term, collaborative process. What Wade seems to be doing with Democratic organizing for TechNet is more like, 'Get it done, and get it done today.' It's a very different style—high pressure, more like a political campaign."

Fazzino sighed. We were hanging out at the TechNet office, where a few young staffers were bustling around, talking on headsets and trying to look like Silicon Valley go-getters. I told him that I'd heard Dan Schnur was angry that Randlett had already "locked up" the loyalties of key high-tech executives for the Democrats. "The TechNet structure's set up to allow our political directors to build these effective programs that are partisan in nature," Fazzino said with a shrug. "The problem is really that Wade's had a yearlong head start, and now the Republican side has to create an effective program fast if it's going to catch up."

Fazzino sounded worn out. I thought that everyone at TechNet understood quite well, without John Doerr's having to spell it out, that nothing was supposed to get in Randlett's way. And though the Republicans would never, over the next four years, manage to "catch up," neither Fazzino nor any other TechNet official would be able to make Randlett slow down to wait for them. "Wade steps on people's toes a bit," Fazzino said. "There are lots of mellow people here in California, and one thing Wade is not is mellow. His style is much more—well, more Eastern. He's not a hail-fellow-well-met, and definitely not laid-back."

Fazzino looked at me and gave a weak smile. Though he was nominally the director of TechNet, nobody in the media went to him for information, and few executives called him when they wanted something done; nor did they call Dan Schnur. Within just a few months, with a behind-the-scenes nod from Doerr and some meetings in Washington, Randlett had branded himself as the man who was really in charge of TechNet.

"I think he could be even more effective if he was a bit more laid-back," Fazzino said somewhat wistfully. "I mean, the guy walks into a room and says OK, now we're going to get the following ten things done, and he gets the whole meeting to sit up straight. He makes it an imperative to act." Fazzino sighed. "But he's hard to challenge, because he delivers."

Not only was Randlett on a roll with his work, but I could see that he was blossoming in other ways, as his romance with Tamsin Smith deepened. The two had met in 1997 through Simon Rosenberg, at a New Democrat Network fund-raiser, and hit it off immediately. "I'd heard Wade had a lot of personality," Smith told me, flashing her wide smile. "But I liked his style. I could talk to him all night." Smith was tall and slender, with sleek hair and a sharp mind; through her work in government affairs for The Gap and her background as a staffer on Capitol Hill, she was fluent in politics as well as business. Together, Randlett and Smith made the perfect young power couple for San Francisco in the boom years: handsome, well dressed, well connected, and successful. And Randlett knew it. "I've got a great girlfriend," he said. "Business is good, I'm doing the kind of politics I love. *And* we're winning."

PART TWO
bugs

CHAPTER six

A few years back, Vice President Al Gore made a speech in which he said something that stuck with me. Launching his proposal for telecommunications deregulation—an issue, in its day, as fraught with political pitfalls as high tech's political debut was now—Gore had declared, "A time comes in any revolution when expectations are high but accomplishments are not yet concrete."

In the winter of 1997–1998, expectations for the new relationship between Silicon Valley and Washington were high indeed. But as the winter wore on, the bugs became harder and harder to ignore. Some of these bugs were predictable, the result of stylistic and conceptual differences between the systems running Washington and Silicon Valley. High-tech business worked on principles of efficiency, rationality, return on investment, and speed. Politics, by contrast, was a slow, chaotic, illogical system, conservative of its traditions and suspicious of innovation. Not surprisingly, the attempt to wire the two systems together into a seamless network was fraught with difficulties.

But other bugs had to do with the growing fractures within each system. The high-tech industry was becoming increasingly more complicated, and it held together less as conflicts sprang up between Old New Economy businesses and New New Economy start-ups; between biotech companies and Internet nerds; between venture capitalists and investment bankers; between San Francisco and New York, Seattle and the Valley.

Similarly, there were long-standing problems inside the Democratic Party, as Old Democrats and New Democrats struggled for control over ideology, money, and machines. There were daily problems in Washington, as the demands of governing crashed into the demands of campaigning for the 2000 race. And there were huge problems, threatening to pull the party apart, as the crisis around President Clinton's impeachment grew.

Not at all surprisingly, it all meant problems for the man who aspired to be the go-between bringing everyone together. And Randlett's personality brought with it his very own set of bugs.

One of the first events in Washington to catalyze the distrust of young high-tech entrepreneurs—and confirm the antigovernment bias of older libertarians from big computer companies—was the furor in the winter of 1997–1998 over encryption. Unlike many other issues on the high-tech agenda, this one did not pit Old Democrats against New. Rather, it pitted high-tech newcomers against the clout of the national-security apparatus and law enforcement—and, as such, it was a serious test of power.

The Pentagon and the National Security Administration had, since the very beginning of the computer industry, set export controls that strictly regulated not only foreign sales of conventional weaponry but also sales of the kinds of high-tech equipment that could be shipped abroad. One of the most sensitive products was encryption software, which the government feared could be used by enemy states or freelance terrorist groups to communicate without detection. The NSA, which oversaw surveillance—satellite spying as well as code-breaking—was horrified by the idea that American companies would ship abroad software that essentially made it possible for anyone to hide from it.

"Privacy," though, had been an early battle cry of the pioneers of the digital revolution. And though commercial Web sites, by gathering data on consumer behavior, were routinely violating individuals' privacy, most high-tech executives saw what the market was doing and what government was proposing to do in a very different light. Corporate data-mining, they felt, was just part of free enterprise; export controls on encryption were examples of unnecessary government meddling. Most Silicon Valley software executives were reluctant nationalists, at best: the Internet, and their markets, had a global reach. Their position was both libertarian and mercenary, and it won wide support from high-tech firms.

The Pentagon and NSA were shocked; they had always been able to bend business to conform to their ideas of national security. A history of working with high-tech companies that were defense contractors, or funded largely through government weapons research, had given the NSA the expectation that high tech would be compliant with U.S. foreign-policy goals. The new high-tech companies, however, were independent of financial ties to the government: they made money not through defense contracts but by shipping their software, as widely as they could, to whomever wanted to buy it. Their sales were threatened by export controls on encryption; they were not impressed by appeals to their patriotism, and they were ready to fight like hell.

Though the high-tech industry firmly supported House and Senate legislation that would essentially end export restrictions on software equipped with strong encryption, the Clinton administration went out of its way to derail the widely supported bills. When Congress went back into session in the fall of 1997, the situation had reached a stalemate. "There's a huge polarization on the Hill between what advocates of very liberal controls want and what law enforcement wants, and it's not for lack of knowledge," an industry insider told me. "They're just knocking heads."

Administration sources said the best chance for peace lay with talks among the interested parties—the industry, civil libertarians, and law-enforcement and national-security interests—with Vice President Gore as a kind of Jimmy Carter–style mediator. Gore, however, did not manage to convince software companies or Congress that he was really on top of juggling the hard-line policy positions taken by the Defense Department, the CIA, the NSA, and the FBI on the one hand, with the less restrictive approach applied by the Commerce Department.

A senior Senate aide involved with the issue said wearily: "I think that hope springs eternal. People in the industry really want someone in charge, and they don't want it to be the FBI director. They want the vice president to step up to the plate and take charge, because they see the administration as optimistic, with a lot more flexibility than they may be able to get on the Hill with the FBI director around."

As the issue came to a head, I went over to Pacific Heights to see lobbyist Beth Inadomi of Podesta Associates. An articulate thirty-four-year-old with precision-cut hair and a diplomat's tact, Inadomi had recently moved to San Francisco when her husband, Tim Newell, was lured out of the White House to become a vice president of Robertson Stephens for Internet and e-commerce companies. "He's joining us because he's very capable, and has a very worldly view," said Sandy Robertson, who had denied to me that Newell was hired because of his political connections. "He hasn't had a lot of investment-banking experience, but he does have a lot of connections with high-tech people." Newell, meanwhile, had said only that he was looking forward to a simpler life in San Francisco. "It's a great company," he told me, speaking of Robertson Stephens. "And they hired me to do business, not politics."

Inadomi had been immersed in the encryption debates for years, and I figured she knew as much as anyone did about the weird, cultish protocol of Hill subcommittees and the political exigencies thereof. I thought she could explain the pressures on Gore around encryption, and the goals of the high-tech industry. But mostly I called on Inadomi because I hoped to hear her laugh. She had a deep, spontaneous eruption of a laugh, full of nuances that her otherwise letter-perfect femininity never hinted at. "Tim said your moving here had nothing to do with politics," I said, settling myself on Inadomi's cream-colored sofa by the huge bay windows. She laughed.

Then we got down to business. "At the end of the year," Inadomi explained, "the [Commerce Department] regs on encryption are scheduled to expire, and the White House is going to be a major player. Ultimately, the President and vice president are going to have to make this call. And it's going to be a political decision, not a technical one."

Inadomi was telling me what I'd already heard from John Podesta in the White House; he had been given the brief on encryption largely because of his experience with technology issues. Podesta was the brother of Tony Podesta, and a co-founder of the firm where Inadomi worked. "I think that the hope for a technical solution that would be a short-term fix for the fears of law enforcement was unrealistic," John Podesta had told me. "We [the administration] stumbled into a quick-fix mentality too quickly, and the industry was overly paranoid too abruptly. The vice president has maintained open lines of communication all along, and is one of the people who understand the issue from both perspectives." Podesta had sounded equally confident when he asserted that encryption battles "haven't poisoned the overall atmosphere" between the administration and the high-tech community. They certainly didn't seem to have troubled his personal relationships. "We just agree not to talk about that stuff," he said.

"John's family," Inadomi said with a cool smile. "But he can't make it all work between the industry and law enforcement. Gore is going to have to build the bridges here." She rose, stretching out a perfectly manicured hand. We kissed cheeks, and I left.

By 1998, the Silicon Valley revolution was lurching into yet another phase—one in which Gore's struggles to mediate encryption would fade in importance. In August 1997, according to the Commerce Department, there were 58 million people connected to the Internet in America; by August 1998, there were 80 million, and they spent more than $101 billion on-line. As what a Commerce Department official called "the Internet tornado" swept across the economy, "changing supply chains and relationships between customers, businesses and suppliers," the real scope of the potential for e-commerce was becoming clear, raising an entirely new set of challenges. Businesses, lawmakers, financial markets, and government regulators would have to sort out their interests and decide how to take advantage of the new situation.

Now CEOs were investing early money in candidates, parties, and PACs; among congressmen, fund-raising jaunts to the Valley were becoming the thing to do. By the end of 1998, high-tech industries overall would spend $25.4 million on D.C. representation, up 30 percent from the previous year. And politics would have to adjust accordingly.

Nineteen ninety-eight was the year I met Tony Podesta, a man who deeply understood the business of politics and the politics of business. If anyone could navigate the cultural divide that still separated the Valley from Washington, and explain the different worldviews that were causing the bugs in the system, I thought it might be Podesta.

"If you don't understand how things work here, you can miss a lot," commented Podesta, advising me early in my explorations. "You tell some Valley guy, 'We're gonna meet with the head of the Office of Information and Regulation Affairs at the Office of Management and Budget,' and he thinks, Oh, nobody important." He chuckled. I decided to follow him and see what else I could pick up.

Podesta was a lifelong liberal Democrat, with a small lobbying firm that brought in around $7 million a year representing some of the most prominent corporations on earth. He'd launched Podesta Associates in

1985 with his younger brother John, an expert on law and technology who worked for the Senate Judiciary Committee. Over the years, Podesta Associates had forged close relationships with big firms like IBM and the biotech pioneer Genentech, while seeking out new Silicon Valley players like WebTV. By 1998, Podesta counted among his clients MCI, Digital Equipment, Textron, Time Warner, and CBS; the Recording Industry Association of America, the National Association of Broadcasters, the PCS Alliance, and *The Washington Post*. Over at the White House, where John Podesta had become deputy chief, then chief of staff, Tony Podesta's services were occasionally retained for sensitive political matters, such as shepherding tricky nominations through Congress. He had also made himself useful advising Bill Clinton's re-election campaign. Among the one hundred top-spending lobbyists in personal political donations for the 1996 elections Podesta ranked number eighteen. And he always urged his clients to join in. "I tell people it's better to be in the game than not to be," he said. "Nobody ever got hurt in Washington from knowing too many people."

Podesta was a gregarious man, quick to show his old-fashioned manners, his raspy laugh, and his temper. He had an intense warmth, shot through with flashes of an odd, abstracted melancholy. Tan and barrel-chested, with finely carved Italian features, he stood out amid the herds of white lawyers trotting dutifully through the city's corridors. "Tony's big," Beth Inadomi had warned me of her boss. "He's large in terms of size and—well, just large. Flamboyant. This is a town where everyone wears navy, navy, navy, and maybe charcoal gray. Tony has been known to wear aubergine. And that's just the suit."

Podesta fed me the first time I met him, heaping garlicky bruschetta on my plate and pouring wine for me. An inveterate host and a passionately knowledgeable contemporary-art collector, Podesta liked to keep his friends up late, cooking for a constant stream of D.C. insiders who savored political gossip and homemade pesto in equal measure at his spacious Adams-Morgan home. Podesta roamed a lot, dropping in at the Venice Biennale, visiting his art dealer in London, and fitting in the occasional trek through some place like Madagascar. In Washington, his social circle crossed party affiliations and the public/private sector divide, bringing together ambassadors and corporate executives, speechwriters and senators, curators and White House wonks. Podesta was wired into the enormous and expanding network of telecommunications heavies who revolved through positions at the FCC, telecom corporations, and lobbying firms. And though I'd never seen him hang out much with the Valley's big boys on their own turf, I knew that he hosted dinners when someone like John Doerr or a TechNet delegation came to town.

Podesta liked to keep his options open, which made him reluctant to accept a group like TechNet as the only voice of a complex industry. "Wade's people have a lot to say, but they don't control the switchboard," he once commented to me. "They don't run the network." He was cordial with Randlett and also with the government-affairs representatives of high-tech companies who worked the Hill. He kept in touch with people like John Perry Barlow, Jerry Berman, and Esther Dyson, promoters and pundits of the early Internet scene; in 1992, he had midwifed the birth of the Electronic Frontier Foundation in his living room, and characteristically remained friends with all its founders after a bitter split. And he stayed on top of the gossip from California.

But overall Podesta didn't seem deeply impressed by technology as such. "I studied at MIT," he admitted awkwardly. "But, uh, I didn't bother to take computer science."

Podesta did have a keen interest, though, in helping politically naïve information-age businesses understand the rules of the influence game. He showed, I thought, a remarkable ability to close deals leaving everyone happy. It was an approach that resonated equally with businessmen steeped in the win-win jargon of negotiating and politicians deep in the pragmatic you-scratch-my-back-I'll-scratch-yours conversations that make Washington run. Jeff Smith, executive director of policy for the White House Office of Science and Technology Policy, had spoken admiringly of Podesta's skills. "We've got a hundred, maybe two hundred people at the most in Washington who really get science and technology," Smith said. "Tony's right up there. He exercises a very influential role in tech policy now."

The first time I asked Podesta about his reputation, however, he demurred. "I'm not so much of a tech guy," he said. "I just help people talk together. What I really am is a translator."

What Podesta regarded as a translation problem had been framed more dramatically by others as nothing less than a war between paradigms. For them, the choice was stark: would Silicon Valley and its speeded-up New Economy change the way Washington traditionally did business, or would Washington tame the geeks? The overblown rhetoric of information-age gurus may have convinced some techies that their reach was unlimited: after the Proposition 211 fight, I'd listened to John Doerr talk with a group of CEOs at Kleiner Perkins about "rewiring government."

But Podesta was a man who tended to take the long view of human events. And his bet was that Washington, built as it was on an enduring and nuanced obsession with power of every kind, would ultimately prevail. "The Valley guys generally start out with the view that politics doesn't have any meaning, and that politicians are bumper stickers traveling as human beings," Podesta said with a shrug, as if to indicate the suicidal futility of such a stance. "They don't understand it's in their interest to pay attention."

I'd heard much the same thing from other lobbyists. "It's a Mars and Venus kind of thing," agreed Michael Maibach, a standard-issue business guy who had spent most of the last fifteen years in Washington as Intel's VP of government affairs.

Unlike Podesta, though, Maibach largely blamed the "machine-age" federal bureaucracy for the culture clash. "The Commerce Department takes twenty months for a patent review," he groused. "That's two months longer than our product cycle."

But in 1998, when the Department of Justice launched antitrust actions against Microsoft—a spectacle that alternately cheered Microsoft's competitors and aroused their fears of more wide-ranging government oversight—Silicon Valley's bluster began to sound hollow. And then when a DOJ case was filed against Intel, the anxiety grew. "The first time a senior FCC official had breakfast with my boss, he said, 'You're lucky you never met me before, or we would have regulated you,' " Maibach recalled ruefully. "Now . . ." he sighed. "In some ways, it was a blessing to be ignored."

Despite the Valley's near-universal dislike of Bill Gates, most high-tech executives found his case instructive. Gates couldn't believe guys who failed high-school physics were judging his software; then he got slapped down hard by politicians who couldn't believe a failure at high-school civics was giving them back talk. "All of a sudden, [high-tech] people began to get interested in what the government could do," Podesta observed. "That's what tends to happen when you get a sock in the teeth."

By the end of 1998, Microsoft would have fifty-six lobbyists working inside the Beltway. "It comes down to a bandwidth issue," said

Podesta, pointing to looming regulatory decisions on encryption, World Intellectual Property Organization legislation, immigration, and obscure but vital tax and securities legislation affecting high tech. "How much time can your company afford to *not* spend on politics?"

All this activity in Washington was worrisome to people like Wade Randlett, who had his own plans for how high tech should be represented there. Traditional lobbying, with "old, tired, government-affairs hacks" and trade associations, might be fine for Old Economy businesses, he said, but Silicon Valley deserved something flashier. Randlett wouldn't hesitate to wield TechNet's stable of CEOs to hammer home the point that his organization deserved top-level attention. And he was ruthless about insisting on TechNet's dominance of "the high-tech political space": he did not want anyone else claiming to represent the interests of Silicon Valley. "We learned from Microsoft how to embrace and extend our strategy in a way that develops strategic partnerships and locks everybody else out," Randlett had told me in TechNet's early days. "We don't want any competition." But Randlett's brashness and his end runs around Beltway protocol had already made him a number of enemies in Washington, and by the time he began to apply himself to "strategic partnerships" his rhetoric was toning down. Podesta Associates, Randlett thought, might be a good firm for TechNet to hire for some routine Hill lobbying. "Tony knows how things work," the younger man said, a bit grudgingly. "I guess he's as good as they come. We can do business together."

"Oh, sure, I'll hold, no problem," Karen Lewis said, as she hyperventilated into her headset. Podesta's super-stressed assistant searched through a pile of papers and took another sip of her Mountain Dew. "Tony's on his way," she said to me, standing up and looking under the pile beside her chair. "Can Dick tell us if we need to reschedule the conference call? OK, I'll hold." Lewis pulled off the headset and sighed theatrically. "I am going to have a nervous breakdown." Another call. "Hello, this is Karen. Yes, Tony got NAB [National Association of Broadcasters] to contribute to the event, and he's working on other people. We'll get back to you."

The downtown D.C. offices of Podesta Associates, with a dozen principals and ten associates, were about as mellow as those of the typical start-up, albeit with wilder art. When Lewis ushered me into Podesta's own office, a canvas of phallic black and white swirls caught my eye; next to them was an ecstatic mural-size painting in pinks and golds. *Artforum* and dealers' catalogs were piled next to *Roll Call* on a twisted aluminum sculpture that served as Podesta's coffee table.

"He's walking in now," Lewis said. "Sit down."

Podesta had just returned from a business trip to Romania on behalf of Textron to see about a weapons deal, with an overnight in Paris to watch the French Open. The night before, a packet of ripe and reeking Mont St. Michel stashed in his briefcase, he'd crossed five time zones, cooked dinner for eight—featuring the Parisian cheese, along with a fine Ligurian pesto—made a few dozen phone calls, yelled at some staff, and answered his e-mail before waking at six to start the day's round of meetings.

Basically, I liked Podesta a lot: at first, because his sophisticated taste in art, his aubergine suits, and his genuine enjoyment of female company had led me to think he was gay. But Podesta said no. "Maybe in my next lifetime," he offered when he saw my disappointment. I decided that it was Podesta's lingering respect for government that made me feel at home: his basic belief in democracy, which, though eroded by years of moneymaking and rightward drift, far surpassed anything to be found among the wonder boys of Silicon Valley. Podesta still felt the need to defend the choices that had led him from hard-core liberal crusader to big-business mouthpiece. "I haven't really changed," he'd insist. "I still believe in social issues like abortion rights and the First Amendment, stopping censorship. I guess I'm maybe a little more economically conservative now, more fiscally responsible. I'm a little more libertarian in terms of what I think government can do."

Wrestling off his jacket, Podesta went to work without ceremony, ignoring me as he skimmed through his long and detailed phone list. A constant stream of calls was rolling in, but first he needed to clear up some details from his trip to Romania. "It's a $33 billion economy and a $2 billion deal," Podesta said in a reasonable tone. He started to pace, gesturing with a free hand. "What I was told is that he's running around trying to undo it. But if we don't end up with the ninety attack helicopters nothing else is possible." He listened for a moment, still walking. "Who do they need encouragement from?" Podesta hung up, and I asked him the story. "The ambassador wants to bring some Romanian software guys to Silicon Valley," he said. "It's just a favor, but I'm going to see if anyone's interested. I'll call Jerry Yang."

Like so many of his clients, Podesta struck me as working an information economy. "Tony's a router," the White House's Jeff Smith said.

"He knows how to get people from A to B." Or, as Podesta put it when he finally hung up, "I'm software. I'm a server, I'm a switch, I'm all of the above." Whatever the metaphor, Podesta made it clear that politics was all about the strength of your network.

"Do you know him?" was the ubiquitous D.C. question; with Podesta, the answer was likely to be yes—even if the person in question was a Republican. "If you're looking for someone who can call Trent Lott at home," I once heard Podesta tell a potential client, "there's people better at that than we are." But then he dropped into the conversation the fact that a Podesta Associates principal named Kimberly Fritts happened to be the daughter of the head of the National Association of Broadcasters (a Podesta client) and a former staffer for Republican senator Connie Mack of Florida (a recipient of Podesta campaign contributions).

"Politics is a business, and you want to understand who's in charge," Podesta explained. "But there are potential allies everywhere, if you understand that you're in it for the long haul. I have my own political views, but that doesn't mean I can't work with everyone."

Making the circuit with Podesta, I tried to see how the game operated. The most instructive story I pieced together was the case of Genentech. Even though most new biotech companies had only a shaky conceptual connection to the larger high-tech industry now, the San Francisco–based Genentech illustrated fairly well how "older" Silicon Valley firms had learned to engage in politics. And it showed how well Podesta understood his business.

The biotechnology giant had been Podesta Associates' first client a decade ago, back when Podesta's lobbying style tended toward the splashy, media-directed side of the game. (One year, when the California Poultry Association asked him to fight legislation that allowed its competitors' frozen chickens to be labeled "fresh," Podesta carried a crate of the icy birds to Congress and set up a bowling tournament with them in the corridors.) Podesta's work for Genentech had begun conventionally enough, as he guided the company through hearings on human growth hormone or numbingly dull negotiations about R&D tax credits. But it was his more "out-of-the-box" tactics that paid off for Genentech in 1997, after nearly two years of dogged lobbying, when he won sweeping changes in the operations of the Food and Drug Administration. "The opportunity to do this kind of stuff comes along once in a generation," said Walter Moore, Genentech's vice president of government affairs. "And Tony provided the bipartisan glue that made FDA reform happen."

"Reform" of the FDA had been on Genentech's agenda from the beginning of the first Clinton administration. Like other biotech companies, Genentech felt crippled by the Food and Drug Administration's laboriously slow drug-testing and approval process, by labeling and advertising regulations, and by restrictions on the experimental uses of approved medicines. Podesta knew that Genentech couldn't get new legislation written through traditional insider negotiating alone, and he launched a brash public-relations campaign that took the fight into the open. "Sure, I know how to be an enemy. But the FDA was well thought of. We didn't need to bash [then FDA head David] Kessler. We just needed to be more energetic and compelling with our message than the agency was."

And biotech's message was loud and clear: deregulate. By the mid-nineties, a rift had opened between older pharmaceutical companies — large, diversified, heavily invested in infrastructure — and the newer, more audacious start-ups churning out not just new drugs but new processes for making drugs. The younger companies, surviving on venture capital, needed to slash through regulations and get their innovative products to market as quickly as possible. Meanwhile, the AIDS epidemic had brought a new force into the equation: educated, articulate, desperate patients who had learned how to work the regulatory system taught themselves advanced pharmacology, chained themselves to the railings outside FDA meetings, and harassed the pharmaceutical companies over pricing and access to medicines.

Podesta saw an opportunity for Genentech "to convert what could have been seen as a deregulation scheme into a matter of patients' rights." And, in an early meeting with Senate staffers, he decided to add the issue of wealth to the issue of health: "I argued that either we were going to streamline the U.S. government, or the most advanced health-technology companies in the world were going to move all their jobs to Europe."

He seized on the 1996 congressional campaigns to launch Genentech's push for legislation to radically overhaul the FDA. "The fact that people are running and want to visit with constituents usually makes their attention span go up," he noted. "Instead of simply testifying in hearings and meeting with staff in Washington, we took it to key players in their own backyards. We got patient groups organized, we got employees of medical-devices companies to meet with candidates on their home turf, we basically ran a grassroots political campaign."

Back in Washington, Podesta identified "three zones of power and authority" in addition to the Congress members writing the legislation: the FDA, the Health and Human Services Department, and the White House. Genentech's Moore recalled watching as the pieces came together. "Tony was able to keep the consensus together all the way through when every word in the bill was contentious," he said. "He knew [Senator] Barbara Boxer. He knew Greg Simon [then the vice president's chief domestic-policy adviser] and Sally Katzen [then at the Office of Management and Budget], who were working on it from the White House. His contacts were everywhere."

Simon recalled hundreds of private conversations and endless meetings on the subject. "Tony was one of maybe two people I ever looked forward to hearing from," he said. "I could actually trust him to tell me not only his client's point of view but what was going on politically." What was going on politically, of course, had been largely stirred up by Podesta Associates' grassroots public-relations blitz, as well as by Podesta's own behind-the-scenes network of friends. "I was the point person for the administration on this," Podesta said. "They'd sit down with the pharmaceutical association, the biotech association, the medical-devices association, and David [Beier, then Genentech's vice president of government affairs]. Genentech was always at the meetings, because I was the one who organized the meetings for the White House."

The deal was finally closed, at an after-hours White House meeting, after Podesta negotiated a final compromise. With offhand modesty, he summed up his entire strategy. "First, you have to make the technical issues into issues people care about, and have voters bring them home to politicians. And, second, you have to be in the conversation enough so that you know who everyone is and what everyone wants." He paused, and then repeated his essential mantra. "You know why I'm good at what I do? I know what everyone needs."

Listening to the story, I understood why the White House had chosen Genentech as the site for its recent announcement of an extension of R&D tax credits. Al Gore had enthused to the press about healthy families and a better future just days before news of breakthrough breast-cancer drugs pushed up both Genentech's and the vice president's stock. "Yeah, we held that event at Genentech to thank Gore for supporting us," Podesta said. And then I also understood better why, shortly thereafter, a new chief domestic-policy adviser to the vice president had been appointed: David Beier of Genentech.

I asked Podesta if he thought his new high-tech clients could absorb the kinds of lessons about Washington that this story could provide. I watched Podesta sit uncharacteristically still for a moment, gazing at a painting on the wall and reflecting. "Yeah," he finally said. "They're visionaries out there in Silicon Valley. But nobody's gonna invent three branches of government and bicameralism."

"Business has the idea that the public sector should be driven by speed and profit," he said. "But democracy is messy, democracy is slow." Podesta shrugged. "High-tech guys just have to learn to live with it," he said. "There are smart people here, and there's a way smart people can do business."

He reached for his briefcase, and we both stood up. "We have no permanent allies," Podesta added. "We have no permanent enemies. We just have interests."

CHAPTER seven

During visits to Washington in 1998 I became convinced that the 2000 campaign would be at the heart of the Democrats' overtures to high tech, and central to high tech's political ambitions. And yet the campaign opened up the potential for even more bugs in the network.

The hot, fast, competitive culture of a campaign is very different from the culture of day-to-day governing. Campaigns aren't about developing the kinds of long-term relationships that Tony Podesta nurtured in his work on the Hill; they're not about formulating the big-picture analyses and policies that Al From and the DLC cared about. In a way, I thought, campaigns had a style that should make them more familiar to the aggressive entrepreneurs of Silicon Valley: anyone who had ever been involved in an IPO could probably appreciate the attitude in a campaign war room.

But the entrepreneurial attitude of campaign staff and consultants depended heavily on an intimate knowledge of the political landscape, and tended, even more than government service did, to exclude all amateurs—even wealthy ones. I could see quite easily how high-tech supporters could be shoved aside, dissed, and trampled in a presidential race, especially during the early pre-announcement and primary periods, in favor of tried-and-true Democratic constituencies. "Let's look at the market," a former DNC official had explained to me once. "There's a very small electorate in presidential primaries, and if you look at that market, and the money behind the voters, it works very strongly against innovation in your message." The official looked pained, and shook his head. "Innovation is a luxury, frankly, that candidates in presidential primaries just can't afford," he said.

We were still a long way from the primaries, but it was easy to see that if I was going to understand the power Silicon Valley would have in 2000, I would have to pay more attention to Vice President Al Gore's plans now.

Nobody could predict the political twists and turns of the next few years, but I did wonder, from time to time, whether Gore's reliance on the most boosterish version of the New Economy message was going to rebound against him if the economy turned down. As Tim Newell had admitted to me, "Gore is strongly associated with the New Economy: that's good, and it's helped him. But if it crashes, he's going to crash, too."

Despite a steadily growing economy, not everyone was without concerns. Laura D'Andrea Tyson, the former chair of the President's Council of Economic Advisers and head of the National Economic Council, had left Washington after Clinton's first term to become a professor of economics and business administration at the University of California at Berkeley. I called her to ask about the New Economy, and Gore, and the general direction of the economy. Speaking quickly but carefully, she made a distinction between "the political and economic definitions of the New Economy." Tyson had not lost her Beltway tact. "I'm compelled by the notion that new technology is enabling us to change how things are produced and distributed and bought," she said. "In that sense, it's a revolution. But what I don't think we know at this point is if we're really in the middle of a structural change—we're unable to predict it."

The technological revolution, Tyson argued, did not automatically provide a simple—if politically attractive—formula for an all-new, perpetually booming economy. "Has the technology fundamentally reduced the volatility of the financial adjustments that cause business cycles? The answer is no," she said. "The same technologies which enabled huge flows of capital into foreign markets can make it flow out at breathtaking speed: the contagion is through the wires!" Tyson paused. "I think policymakers should have more caution and try to make gradual changes," she concluded.

But Tyson's was a minority voice—and politicians like Gore, in any case, were less concerned with economic theory than with the advantages offered by a boom period. And Gore was busy setting up the practical infrastructure necessary for his next political steps.

From the moment Al Gore was sworn in as Clinton's vice president in 1996, there was essentially no time that he was not running for President. Seemliness was one thing: Gore was a consummately loyal man who had managed, in his first term, to carve out a role that was simultaneously dignified and deferential. The fact was that Gore shared Clinton's politics, and saw himself as part of a New Democrat team; he had no interest in undercutting Clinton or competing with him.

Practicality, though, required Gore to think ahead. Given the huge, ever-growing influence of money on campaigns, he needed to build up his piggy bank long before he could officially raise money as a candidate for President. Gore could not raise money for a presidential bid in 2000 until he announced his candidacy, at which time federal limits of $1,000 per individual contribution would kick in. But there was no limit on the amount of soft money the vice president could raise for his party.

Silicon Valley's general distaste for politicians—"Uh, uh, uh-oh, White House, black box, no good, abort," as one fund-raiser mockingly described high tech's attitude toward Washington—led me to expect that questions about the propriety of some of Gore's past fund-raising might sour would-be supporters from the industry. Gore's four dozen fund-raising phone calls from his White House office during the 1996 campaign, and his fund-raising efforts at a Buddhist temple in Southern California, were widely criticized; I knew there was probably much more that the Valley could find to condemn. But both Democrats and Republicans in the tech sphere were surprisingly nonjudgmental about Gore's high-stakes arm-squeezing. Dan Schnur, the Republican political director of TechNet, was blunt when I asked him about it. "It's what's expected of politicians," he said, unperturbed. "Birds fly, fish swim, and Gore raises money—that's all people think about it."

But Gore was also raising an even more important kind of political capital through favors to different sectors of the industry, friendships with well-placed individuals, and general polishing of his good-science, future-friendly image. By helping biotech executives "reinvent" the Food and Drug Administration, trolling through John Doerr's Rolodex for potential dinner guests, or telling the media how much he regretted trading his Macintosh laptop for a boring old PC, Al Gore was campaigning hard. So from the very beginning of his second term, the man who would be Technology President laid cable for a power-savvy, technologically hip, and thoroughly modern version of a political machine.

Randlett just laughed when I said the word. "It's not a *machine*," he corrected me. "That's such an old-politics term. It's a *network*."

In February 1998, after months of planning, Gore officially launched his Leadership '98 PAC, and announced his plans to raise between $2 and $4 million, which he would disperse to the Democratic Party candidates of his choice. The vice president could now enhance both his visibility and influence by amassing large amounts of soft money, and spreading it around in areas where he needed friends, or might want favors later on.

To this end, Gore had enlisted the advice and support of Peter Knight, his former chief of staff and campaign director. Knight, a lawyer and a powerful Washington lobbyist, had survived a fundraising controversy related to his role as chair of the 1996 Clinton-Gore re-election campaign. Cleared of wrongdoing, Knight had settled back into his lobbying work and what Tim Newell called "the care and feeding of donors" to the Democratic Party.

Knight was more than simply a moneyman; he worked closely with the political advisers assembling around the vice president, whose job was to lay the foundation for a Gore presidential campaign. These included three other former Gore chiefs of staff: Roy Neel, Jack Quinn, and Craig Smith; Bob Squier, elder Democratic adviser and media master; Tony Podesta's old friend David Beier; and lobbyist and former New York congressmen Tom Downey. None of these people wanted to talk to me—except for Squier, a loquacious and intellectually curious man who enjoyed discussing political strategy the way others enjoyed playing golf. Knight, probably because of his previous experiences on the wrong end of campaign-finance investigations, was especially close-mouthed: after forty minutes on the phone with him, I'd come away with little more than his name, age, and the strong impression that I'd been talking to a lawyer.

But maybe there wasn't all that much to say. I began to understand that when it came to Gore 2000 intrigue, there was really no tightly controlled central cabal with a specific master plan yet. Knight's seemingly vague statement that Gore was only "building relationships with like-minded people" was a fairly accurate representation of the facts. "He's making friends, he's lining up donors, he's putting pieces together," Tim Newell explained to me. There was a huge amount going on, but it was the real stuff of politics: no smoking gun, no handshake deals, no historic moments; just a slowly accumulating set of relationships.

But there was a bug inside the system. Thanks to Gore's boss, the entire set of Democratic Party relationships—and perhaps the success of the party's 2000 presidential campaign—was likely to blow up at any moment.

Politics, almost by definition, is the practice of the real, the disappointing, the unselvaged edge. But I liked, from time to time, to look at the big picture anyway. This meant looking at politicians' moves as if they were actually based on principles and strategic considerations, and not on expedience, clumsiness, or vanity, which were much more likely to rule political decision-making.

During 1998, I was searching for the big picture because practicality had seemingly disappeared from the political scene. Over more than a year in which it unceasingly tried to dump President Clinton, the Republican Party's actions were so illogical, so hysterical, so devoid of the slightest grain of common sense that I was almost compelled to think there must be a strategy—if a perverse one—at work.

Maybe, I thought, it went something like this:

The Republican Party, having done the very best it could in 1992 and 1994 with the election of a majority of true-believing, God-fearing Contractors with America, had nonetheless been unable to checkmate the mysteriously popular Bill Clinton. It read the writing on the wall: that Republicans seemed doomed to be a minority party in terms of the electorate at large, even if a controlling one in Congress due to the district reapportionment of 1992. It understood that Republicans could win seat after right-wing safe seat in the House in perpetuity and still not convince their fellow Americans to vote another Republican into the White House.

So perhaps, looking toward the future, the Republicans had decided to go after Clinton without caring if they weakened not just this President but the presidency itself. They could deploy the tools used against Richard Nixon—special prosecutors and independent counsels—to erode Bill Clinton's power. They did not have to be concerned if their attacks wound up shifting power away from the presidency and toward the legislature, because they knew would have a hard time winning the White House anyway. The Republicans could continue their determined march away from the center, which elected Presidents, and concentrate on winning power in an ever more powerful House.

This was the big picture. I was pretty sure it was wrong. But I couldn't, otherwise, understand what the Republicans thought they were doing. What I could understand was the growing rift that the Republican attack on Clinton was causing among Democrats. In part, this was because a number of New Democrats—including Senator Joe Lieberman, who delivered a blistering attack on the President, and some of Simon Rosenberg's tech-friendly House members, like Jim Moran and Adam Smith—didn't seem to want to take the chance that their districts would perceive them as being soft on adultery. "Look, they're scared," Simon Rosenberg said. It was the summer of 1998, and he and I were sitting in a sweltering outdoor café discussing the fall elections. "Our members are facing election in some of the toughest swing districts in the country, and they're nervous."

But there was more. Despite the fact that Clinton was the first DLC President, that he had jump-started the New Economy with a pro-business, antiregulation agenda, that his administrations had set new records for Democratic centrism overall—nonetheless, Clinton had proved himself to be more wedded to winning than to principle. From his first term onward, he'd abandoned whichever constituency—liberals or New Democrats—he'd needed to as circumstances demanded. He'd cut deals in order to bolster his own opinion-poll ratings, and dropped policies that threatened to be unpopular. I remembered how Rosenberg had told me in 1997 about NDN members' chronic fears that Clinton was "backsliding" on their agenda, and how he presented the New Democrats and the Old Democrats as perpetually locked in "a battle for Clinton's soul."

The impeachment scandal justified, even hardened, many New Democrats' long-simmering mistrust of the Man from Hope. Having spent years being anxious about Clinton's ideological slipperiness, they now had to confront the facts of another kind of philandering. And it all made them nervous. "I think a lot of our folks are seen by the White House as abandoning him," Rosenberg admitted.

The President's staunchest defenders turned out to be hard-core Old Dems, stone liberals like the Vermont socialist Bernie Sanders and the fiery Maxine Waters from Los Angeles. The Reverend Jesse Jackson, the Congressional Black Caucus, and the AFL-CIO stood by their man—the very one they'd condemned a year ago for his Third Way gutting of welfare and his abandonment of health care. But these were Democrats who could never make common cause with Republicans, who owed little to the suburban swing voters courted by the New Democrats. These were people who had been elected by a base that was reflexively and self-defensively Democratic. The New Democrats could co-opt Republican ideas, undercutting the right wing by adopting its pro-business agenda. The Old Democrats, on the other hand, hated Newt Gingrich and everything he stood for. They now saw their President in danger of being destroyed by the same right-wing forces of evil that had attacked their unions and their affirmative-action programs and their rights.

Slowly, as the battle raged and partisan lines hardened, the right wing of the Republican Party and the left wing of the Democratic Party would each become stronger, forcing significant changes in the political landscape. Clinton's State of the Union speech in 1999 would mark, according to Simon Rosenberg, "a remarkable shift leftward," and by the end of the year, with the articulation of new administration positions on Social Security and Medicare, that shift would dramatically affect Al Gore's political positioning. After the impeachment, the administration would, as Rosenberg put it, "soften its line against the old party," with the result that Gore, no matter how much he might have sought the center a year earlier, "had to live in that new world." But it would be long, agonizing months before all the real political consequences of the Starr investigation emerged.

Meanwhile, detail by sordid detail, the scandal was consuming Washington. By the time President Clinton was formally impeached, most of the country would be thoroughly exhausted by the affair: political discourse would be almost entirely replaced by dirty jokes, conspiracy theories, and a barrage of media punditry so simultaneously prurient and pompous that I found myself regularly apologizing to strangers for my profession.

Yet, during it all, the Valley seemed uninterested. At first, the scandal just confirmed most techies' naïve but visceral distaste for Washington, and their belief that all politicians were corrupt. More to the point, Silicon Valley saw the scandal as irrelevant to its main preoccupation, which was making money in an ever-expanding, almost scarily soaring economy.

But Wade Randlett, who wanted to remain in his position as the go-between and kingmaker, needed the Valley to care about politics, if not the impeachment. In August 1998, Randlett started pushing hard on one of the few political issues that did matter to the majority of CEOs of TechNet, Republicans and Democrats alike: allowing high-tech companies to bring in more foreign workers on temporary visas.

California had always run on the energy of immigrants, but the high-tech boom of the 1990s was turning Silicon Valley into a magnet for an astonishing number of foreign-born engineers and entrepreneurs. The Dick and Jane subdivisions radiating out from San Jose had lost the blond, suburban homogeneity that reigned even twenty years ago: Silicon Valley now had corner stores where Bengali engineers stopped in for cricket news; movie theaters with samosas stacked up in the concession booths; gas stations that sold tapes of cheesy pop music in Korean and Mandarin. The malls were full of Pakistani families and Taiwanese students and bleary-eyed, turbaned engineers on temporary visas buying cell phones for their relatives back home. By 1998, less than 4 percent of Santa Clara County's inhabitants were African-Americans—but fully 28 percent had been born abroad. And those were just the legal immigrants.

It was still not enough for most Silicon Valley employers, though. At a time when California ranked fortieth among the states in spending on its elementary schools and California's once-glorious university system was overcrowded and understaffed, companies complained that it had become harder and harder to hire qualified technical people at home. They began casting their nets wider, drawing in not only the kinds of Americans who had always migrated to the West Coast looking to make their fortunes but young adventurers from abroad. India's state system of technical colleges and universities, in particular, was an incredibly rich source of talented engineers, whose education and training had been subsidized by someone else, and who were willing to work harder for less money than were comparable American techies.

TechNet argued the case for expanding visa opportunities for skilled immigrants, through the H1-B visa program, which allowed qualified technical workers into the country on temporary visas to work at specific companies. As things stood now, only about 65,000 six-year H1-B visas were allotted each year, and employment-based permanent-resident green cards were limited to 140,000. Studies underwritten by the industry claimed that as many as 200,000 high-tech jobs were open and going unfilled, though a General Accounting Office report questioned the numbers. Pointing to the tight labor market in Silicon Valley, and the growing shortfall of U.S. engineering graduates, TechNet asked for the immediate expansion of visa slots, as well as a review of rules to allow high-tech companies to bring in foreign workers as needed.

Labor unions, on the other hand, resisted expanding the H1-B visa program on principle, fearing that employers, as in other industries, were simply interested in using immigrants to drive down compensation for American workers. Because the immigrants' legal status depended on special visas provided by companies, unions said, the immigrant workers were essentially indentured, unable to switch jobs or jump from start-up to start-up as ambitious young Americans did. Nor did the immigrants require the expensive benefits paid to older engineers who had seniority. Some professional associations, like the American Association of Engineers, pointed out that American engineers in their forties and fifties often found it difficult to get work. The argument for expanding visas, they said, boiled down to self-interest: it was simply less expensive for Silicon Valley to hire cheap young Indian labor than to retrain older American engineers in new technologies.

I had to agree with Wade Randlett's scornful dismissal of the unions' position. "Come *on*," he said to me, irritated. "Nobody can possibly believe this is the cruelest economy out here, that people are being left for dead by the roadside." High-tech companies competed fiercely for engineering talent, waving enticing packages of stock options at them, putting up huge billboards along Highway 101 to lure them in, poaching one another's best hires. Immigrant engineers, like their American counterparts, expected high salaries; the industry had simply grown so fast that there weren't enough people to staff it.

One morning in mid-August, I went up to see Randlett at his temporary offices at Hambrecht & Quist, in the heart of San Francisco's financial district. The investment bank had a number of executives— Nancy Pfund and the CEO, Dan Case, prominent among them—who had long been big boosters of TechNet, and they'd lent Randlett space on the eleventh floor.

Randlett was sitting in a swivel chair with his gray suede loafers up on the desk and his back to a huge window. He waved at me and kept talking into his headset, cleaning his nails. "The way the whole economy out here's working," I heard him explain, "is the big companies aren't big companies, they're a lot of little projects under one roof. They're firing all the time, laying people off, starting up some other project. And the people who get fired don't go to the ash heap of history or start flipping burgers at Burger King. They go to Sun."

Randlett paused. "Sure. I'll hold," he said.

"Who's on the phone?" I asked. "Labor?"

Randlett rolled his eyes. "White House," he said. "They're getting pushed hard from the left." He started tapping on his laptop keyboard. "Hi, no, no problem. I just wanted to make sure you understood that 'total compensation' means total compensation, right? We're not trying to get cute with that. OK. OK, we'll talk tomorrow."

Randlett took off his headset. "Labor decided to fight a losing battle the wrong way," he pronounced. He had never been shy about his opinions, but I'd come to recognize a certain tone of utter certainty that kicked in when he was trying to convince Washington that his high-tech forces would prevail. It was a stance that relied partly on evoking a mystique about the Valley—"the way things work out here"—and partly on sheer bullheaded aggression.

"Labor's whole 1982 view of the world is that it's business versus labor, that business wants to fire workers and hire cheaper ones," he said. "But try to apply that to high tech, where they're creating sixty thousand jobs a year. Try to explain how it's bad for labor to work at a company that's growing jobs. Try to show why it's exploitation to make workers into owners." Randlett laughed sharply. "If you really believed 'workers of the world unite,' that crap I have to hear all the time, you'd be trying to get Indian engineers *more* jobs with stock options."

So why weren't the Republicans stepping in on H1-B visas and seizing the chance to make themselves the antilabor standard-bearers of the high-tech economy? Virginia Postrel, the utterly modern and articulate conservative who ran *Reason* magazine, had been fuming about her party's stupidity vis-à-vis high tech for a while. I found a piece she wrote in *Reason* in July 1998, subtitled "An Alienated GOP Hands the Future to Al Gore," and it explained a lot.

In the article, Postrel tore into the reactionary cultural conservatives who cared more about banning pornography on the Internet than about courting high tech—"the Bauers and Bennets, Kristols and Dobsons," she wrote, "all the pundits and activists for whom the party is a vehicle to attack contemporary America." She lamented that Republicans failed to understand the deep cultural identity of high-tech executives. "The people *Wired* identifies as 'the connected' . . . are defined neither by their gadgets nor by their money," Postrel wrote. It was the same analysis I'd heard in the New Democrat study of "wired workers," and from strategists at the DLC. "They value learning and achievement," Postrel noted. "They look forward to the future. They believe in creativity, enterprise, and progress."

Postrel railed against Al Gore and the Democrats as "Washington bureaucrats" with "an impulse to slap regulations on technologies old and new." Yet, she admitted, "Gore courts innovators, says they're important, affirms their values. Bill Clinton does the same. The Democrats may be lying, but the national Republican Party is hardly even trying. It is too busy appeasing activists who think Ralph Reed is a moderate squish. It is too busy heaping contempt on the people who are inventing the future."

Postrel's analysis of the Republican Party resonated strongly for me: the battle between Old and New was clearly playing out not only among Democrats. And her argument made sense when I saw the consequences of those conflicts. "The Republicans in Congress decided H1-B was gonna be their issue," Randlett said during the legislative battle over visas. "But that was fucked up by [Republican conservative] Lamar Smith, who decided he didn't like immigrants." Randlett had always been convinced that Republicans were so congenitally dumb that he could afford to make mistakes, since the GOP would inevitably make worse ones. By now, I'd almost given up thinking that was a risky attitude: even Postrel had written that "the GOP has reclaimed its old status as the stupid party, deaf to the language of achievement and hope." But I did wonder how long the Republican Party would stay agreeably Neanderthal for Randlett's convenience.

In California, where Gray Davis—a breathtakingly dull technocrat with textbook New Democrat politics—was fighting hard-right conservative Dan Lungren, the state's attorney general, to become governor, the Republicans were under pressure to change. Randlett's old colleague Dan Schnur had left TechNet, perhaps discouraged by Randlett's superior ability to organize TechNet's members for the Democrats. Schnur was now advising Dan Lungren's campaign, and had tried to claim H1-B for his candidate in order to use the visa issue against Gray Davis. Schnur still had a lot of friends in high tech, and he was way too sharp to think he could win Silicon Valley by promoting Lungren as a socially conservative immigrant-basher.

But Randlett beat him to the center first. "Dan Schnur thought he was real clever, because the White House was still waffling on H1-B," Randlett sniffed. "So he thought he'd stick it to Gore by making Davis choose between the White House and high tech. But at the local level we'd got to Davis already, and Davis was like, 'H1-B's great, it's the right thing for the state, I'm happy to tell the White House so.' Stopped him cold."

The H1-B battle stretched out over several weeks, during which I'd stop by to see Randlett occasionally and check in on the status of events. I asked him one day why, if the New Economy logic of growth was so obvious, and its political benefits for California and the administration so clear, the White House couldn't see the light and unequivocally promote the TechNet line on H1-B visas? Randlett started to rant about "entrenched bosses" and "the old model," but his phone rang again.

"John!" he said warmly. "How are you? Yeah, I really feel bad for him, and Hillary and Chelsea, and all the crap they have to go through." And then he was off, talking to John Doerr about Clinton's troubles, and discussing plans for an upcoming TechNet dinner with Al Gore. It took me a few hours of lounging around and half listening in while Randlett breezed through a couple dozen more of these apparently unrelated phone calls before I began to piece things together.

As far as I could tell, from a Beltway politician's point of view right now, the information age that Randlett was touting so enthusiastically was notable mainly for having unleashed Matt Drudge upon the world. Back in Washington, the Monica Lewinsky scandal occupied the center of the universe, and every piece of political maneuvering in town revolved around the crisis. Thus President Clinton and the Democrats had two overriding, and related, concerns: saving Clinton from impeachment and further political damage, and saving other Democrats from defeat in the fall 1998 elections.

The White House was especially invested in California. A Democratic governor in California would preside over two events that were crucial to the interests of the party: the redistricting following the 2000 census that would set the stage for the November 2000 congressional elections, and the vitally important California presidential primary in March 2000. Gore, in particular, was eager to see Davis elected. He obviously shared an ideological affinity with Davis: the success of Davis's centrist message would be a good indicator for Gore's own chances with California voters. The vice president's strategy for getting the nomination depended on winning key states from the start, and arriving at the convention with a solid majority of delegates. Getting Davis in place and stumping for him would go a long way toward helping Gore lock up California.

Randlett knew all this, which is why he was combining tough talk on H1-B visas with some strategically dangled carrots. Silicon Valley, he had decided, should weigh in for Gray Davis in the governor's race, and show the Democratic Party that it was a constituency worth courting. It should demonstrate that it was above the petty politics of impeachment, and that it would stick by Clinton in return for action on its issues. His high-tech friends could also, through donations to the Democratic Congressional Campaign Committee — "the D-triple-C," Randlett had taught the techies to say — show how helpful they could be in a pinch. "The thing about having a guy like me around is I don't mind asking for money," he told me modestly.

Randlett picked up the phone, and was soon heavily into shoptalk with a Democratic Party fund-raiser. "I can fax you the list of targets we talked about," he said. "We're making extra effort with Dan Case and Eric Schmidt but if there are other folks where a call would make a difference, we should put them on Gray's call list. And hey, thanks for helping out on Indiana. I appreciate it." He hung up, then started going over Senator Barbara Boxer's endorsement list.

A few minutes later, Randlett was calling a high-tech executive about the California gubernatorial race and trying to wring money out of him. "Gray was great at 3Com," he said. "He said he agreed with high tech on H1-B visas, and when we asked him if he'd tell that to Clinton, he said sure." Randlett paused. "Yeah, Gore's coming out on the twenty-seventh to do an event for Gray," he said. "We're trying to get one of those famous clutches put together for the same time. I want to tie you in so you're in at ground zero, want to get a couple names of people you think should join us." Randlett laughed. "Yeah, if you like them and they're nice, they're Gore supporters too, right? Thanks. You're a trouper."

Randlett hung up, and we went out for coffee. While we stood in line at Starbucks, he told me about his next project: organizing a new round of Gore-Tech meetings to cement the support of key high-tech executives in the Valley and around the country. "We've been pretty successful in creating a fear of being left behind," he bragged. "I'm going after a bunch of guys who might like Gore, and trying to convince them that early is better than late." Randlett started rattling off names. "Jim Bidzos at RSA, Benhamou at 3Com, they care a lot about e-rate; they aren't really hard-core Republicans. Roger MacNamee, the VC, he's on; Scott Cook—he's a TechNet guy, we own that part, but we want him to do the right thing with Gore. Uh, Dan Case from H&Q, Peter Curry from Netscape, Gary Patterson, he's a gay activist—we need to take all the women, gay, black activists who aren't in spraypaint mode, and sign them up—and maybe Sky Dayton from EarthLink. Who else . . ."

Randlett flipped back and forth so casually among his multiple identities as TechNet political director, Gore-Tech organizer, Gore fund-raiser, Gray Davis fund-raiser, and general Democratic Party cheerleader that I often got confused trying to follow what he was up to in any single conversation. But the density of detail didn't mean that Randlett lacked purpose. "There are just two things worth doing right now," he said. "Raising money and putting it in Gore's hands so he can start using it. We need to be the dominant player for Al Gore in the earliest primary, which is the money primary."

The same dynamic was at work for Randlett himself, who stood to gain influence and stature, and help secure himself a place in Gore's inner campaign circle, if he could personally raise a lot of money for the vice president now. "I committed to $250,000 for Gore, which will put me in the top 1 percent of fund-raisers for the leadership PAC," he explained. Ever mindful of the need to step lightly among the competing egos that surrounded Gore, though, Randlett added, "I've done a good job so far making sure I'm not in anyone's path to success. People who aren't trying to muscle you out are always a double-word score."

What Randlett still worried about was skepticism from Gore's advisers, who would be looking at all the contributions coming in from different fund-raisers around the country. "Political stock works the same way as stock," he said. "It depends on the present value of your future earnings." If Randlett failed to meet his $250,000 goal—if he made a merely respectable, rather than a spectacular, showing, then the buzz around the Valley's importance would fade. "Then, it's likely they'll say the tech guys are overrated, a lot of hype, no show," Randlett said. "They'll say the unions and trial lawyers are always there, and these are guys who could go either way—so why should Gore break his back to get close to them?"

And Randlett also worried that Gore's people were more interested in the money he could raise than in his political advice. The CEOs

Randlett was approaching liked to toss off ideas for reinventing politics: new Web sites, Internet campaigning, running politics "like a start-up." I wondered how disillusioned his new high-tech recruits would be if their checks were cashed but their suggestions were ignored. "Same old story," Tony Podesta had commented once to me. "It's like Hollywood. Hollywood was convinced that they understood the American people better than Washington did, and they had lots of advice for candidates. The movie stars and studio guys, they all wanted to be loved for their minds, and it turned out we just loved them for their money."

All through the summer of 1998, Randlett kept juggling his fund-raising work for Gore, Davis, and the DCCC while keeping his eye on Washington deals—H1-B visas, a new bill on Internet taxation, and the perennial question of who was in charge inside the White House.

The impeachment scandal was continuing to stiffen the resolve of the hard-right wing of the Republican Party, whose members remained uninterested in courting high tech when they could be railing against sinners instead. This should have made New Democrats in general, and Randlett in particular, confident that they could continue cozying up to high tech unimpeded by competition from the GOP. But the scandal had its own dynamic, one not entirely subject to reason.

I found Randlett skittish about discussing the looming issue that, at any moment, could still upend all of Al Gore's plans, torpedo the Democratic Party, and recast the entire electoral landscape for the fall. "Hi, it's Wade from TechNet," he'd say casually, phoning a high-tech mark. "I really want to see you take a leadership role with the vice president, because I think the fit's just right. Yeah, let's sit down and talk about organizing, what we need to do." But he wouldn't bring up Clinton, unless the other person did first, and then he'd try to play it lightly, as if sophisticated people knew the idea of impeachment wasn't really important. "Sure, there are gonna be some rats jumping off the ship," he'd say. "But I know you're one of the guys who're gonna stay on. I appreciate it." In general, the only way I could tell whether Randlett was having a hard time was through his tone of voice: when things were going well, he was loud and profane; when he was angry or stressed, he got quiet and very polite.

"Tell me who he reports to and I'll call his boss—he's a yutz," Randlett was booming when I walked into his TechNet office in Palo Alto one afternoon in August. I figured things were going well. Despite all the equipment—phones, computers, a Palm Pilot, and a printer—crowding his desk, Randlett's most essential tool seemed to be a yellow legal pad, on which he was scribbling frantically. When he hung up and I asked him about his efforts to sell the Gray Davis–Al Gore fund-raiser, he was proud.

Marc Andreessen, the billionaire boy wonder, had agreed to open up his Palo Alto home for the event, and Randlett was thrilled. Andreessen had developed Mosaic, the first effective Web browser, in 1993 while he was still an undergraduate student in Illinois. Two years later, led by ace Silicon Valley businessman Jim Clark, with help from John Doerr, Andreessen launched Netscape—a technological and business breakthrough that effectively ushered in the entire Internet era. He'd been a key player in the "browser wars," pitting Netscape and a coalition of John Doerr's friends against Microsoft. He'd made an insane amount of money while keeping his reputation as a cutting-edge software genius. Now he was in the process of selling Netscape to AOL, and torn between taking a high-level executive job at AOL or launching another innovative start-up.

Andreessen was someone Randlett had long been cultivating for his money and name, but the two men seemed genuinely friendly as well. They were about the same age, and equally quick-witted: while Andreessen was Midwestern and blond and amiable, he was hardly the big lunk he looked. He lacked Randlett's political cunning; in fact, his expressions of interest in political affairs seemed to spring largely from an effort to be polite. But he was glad, he said, to offer his home—a sprawling stucco mansion tucked behind high walls on a quiet Palo Alto street—for whatever Randlett wanted.

In preparation for the Gray Davis fund-raiser, Randlett had written up some remarks for Andreessen to make, and sent Gore's staff a note reminding them that Andreessen, who would be turning twenty-eight the day before the event, was devoted to his bulldogs. "They should pay him some personal attention," Randlett said. "The guy has made a decision to do the right thing. He's rock-solid, and they shouldn't fuck this up."

As it turned out, they didn't. A few hundred people gathered on the lawn, laughing dutifully as Gray Davis and Al Gore exchanged predictable jokes about their images: "He's my charisma consultant," Davis said, pointing to the wooden vice president. Both politicians made fawning reference to Silicon Valley "where the future is being invented every day," and Davis added some words about "the almost mystical belief that all things are possible in California, because we are a people of destiny." After the speeches, Davis, as socially tone-deaf as the archetypal geek, introduced Andreessen to the vice president. "Al, you should probably meet Marc," Davis said, without much enthusiasm. "He's the youngest and richest man here." Gore pumped Andreessen's hand warmly, and delivered birthday greetings from President Clinton.

Andreessen, in a new gray Armani suit, beamed hospitably. Figures had just been released by the University of Texas that showed the Internet economy had grown, from 1995 to 1998, at a rate of around 175 percent, compared with 3.8 percent for the overall U.S. economy. For the man who had made consumer access to the World Wide Web possible, this must have been gratifying.

Andreessen's bulldogs managed to stay indoors until the end of the fund-raiser, when they ran out past the Secret Service guards and peed by the dessert table. "Nice," said Randlett, thanking Andreessen as the waiters packed up. "Thanks so much, pal. We'll talk." The net for the afternoon was going to be around $350,000, Randlett thought.

If fund-raising were the only measure of Randlett's success, then the "branding" of Al Gore as the standard-bearer of high tech had continued without incident—proving that Gore's identification with Clinton, and even the Democratic Party's identification with Clinton, was not yet a huge impediment. But as the fights over H1-B visas showed, and as the power struggles inside the Gore campaign suggested, real politics were much more complicated than fund-raising. Holding together the alliance between Gore and high tech would take a lot more than setting up yet another dinner. And there were other bugs in the system just waiting to show up.

CHAPTER eight

Even as what an old-fashioned friend of mine liked to call "the Year of Presidential Shame" wore on, the economy continued booming, keeping Clinton's approval ratings higher than any of his enemies—or even his friends—imagined possible. Unemployment was the lowest in nearly three decades; there was a budget surplus of $70 billion; and an overheated obsession with making money had moved out of Silicon Valley and into the heart of America's mainstream.

The hype made me think about some fourth-graders I'd taught, for whom every number bigger than twenty was automatically "a million," "ten million," or "eighteen bazillion million." We'd spent a whole week taping pieces of graph paper to the wall and counting off squares, so that the class could look at an actual million of something. It didn't cool down the kids' rhetoric, of course—"I bet there's *ten million* ants in that sandwich"—but it helped me understand the figure. Now that grownups tossed off "a million" the way eight-year-olds used to, though, I was having serious trouble with math. I just couldn't grasp the market capitalizations of the companies—new companies—that kept popping out of the IPO gate. They had no earnings. They had about twenty-three employees each. And they were all making a bazillion dollars.

Wade Randlett's interest in these new high-tech companies, though, wasn't *all* about money. His political work, he assured me in August, was intended not just to fund-raise from high-tech millionaires but to organize, to "claim these guys for the forces of light."

But one of the main problems that Randlett was confronting now was that high tech, even as it took control of the economy, was becoming too big, too diverse, and too fractious to be contained by a single political identity. Everyone knew it, and Randlett himself admitted that "high tech" was far too broad a category for the thousands of New Economy businesses that had sprung up in the last year.

But neither did Randlett want to cede the space he'd carved out for himself, as political adviser to and spokesman for the fracturing categories of high tech and the New Economy. He wanted to "own" the politics of high tech; he wanted to be seen as the person who understood the interests of the industry, the interests of the Democrats, and who could make the matches. He didn't want to risk letting Republicans in, or business competitors to his friends; he wanted to keep control. Randlett—and, behind him, the shadow of John Doerr—still wanted TechNet to represent it all.

Randlett offered to let me accompany him on an organizing trip to Seattle, where he was planning to promote TechNet and recruit a handful of well-placed, high-tech capitalists for Gore. It was one of the visits around the country to high-tech centers that he'd been talking about making for a year; now that places like Austin and San Diego and Salt Lake City and North Carolina had their own share of Internet millionaires and hot start-up companies, Randlett knew that he had to expand his network out of the Valley. Still, he'd been putting it off for as long as possible. "Seattle is like we were in the Valley in 1995 in terms of political involvement," he said. "It's like an archaeological dig."

I thought the trip would be an opportunity to see, firsthand, how far Randlett's reach could really extend, and whether he and TechNet could continue to paper over the actual differences among high-tech companies and incorporate them all into one political entity. I wanted to see whether the vision of a unified political force—one oriented toward Gore and New Democrats—was still possible, or whether money and growth had pulled the industry too far apart.

The Seattle trip would be another of Randlett's blended missions: part ongoing Gore-Tech work, for the vice president's office; part unofficial preparatory work for Gore 2000 and fund-raising for Gore's

Leadership '98 PAC; part TechNet proselytizing; and part network-building and general schmoozing on behalf of New Democrats.

And it was another of Randlett's undertakings that seemed mysteriously oblivious to factual reality. In the late summer of 1998, it was just as weird, I thought, to go to Seattle without paying a call on Microsoft as it was to work in Democratic Party politics without mentioning Bill Clinton's possible impeachment. The landscape of the entire American high-tech industry, it could convincingly be argued, was dominated by Bill Gates and his empire, but certainly in Microsoft's hometown the company should be impossible to ignore. The city was crammed with tens of thousands of Gates's employees—and with thousands of Microsoft millionaires who had retired in their thirties. Gates's ongoing feuds with other CEOs were staples of local chat. The company's exploits rated almost daily coverage in the local newspapers, as did the philanthropic activities of Gates's foundation. Not to mention, of course, the small fact that the Justice Department and twenty states had, a few months earlier, launched a landmark antitrust case against Microsoft that marked the single most significant intersection of the high-tech industry and the government to date.

The entire case, I believed, was inextricably bound up with the politics of the Valley, insofar as it was bound up with the ambitions of TechNet's co-founders, John Doerr and Jim Barksdale. Barksdale's general counsel, Roberta Katz, had drawn up a brief against Microsoft detailing its alleged anticompetitive practices and submitted it to the Justice Department; Barksdale himself would be a key witness for the government against Bill Gates. Doerr's role would be much less public, but it was obvious that Microsoft was at least as much a competitor to him and Kleiner Perkins as it was to companies like Netscape. Microsoft was a major investor in promising software and had spread its millions around relentlessly in the attempt to preempt, co-opt, and own new technologies. As more and more capital flowed into Silicon Valley, venture capitalists like Doerr had been forced to fight harder to become the lead investors in promising companies—and they frequently found themselves competing with Microsoft. So, though TechNet as an organization had remained what it called "agnostic" on the subject of the case against Microsoft, it did not take much to see that TechNet was run by people whose every interest lay in helping the Justice Department weaken their powerful competitor. But on this trip, it seemed, Microsoft would be missing from the conversation. Randlett was talking about visiting only a handful of young entrepreneurs with Internet start-ups, a biotech guy, and Jeff Bezos, the CEO of Amazon.com.

It turned out that Randlett's girlfriend, Tamsin Smith, was also arranging to come to Seattle, in an attempt to wring some private vacation time out of a business trip. She was as hard a worker as Randlett was, and her job for The Gap kept her on the road a lot; this would be a chance for her to connect with Randlett. "I'm done by five both days," Randlett vowed, as he and I went over plans. "I'm in deep shit if we don't wrap up the meetings in time for me to take Tamsin to dinner." I nodded understandingly: my girlfriend was coming, too. In a perverse way, I rather enjoyed these male-bonding exercises with Randlett, though I did have pangs of sympathy for Smith, who was an impressively good sport about his chronically impossible schedule. "I'm with you," I said. We booked the tickets.

We were staying with friends in a rainy, run-down, rose-covered neighborhood dotted with black storefront churches and Vietnamese noodle shops. I picked up Randlett at his downtown hotel, where well-dressed men carried laptops and cell phones through the lobby and copies of *The Wall Street Journal* lay next to local papers in the lounge. Smith was off at a meeting of her own, so as we walked to breakfast Randlett rehearsed for me what he was planning to say.

First was the question of issues. For all TechNet's hype about "the high-tech agenda," it was difficult to tell what the Seattle executives actually cared about—and to what extent they shared the concerns of their counterparts in Silicon Valley. Half to himself and half to me, Randlett mused aloud about which issue he would use to grab their attention. "Could be FASAB [the Federal Accounting Standards Advisory Board], could be education, could be stem-cell-tissue research," he said. I looked dubious. I thought FASAB, in particular—which was under pressure from the industry to revise its rules on whether stock options should be treated as compensation—was a cause unlikely to drive people to the barricades. But then I recalled a rally Paul Lippe had organized back in 1995 about accounting standards. Lippe's event had drawn hundreds of incensed managers and executives to a parking lot in Mountain View, where they shouted at Senator Dianne Feinstein and threatened civil disobedience. Maybe there were other issues, equally unobvious, just waiting to be identified.

Randlett continued. "The point, anyway, is to get them to say what's the single most important thing, then present it to Gore, so he can give it back to them. You want them to feel like he's nailed it, he understands."

The same process of consultation that would draw executives to Gore, he said, also worked in recruiting for TechNet. "I ask them what they care about, then explain that we can be enforcers for it. Until TechNet came along, there was nobody who, if politicians crossed us, was gonna push back." Randlett chuckled. "These guys in Seattle are all about efficiency," he said. "I want them to understand that we get things done."

Things simmered along slowly for the first few meetings, with slightly bemused executives listening to Randlett brag about the influence of TechNet. Many Seattle high-tech companies already belonged to industry associations, including the Technology Alliance, chaired by Bill Gates, Sr., and the Business Software Alliance; they didn't seem to understand why they should join another. Randlett explained that TechNet wasn't really a threat to anyone, though he couldn't entirely stop himself from bragging. "We don't compete with industry associations," he'd say. "We don't hire hacks and hope they do a good job. We develop relationships with the most important people, and get executives into meetings with them. We're not about lobbying; we're about a different kind of politics."

And those politics, Randlett said, taught that "you don't win because you're right—you win because you're strong. We build your political capital so that when it comes to the crunch, he takes your call." The "he" Randlett was referring to could, of course, be construed in a bipartisan way. But he deftly worked in the fact that the Democratic side of TechNet and "our group of guys in the Valley" had already developed a strong relationship with Al Gore—and then he would segue into the next item on his list, getting support for Gore. Once again, he skated over the question of his own multiplicity of roles, and presented himself as the go-to guy for the Al Gore 2000 campaign. Smoothly, he offered the Seattle executives the chance to join the club.

"It's hard to overstate how tough it is to get involved in a [presidential] campaign late in the game," went Randlett's pitch. "Right now, I've got a core group of business people, real live capitalists, who are putting their money on Gore, and who are making sure that their message gets out." Randlett had a sincere, we-understand-each-other tone. "Al Gore used to have, as tech advisers, people from the universities," he said. "But with all due respect, if you want to win important political battles, you don't start with the universities. We want to make sure we're in there at his side—better us than the trial lawyers or the teachers' unions."

Not everyone got it. One twenty-nine-year-old software entrepreneur, an angelic Seattle punkster with a tentative goatee and slouchy clothes, had to have Randlett clarify for him what a "primary" involved, and most of the executives seemed somewhat befuddled by the rules governing PACs. I thought Randlett made a thousand dollars for a chance to "get in early" at Gore's side sound like a pretty good bet. The executives were hardly political insiders—but they weren't fools, and I didn't think the gist of Randlett's message would be lost on them. *We have power*, it said. *You can share it. Get on board now.*

It was late afternoon when we arrived at the offices of Amazon.com, the Internet start-up turned phenomenon that had made "e-commerce" a phrase that even Washington had to care about. In a little more than three years, the pioneering on-line bookstore had earned Jeff Bezos nearly $9 billion, and changed the way consumers thought about shopping.

Randlett wanted to make this visit productive, though less by getting Amazon.com to become an active player with TechNet than by recruiting its chief executive for Gore. Bezos, a former computer whiz and Wall Street hedge-fund manager, had started Amazon.com in his Bellevue, Washington, garage in 1995. Almost immediately, it began a prodigious rate of growth, becoming the world's biggest on-line consumer merchant, quadrupling sales by its third year and attracting more than 4.5 million customers. Bezos was a prize worth getting. If Randlett could snag e-commerce's hottest executive for Gore—winning his money, his endorsement, his help—it would go a long way toward cementing his reputation as the most important go-between for the worlds of politics and of high tech.

Jeff Bezos came down to the reception area of Amazon.com, a desk plopped in a scruffy corner of the ground floor of an old hospital building, to meet us, and led us up a dimly lit flight of stairs to his office. Bezos, a small guy dressed in khakis and a denim shirt, had an eager, open face and an irrepressibly bouncy demeanor. His tiny room was crammed with papers and books spilling off every surface; he pulled up some beat-up folding chairs and sat down, leaning forward. "I don't want to waste your time, Jeff," Randlett began. Bezos nodded impatiently.

Randlett had two things he wanted from Bezos: his endorsement of Gore, which had to do with Bezos's image as the most successful entrepreneur in cyberspace; and his advice for the vice president, which had to do with his actual smarts.

Oddly, Bezos turned out to be far cagier about the first request. "I just want you to know who's on board," Randlett began, rattling off the names of executives whose prominence and cool he thought would appeal to Amazon.com's iconoclastic leader. "Jerry [Yang], Marc [Andreessen], Joe Kraus, Halsey [Minor]."

I tried to stay expressionless. The two men were facing each other, close-up, and I was in a chair slightly off to one side, enjoying their benign neglect, so Bezos probably didn't notice how startled I was at the mention of Minor. The CEO of C/NET was, I knew, a Republican at heart, and though he'd been a generous host to various New Democrats, and a cheerful supporter of TechNet, it seemed highly unlikely that Minor had really signed on already to support the vice president. (Two years later, in fact, he would become a vocal supporter of Republican candidate George W. Bush.) Apparently, Randlett was following standard campaign practice as he gave Bezos names: in the absence of explicit rejection, it was perfectly ethical to claim someone's support and to do it as early as possible.

None of the name-dropping seemed to matter, though: Bezos had already demonstrated, in his approach to business, his utter lack of interest in following the crowd. Now he was nodding and making hand motions, as if to speed up Randlett's presentation.

"OK," Randlett said without missing a beat. "The next thing is, nobody in politics knows how to sell themselves on the Web. How do you get e-mail to a million people without being a spammer? How do you build a strategy for a cyberspace campaign?" He paused, then slipped in a sly, pointed question. "How can we get Amazon.com people to Gore?"

Bezos blinked, as if debating whether to fully turn on his attention. "The thing about Gore is he *has* to win the Web," Randlett confided. "He's the technoguy, he's got the rep for being Mr. Internet, it's his to lose. The stakes are so much higher for him. The other guys—nobody expects them to know their way around the Web. If Gore's on the Web, everyone says yeah, fine. But if Bush stakes out the Web first, Gore's in deep shit." Randlett took a deep breath. "Gore doesn't just have to have 'a cyberspace strategy,'" he concluded. "He has to *be* the Web."

Now Bezos was on. His slightly goofy, elfin face lit up, and he thought for at most fifteen seconds before blurting out a marketing idea. "Lawn signs," he said. Randlett looked at him quizzically.

"The lawn sign in cyberspace," Bezos said a little impatiently. He was thinking aloud, describing his concept. "It'll look a little crooked, handmade, a little grass under it. It'll say 'Gore 2000,' or 'Geeks for Gore.' And if you click on it, there's a link to how you can get one for your own Web page. And a link to Gore's page. Or to another statement about why I support Gore—" he broke off. "Nah, too fancy," he said. "Just lawn signs. The point is, you don't pay for them—they're not commercial. They're the hip sticker to stick on your own Web page."

I'd seldom seen Randlett so genuinely excited. "Yeah," he breathed, spinning out the idea. "People see lawn signs on their friends' sites, they say, 'Hey, that's cool. Where can I get one?' Everyone wants one, they spread . . ."

Bezos and Randlett were smiling at each other, while Randlett calculated aloud. "Millions of people have Web pages," he figured. "You don't want him on Yahoo! That's like a TV ad; this has to be grassroots. Go to Geocities and AOL instead . . . Say we get ten million of them to put a lawn sign up for Gore. By the time Gore launches his campaign, we *own* the Web." He shook his head admiringly. "Jeff," he said. "Man, Jeff, you're a freakin' genius. Bob Squier will wet himself when he hears this."

Bezos looked happy. "All you need is a thousand of them up," he said. "Then traditional media will pick it up, do your marketing for you."

"I want you to sit down with the D.C. folks making this happen, and get the right info flow to them," Randlett said. He pumped Bezos's hand. "Jeff," he said with a grin. "Thanks."

As we walked down the stairs, I asked Randlett why he hadn't asked Bezos for a contribution. He looked irritated, and I could tell that in the excitement of the moment he'd just forgotten. But he rallied. "I'll call him tonight and thank him again for his help," he said. "Then I'll explain how giving money is like putting a sign up, so that when people sift through the finance records they know the Web supports Gore. And how you need to establish yourself—so when you give them a good idea, like Jeff just did, they'll execute on it."

I turned it over in my mind. Actual lawn signs, as far as I knew, had never been decisive in elections, and virtual lawn signs on Web sites would probably look like just more advertising junk. I wasn't particularly impressed by the concept, but I kept quiet. The point for Rand-lett, I realized, was probably not to extract a really good campaign idea from Bezos—who, after all, knew nothing about campaigns, even if he was supposed to be a retail genius. The point was to get Bezos to care about Al Gore, and to exploit the universal human tendency to commit to people who ask for your advice.

But Bezos's idea was doomed to be lost, as were almost all of the contacts in Seattle that Randlett had tried to forge. Much bigger forces were at work in the world of politics, and in the next few months Rand-lett's efforts to pull Seattle into his orbit weren't going to get much attention from the White House.

CHAPTER nine

D ecency," Tony Podesta was saying, "dictates that we talk about politics tonight." It was a breezy September evening, and Podesta had just kissed Senator Carol Moseley-Braun goodbye at the door of an upscale Italian restaurant in downtown Washington, crossed the room shaking hands and greeting power diners, and sat down with a sigh. A few blocks away, in the Capitol, independent counsel Kenneth Starr's thirty-six boxes of documents were stacked under guard, emitting vibrations strong enough to disturb the atmosphere at every table in town. Podesta ordered a bottle of Amarone and leaned toward his guest, John Williams, the CEO of Biztravel.com. "I'm afraid your testimony at the Aviation Subcommittee just might not get a lot of press tomorrow," he said dryly.

The Podesta brothers had pulled even closer than usual as the impeachment scandal built. Both were solid Clinton loyalists: Tony had run the Clinton-Gore campaign in Pennsylvania in 1996; and John, dubbed "the Secretary of Shit" by colleagues during Whitewater for his damage-control role, had fiercely defended the President as each new allegation surfaced. When John was summoned in the summer to testify before the grand jury investigating the Monica Lewinsky affair, Tony had spirited his brother's children off to Italy for a vacation with their grandmother. Now Tony Podesta was calmly going about his business with clients, congressmen, and Democratic Party bigwigs, while his brother coordinated staff response to the scandal, and the mood inside the White House lurched from anxiety to hysteria.

I'd heard that Tony Podesta was showing up at the White House on Saturdays and evenings to help with strategy. "I don't know much, of course," Podesta said, sounding unworried when I asked him how John was doing. "I haven't wanted to ask." He smiled gamely and raised his glass. "Cheers," he said. "To the Republic. God help us."

The next night I had a not-for-attribution dinner with a New Democrat congressman. "He's losing altitude," said the congressman, chewing his beef. "Fast."

I didn't need to ask who "he" was: Clinton's precarious position was all that anyone in Washington could talk about. "How could someone who had all these amazing political gifts throw them away?" the congressman demanded. The House New Democrat Network, with Clinton's cooperation, had been using New Economy issues to drive House Democrats to the center, and now the congressman saw all the New Democrats' work in danger. He sounded furious, then depressed. "I'm afraid we could lose the party," he said.

The congressman buttered his bread angrily and reviewed the state of the Democratic Party as he saw it.

"Look," he said, "I have a blue-collar Old Democrat district, and I see why high tech frightens these guys. But I'm a New Democrat. I think we can't go on the old way. Yeah, I think Clinton was right to run Jesse Jackson out. He was right on welfare, right on trade. He knew we have to move to a high-tech, information-age economy. But he also knew the Democrats can't afford to lose all those people in the unions." He sighed. "Basically, I think Bill Clinton saved our party."

But now, I asked, where did Clinton's troubles leave the Democrats? The congressman looked glum. "Gore has a kind of inevitability for 2000, because nobody else has a machine, or people, or money," he said. "But Gore can't promote the New Economy because he can't convince people that they won't be left behind. The Silicon Valley guys sure can't do it, because they're elitist, arrogant; they say you're stupid if you disagree with them on anything. Al Gore just doesn't have the knack that Clinton did: he's a technocrat, he has no soul, he can't carry the different parts of the party. Clinton was the only one able to bring all the Democrats together."

I noticed that the congressman was already referring to the President in the past tense, and pointed it out to him. He shook his head, tight-lipped. "If you look at it from a distance, a literary distance, it's really tragic," the congressman said. "It's a tragedy."

Back in Silicon Valley, the period leading up to President Clinton's September 25, 1998, dinner with high-tech executives was developing into what Randlett called "the worst time of my political life."

Randlett recounted the sequence of events to me one afternoon in his TechNet office, where he sat sprawled under a message board that featured, tacked up in the top corner, an inspirational thought attributed to Henry Kissinger. "There cannot be a crisis next week," it read, "because my schedule is already full."

The dinner, a fund-raiser for the Democratic National Committee, had been planned as a way to inject badly needed cash into the party, and at the same time show that the President retained strong support from the business world. John Doerr, who remained as loyal to the administration as anyone, had committed to hosting the fund-raiser, despite growing speculation in Washington that Kenneth Starr's investigation of Clinton was about to draw blood. "There was mostly cocktail chatter, but that kind of chatter can matter a lot in certain contexts," Randlett said. The President's public appearances were becoming more and more restricted, partly to fend off the press and partly because of angry anti-Clinton demonstrators who dogged him, holding up signs that read "Liar" and "Shame." Concerned, Randlett and Doerr had decided to move their dinner from Doerr's home to the less personal but more secure site of the Technology Museum in San Jose.

What Randlett termed "two weeks of hell" followed, as the scandal snowballed nearly out of control. "The President was in free fall, and it honestly wasn't clear if he was going to be President on September 25," he said. "Then on the sixth and seventh the cigar stuff blows up, there's Monica all over TV, and everything went steeply downhill."

Even in Silicon Valley, executives who had dismissed the scandal as an old-fashioned, overblown Washington fuss began to feel a need to assert their outrage. "I was the nearest phone call these guys could make to complain about Clinton's morals," Randlett recalled. "People were getting beat up by their wives, their colleagues, their swim coach—'How can you eat dinner with this man? You have kids of your own.' " Randlett sounded disgusted. "Right, you have a daughter who might grow up to be a stalker like Monica," he said with a sneer, echoing the ugly White House whisper campaign against Monica Lewinsky. "Give me a break." He rolled his eyes. "But I'd say, 'Yeah, yeah, I know, you're right, it does suck. There is no excuse for it. It *is* bad, that's why it's called a bad situation.' "

Four days before the event, and "just forty-eight hours before the Secret Service deadline to clear the guests' names," Randlett continued, "they announce the release of the video [Clinton's videotaped grand-jury testimony], which freezes everything. We only had $300,000 in commitments, and we needed a minimum of five. We'd done six the last year, and anything less would be reported as losing support. We had no new bodies, no first-time commitments. Some people said no outright, some said they were waiting to see what happened with the tapes. People from Regis [McKenna] to Halsey Minor were giving us soft nos to soft maybes. At that point, John went into gear."

Local reporters were seizing upon Clinton's failure to attract big-name Silicon Valley donors to the event at the Tech Museum. The *San Francisco Chronicle*'s story, headlined "SCANDAL SPOOKS HIGH-TECH DONORS," had Randlett denying rumors that Doerr was "scrambling to find people who would pay to attend," and that high-tech support for the President had "eroded."

But the sex scandal had not entirely overshadowed real politics, and on September 23 the climate changed. For a month, there had been a stalemate over legislation designed to increase the number of H1-B visas, with the White House, under pressure from labor, indicating that it might veto the bill. As the impeachment drama spiraled downward for Clinton, and his fund-raising event in the Valley drew closer, there was a shift in the White House's position.

On September 23, Clinton announced a "compromise," saying that the H1-B visa legislation had been amended to include funding for re-training programs for American workers. And the number of H1-B visas would be doubled.

It was a clear choice by Clinton in favor of New Democrats and against the interests of the Old: it was, crowed a TechNet press release, a "victory" for Silicon Valley. And a number of executives who relied on immigrant engineers suddenly found themselves much more disposed to letting John Doerr talk them into attending a fund-raising event with a moral degenerate.

The dinner at the Tech Museum allowed Silicon Valley to experience, firsthand, the seductive magic of the embattled Bill Clinton. Those who attended the dinner realized that Clinton's political skills— demonstrated both by his behind-the-scenes dealmaking on H1-B visas and by his virtuoso public displays of charm—could keep him in office despite attack, humiliation, and impeachment. "The thing about these events is that they're always perfect," Randlett reflected. "Bill Clinton sits there with his big think face on, and everyone's locked in on him. There are protesters outside, counterprotesters, reporters, there's a red carpet, and everything is imploding on a dark star of itself. I mean, it's a fix you can't get anywhere else." Randlett shook his head admiringly. "We're the friends, we're inside. We can talk about what's on the front page every day. The President gives the sense he's really there, really listening, and you just feel inside the center of the world."

Doerr, himself quite a master at communicating the sense that he offered entrée into the center of the world, had succeeded in making the event a record fund-raiser, pulling in more than the $600,000 raised at Clinton's Silicon Valley dinner the previous year. For the time being, Clinton had won the support, if not the complete respect, of his high-tech backers. All in all, it was the kind of performance that drove Clinton's enemies completely berserk.

The election itself, six weeks later, made them even crazier. Despite— or, as it began to seem in retrospect, because of—the Republicans' incessant hammering at Clinton, the Republican Party lost a net of five congressional seats in the midterm elections, narrowing their already narrow governing majority in the House even further. Republicans won twenty-three of thirty-six contested governorships but sustained a net loss of one. (A significant victory was in Texas, where George W. Bush, with his mantra of "compassionate conservatism," and his support from software companies in Austin, had ignited speculation that he was the heir apparent to the Republican presidential nomination in 2000.) Though President Clinton still had the threat of impeachment and removal from office hanging over him, the election made it clear that voters, whatever they thought of the man, were unwilling to reject everything the President stood for. "The results are clear and unambiguous," Clinton declared, calling the election a vindication of his centrist policies.

Accepting some of the blame for his party's poor showing, Speaker of the House Newt Gingrich was frank. "I mean, I totally underestimated the degree to which people would just get sick of twenty-four-hour-a-day talk television and talk radio and then the degree to which this whole scandal became just sort of disgusting by sheer repetition," he said.

In California, several New Democrats who had been vocal supporters of high tech triumphed, including Ellen Tauscher, Anna Eshoo, Zoe Lofgren, and New Democrat leader Cal Dooley. Gray Davis defeated California's right-wing attorney general Dan Lungren, winning handily with 58 percent of the vote and claiming a victory for "the moderate path to the future." Democratic senator Barbara Boxer was re-elected. Overall, Democrats swept the state, gaining a major advantage for 2000, when California's enormous House delegation—measuring an eighth of the entire House of Representatives—would go through redistricting. It was, everyone agreed, a huge boost for Al Gore.

There were conflicting interpretations of the politics of Democratic victory, however. "The Clinton–New Democrat redefining of the center has finally taken hold," said DLC chairman Al From, sounding happier than he had in months. But others argued that the elections showed a resurgence of Old Democrat values, pointing to high turnouts among traditional Democratic constituencies like labor, African-Americans, and women. In California, AFL-CIO president John Sweeney pointed out, union households had gone definitively for Gray Davis—and union troops had done more than anyone else to get out the vote. Liberals insisted that, just as they had proved their loyalty to Clinton and their antipathy to Republicans during the scandal in August, they had made the difference by coming out to vote their convictions in November. "[The election is] proof that the party made a mistake when it said push away from labor, push away from blacks," the Reverend Jesse Jackson argued. "When we got our full team out on the field, we won."

Wade Randlett laughed at the claim. "Well, yeah, when Republicans are stupid, everyone votes against them," he said. Randlett believed that he and his Silicon Valley machine—no, *network*—deserved their share of recognition for their part in the victory, and started counting up his chits. He had succeeded in being one of the two largest fundraisers for Al Gore's Leadership '98 PAC—"me and one cigar-chomping guy from New York," he said, laughing. It was only a temporary plateau, and it didn't guarantee him a permanent place in the campaign, but he was enjoying the moment.

"I'm fundamentally a staffer," Randlett admitted. "And that's not gonna change. But I went to this dinner with Gore and the Leadership people, and guys like Mitchell Berger, this big deal in Florida, were at the end of the table. I looked at the place cards and couldn't see where I was supposed to be. I was halfway around when Gore calls out, 'Hey, Wade, you're over here,' and sat me to his right." Randlett smiled, relishing the memory.

But the quid pro quo is only part of politics. No matter who raised how much money, by 1999 the politics of the Democratic Party would become, once again, wildly complicated. Bill Clinton would survive impeachment, largely because of his ability to rally both Old and New Democrats against the increasingly unpopular House Republicans attacking him. In early February 1999, I read a newspaper account of House manager Ed Bryant's examination of Monica Lewinsky. In the transcript, Bryant asked his witness if she thought Bill Clinton was "a very intelligent man." Lewinsky replied as condescendingly as a Valley Girl responding to the stupidity of a parent. "I think he's a very intelligent *President*," she said. The clueless Republican was jubilant: "OK, thank goodness this is confidential," Bryant said. "Otherwise, that might be the quote of the day. I know we won't see that in the newspaper, will we?"

Clinton, undeniably, was a very intelligent President. But he would wind up in new relationships with the different wings of his party. Clinton the New Democrat, though bolstered by the fund-raising efforts of his friends in Silicon Valley and elsewhere, would be increasingly leery of political alliances with the New Democrats who had condemned him. And he would reach out anew to reward others who had done more for him—the Old Democrats whose moral, political, and electoral support had grown stronger under Republican attack.

CHAPTER ten

Back out West, the competing forces of Old and New Democrats were vividly on view, playing out as California, flush with money, ran toward the Internet—and thus the New Democratic—age. The Old Economy, though, no less than California's Old Democrats, was still at least as real a presence there as the vivid, slightly hallucinatory, new moment. As 1999 began, with clashes and lapses, conflicts, and missed opportunities to connect, I watched as the bugs in the system to date revealed themselves.

There had been a frost overnight in the Delta, and driving toward Sacramento early on the morning of Gray Davis's inauguration in January 1999, I could see citrus farmers cursing their way through the stiff mud of their orchards as they loaded smudge pots onto tractors. It had been sixteen years since a Democrat was governor of California, and Vice President Gore, along with party luminaries, would be there to celebrate as Davis took the oath. Downtown, state troopers ringed Memorial Auditorium, clutching take-out coffee and blowing on their reddened fingers.

Kim Alexander, a historian and journalist who ran a nonprofit Web site aimed at educating California voters, had warned me about the gap between the ethos of Sacramento and the booming businesses of the

New Economy. "It's the history of California repeating itself," she said. "Remember, the gold rush was the largest voluntary migration in history. People were in such a rush to get rich that California went straight to statehood without a history of self-government, because businesspeople didn't want to stop and participate. Right now, Silicon Valley's the same. People are moving here in droves, and all they care about is making money. There's no civic tradition to build on—just Californians' inherent mistrust of government."

The old auditorium's ceiling was high, framed with delicate, faded gilt stencils. On the stage in front, a hideous riser with wedding-cake white plastic columns draped in bunting was stuffed to bursting with the new governor's blond nieces and assorted county officials. Everyone stared uncomfortably at a limp American flag and waited for the glockenspiels to finish so that festivities could start.

I looked around. This was hardly the California of the New Economy, the home of digital cool, a virtual entrepreneurial cybergarage where adolescent nerds, daring capitalists, and bright-eyed immigrants worked late into the night inventing the future. This was a much older place.

Sacramento is basically an ag town, and ultimately none of the money that runs it feels very far removed from the stink of cows. Sacramento's men tend to wear bow ties or bolos; the women carry handbags and eat Waldorf salads at annual luncheons for the growers' lobby. I wondered what the Valley boys would make of the slightly defensive, overcompensating protocols of the political class here, and how they were planning to do business in the capital of their state, where two grand rivers meet in the shadow of a feed mill.

Business was being done. The sugar daddies behind the inaugural events—or "co-chairs," as the program described them delicately, in gold script—included the California Canning Peach Association, the Bank of America, the California Building Industry Association, and an assortment of waste-management, real-estate, and utility lobbies. "Patrons" and "Benefactors" ran to insurance companies, unions, the dairy cartel, and a handful of Indian tribes looking to enhance their clout vis-à-vis gaming laws. While Microsoft, Hewlett-Packard, and Gateway had all duly chipped in as "benefactors" for Davis's big day, there wasn't a peep from the hot young Internet companies whose growth had provided so much of California's boom since 1992. Nobody I had talked to in the Valley had shown interest in attending the inauguration.

Clusters of lobbyists moved among the folding chairs, shaking hands. Looking at their satisfied and polished faces, it was hard to believe that the businesses Randlett and his gang dismissed as "Old Economy" were going to wither away anytime soon—or, for that matter, that the Old Democratic politicians had any intention of yielding ground to the New.

Willie Brown, currently the mayor of San Francisco and for twenty-three years the single most powerful Democrat in California, was an excellent example. Brown, referred to alternately as Sacramento's Speaker for Life and as Ayatollah Brown, enjoyed describing his first encounter with the mores of the state capital in 1971. A vain, hugely ambitious young black transplant from Denton, Texas, Brown had arrived flaunting a political style that evoked equal parts LBJ and Huey Long. His sartorial style was equally impressive. "I showed up in a blue leisure suit with a pointed collar and an Afro," the mayor recalled with satisfaction years later. "God∂amn! Those goddamn farmers had never seen anything like me before."

Now Brown, dressed in a more contemporary outfit from Wilkes Bashford, strolled onto the stage, smiling wolfishly. A parliamentary strategist of unmatched shrewdness and an unforgiving enemy, Brown had built a kick-ass Old Democrat machine that still, three years after his departure from Sacramento, cranked out legislation according to his specifications. And since Brown tended to raise and disburse around $7 to $10 million each election cycle, most of it tribute from Old Economy tobacco and oil companies, the assembled politicians rose as one to applaud his entrance.

Brown was followed by the governor-elect, who launched into his inuagural address with the same stiff affect for which he'd teased Al Gore during the campaign. Holding his forearm at a strict ninety-degree angle to his waist, Gray Davis hacked the hand up and down and intoned slowly, "My friends. Choose not indifference. Choose hope." The crowd applauded wildly. "Choose lasting values like duty, honesty, service." More berserk clapping. Davis paused for emphasis, as if to make an extremely pointed remark. "We *will* be pragmatic," he said. The point was lost on me, but it was obviously a hit with the audience, and received sustained cheers.

It made me remember how a friend who'd moved from New York to Minnesota described the epiphany she had about her new home when she first heard Garrison Keillor's "Prairie Home Companion" in situ. The radio show was not, as she had always assumed, an ironic, gently mocking exaggeration of the oddities of an archaic rural culture but an utterly literal report. "When he says the big news this week is that everyone's kids are giving their piano recitals, the reason they respond is because everyone's kids *are* giving their piano recitals that week," she explained. "And it *is* big news."

Sacramento was the same. There was no hidden message behind Davis's flat delivery, just a literal-minded recitation of platitudes that everyone agreed with. The crowd of Californians embraced their new governor's dullness with such enthusiasm that by the time Davis reached the pinnacle of his rhetoric and called himself "a centrist," I was prepared for the standing ovation.

I was less sure that Davis represented a triumph of New Democrat values that was about to be replicated nationally: in Washington, as in Sacramento, there were plenty of signs that Old Democrats and the Old Economy were maintaining their powerful grip. And there was still another glitch that Wade Randlett was facing. Not only did the would-be kingmaker have to go up against the forces of history and inertia in order to forge his alliances but he had to go up against himself. In the months to come, Randlett would have to confront the fallout that came from his own personality and his way of doing business — a style that managed to be both too aggressively East Coast political for California and too brat-pack nerd millionaire for the Beltway.

It was, everyone around Vice President Al Gore told me, "way too early" to be thinking about the 2000 elections. I ignored this. It had not been too early for Al Gore's advisers to think about the 2000 elections a year ago, and I knew well that they were not slowing down now.

Not that I could follow what was going on. Even the most insidery people in Washington had been reduced to sniffing out hints and guessing about direction from a scant number of vague clues. Partly, of course, this was because there was no formal campaign structure, no overall political strategy, no staff. By the time Gore's official campaign launched, in April 1999, newspaper stories would describe "chaos" in the campaign, and an "incoherent," "nobody's home" public image.

But even though positions in the Gore camp were still unofficial in February, and even though it was common knowledge that, as one aide told me, "a whole lot of heads will roll before this thing is over," plenty of people still wanted to establish themselves from the start. Some constituencies — those with long-standing, assumed ties to the administration, like labor—felt little pressure to declare their love and fealty to any presidential candidate so early, and were willing to be coy for a while. Others, like Simon Rosenberg and his House New Democrats, felt that their immediate political battles on the Hill were too demanding to allow much long-range focus on Gore. But high tech was different.

Wade Randlett had always tried to impress upon me the value of his mantra "Early is better"; his efforts to get high-tech stars close to Gore had been a central part of his political work since 1996. Others might argue that the best way to influence the Democratic Party in general was by supporting various congressional candidates around the country, or by focusing on specific issues. Randlett certainly believed in spreading his influence around, and for 1999 he had a political strategy that would include expanded work with the Democratic National Committee and the New Democrat Network. But he wasn't about to miss the opportunity to position himself for 2000. Silicon Valley had a lot to gain by elbowing its way in to Gore from the outset.

Silicon Valley also had plenty to lose, and to many in Washington this was largely because of Randlett, whose incessant arm-twisting and self-promotion had caused him problems from the beginning, alienating a number of his political allies as well as his ideological enemies. "He steps on a lot of people's toes," mourned one Democrat, who was left picking up the pieces once, after a "hard-ass" Randlett had stormed through several representatives' offices, demanding their votes on H1-B legislation. "It's not 'How can we work with you?' but 'This is the way it's gonna be.' He doesn't understand that people need a lot of stroking. He doesn't get the idea of compromise."

I thought Randlett, for sure, was riding for a fall. His incredible hubris—failing to see that members of Congress, for example, had egos at least as big as his, and needed coddling—and the get-it-done-now attitude he'd picked up from his Silicon Valley friends were a dangerous combination. Randlett wasn't an easygoing guy. But I also saw a lot of simple jealousy in the way Washington treated him, and in the way people in the Democratic Party dissed him. It was the classic resentment that the Old Guard shows to newcomers who come to town and win.

This second interpretation was, naturally, the one Randlett preferred. As he saw it, his entire career with TechNet had been about challenging what he referred to as "Old Politics," and he didn't mind being unpopular for it. In fact, being disliked made him more convinced that he was winning.

One afternoon, over beers at a Mexican restaurant in Palo Alto, Randlett gave me a capsule version of his efforts to date in lobbying for TechNet—a self-serving, angry but not altogether inaccurate history.

"In July '96," Randlett began, "it was, 'Ha, look at all those Valley guys coming in against 211. They're gonna get their butts kicked.' We raised $40 million, turned the President of the United States around, kicked *their* butt. They said, 'OK, that's initiative politics, the tech guys are learning to crawl now, they're at the primate level.'" Randlett paused for a minute, and sipped his Corona. "But the size of the money we raised sure got attention," he said. "I remember that Bob Squier told John Doerr we were his favorite kind of client—we paid for a landslide."

He went on. "OK, then it was [House legislation] on uniform standards [for securities litigation] and once again it was, 'Come into my lair, little child.' We steamed them totally. They said, 'Hmm, not bad. Wait until they get into real politics, wait till they have to fight a real union.' So then it was charter schools. In forty-nine days we broke a five-year logjam and got the teachers' union on board. The pols were like, 'Well, it wasn't perfect.' So the final nail in the are-these-guys-real coffin was H1-B, when we had to fight organized labor. We started late, and in less than three weeks we blasted them. The trial lawyers, the teachers' union, the AFL-CIO—we knocked them all down in a row."

Randlett gazed off into the distance, where a pigeon was circling above the rooftops, and smiled. "A while back," he said, "I heard that Brook [Byers, of Kleiner Perkins] talked to David Beier at the White House and [Senator] John Kerry, and they said, 'Geez, you guys decide you want to get something done, you do it. Being on the other side of you guys sucks.'"

Randlett laughed. "I've raised the bar, and now they all have to go up. I have a critical chunk of people with cash. I can go to Doerr and ask for $50,000, we can make things happen for a politician. It can be painful if they try to screw us." He took the last swallow of his beer. And then, with the complete lack of humility that had earned him so much animosity in Washington, he summed up his work. "We're not trying to take over politics," he said. "Just our part of it."

But if Randlett intended his "part" of politics to be Al Gore's presidential campaign, he had a lot of fighting to do. To begin with, the core group around Gore was still struggling to define itself, and its overall strategy was murky. And Gore's difficulties in putting together a team reflected larger political problems for the Democrats. The normal sparring among the White House staffs of the President and vice president continued, as did the back-and-forth among the different departments of the administration. Competition was once again accelerating in the wake of the 1998 elections, now that "unity" was less at a premium and short-term factional gain more important. After the impeachment, questions about Clinton's ability to reconcile the different wings of the party had become more pressing. On issues where it seemed likely that New Democrats and the businessmen of Silicon Valley might line up against Old Democrats and labor, consumers, and ethnic minorities, there was no unifying leadership at the top of the party to force constituencies to compromise. Meanwhile, despite Clinton's amazing ability to raise money for his own legal-defense fund, for the DCCC, and for the party, financial pressure on the Democrats had not abated.

In the face of so much complexity, a humbler man would have asked questions, or had long discussions with others, or simply waited. Plenty of regulars in the Democratic Party were doing just that. Simon Rosenberg, who had been suffering through the political fallout in the party from Clinton's impeachment and the strains of the 1998 House races, was trying hard to rebuild his network of New Democrats, urging them to "keep your eyes on the prize." Rosenberg refused, for now, to get caught up in the politics of the 2000 campaign; his work connecting the House New Democrats to high tech was concentrated on crucial, if less glamorous, legislative battles. Understanding the bugs in the system, Rosenberg had opted to work in a classic Washington style: low-key, steady, eschewing permanent enemies and allies in favor of developing, over time, what Tony Podesta had called "interests."

Wade Randlett was following a different timetable. Like a Valley entrepreneur, he wanted to build his business up fast, capture "market share," and go public as quickly as possible, with a splash. A series of brunches with mild-mannered congressmen was fine, but it was not Randlett's first priority. He wanted to select one or two issues that he could sell to both Washington and the Valley, then muscle his way in to the battles and win them. And he wanted to go as high-profile as possible with his network—which meant, according to the strategy that had already worked for him in 1997 with the Gore-Tech group, focusing on Al Gore and the White House, bugs or not.

PART THREE
workarounds

CHAPTER eleven

If the first stage in the romance between Silicon Valley and the Democrats had to do with wiring up the network between them, and the next stage involved discovering the bugs, the third stage was characterized by a process familiar to computer geeks everywhere, and adopted enthusiastically by Wade Randlett: workarounds. The Jargon File, a document on the Web that cataloged the slang of engineers and computer hackers, defined *workaround* as "a temporary kluge used to bypass, mask, or otherwise avoid a bug or misfeature in some system. Theoretically, workarounds are always replaced by fixes; in practice, customers often find themselves living with workarounds for long periods of time." Alternatively, the Jargon File noted, a workaround could mean "a procedure to be employed by the user in order to do what some currently non-working feature should do."

Both definitions of the word, I thought, accurately described Randlett's attempts in 1999 to realize his ambitions. By trying to engage in huge, preemptive fund-raising for Al Gore; to build the Gore 2000 Web site; to rewire the Gore 2000 campaign infrastructure, and to design an "e-Party," Randlett would try to circumvent the bugs that had emerged in his political network. In so doing, he was trying to compensate for what he perceived as the failures of existing Democratic Party structures—"currently non-working features."

At the same time, Randlett's efforts would lead Simon Rosenberg to design his own workarounds. From the Washington side, Rosenberg would try, through a legislative fight over Y2K issues and by setting up a New Democrat Network conference in Silicon Valley, to make the network work without really fixing the problems that had emerged.

Workarounds are noble, if inelegant, efforts. I had a lot of admiration for Randlett's eternal willingness to forge ahead, and for Rosenberg's less brash but equally energetic work. It would take months, though, before I would be able to tell whether their workarounds would prevent—or just temporarily stall—a crash of the entire buggy network.

It was early March 1999. We were sitting in Randlett's office at Hambrecht & Quist, looking out at the rain. Randlett was avoiding Palo Alto these days, and often worked from San Francisco instead. He said it was because of the commute, but I thought it might have something to do, as well, with making sure his identity didn't depend entirely on TechNet. I asked him how he saw his strategy for the next few months.

It shouldn't have been surprising that Randlett's first attempt at finding a workaround to transcend grubby, buggy politics had to do with the promise of a liberating technology. Back in 1994, when I first started talking to pioneers about the World Wide Web, everyone knew the Web was going to change everything; they just didn't know what to do with it. They came up with predictable ideas like porno sites and nutty ideas like Web television and instantly popular ideas like personal home pages. Their ideas showed some confusion: Was the Web a new kind of television station that could provide around-the-clock news? Was it an underground ham-radio network waiting to be filled with the ravings of self-published zine queens? Or was it virtual real estate where corporations could paste up billboards advertising themselves?

At first, the technology was fairly primitive, and Web pioneers spent a lot of time figuring out the conventions: how to navigate a site, when to link out to other sites, how to add audio and video without crashing things hopelessly. Their ideas about e-commerce were equally vague, but it didn't matter: investors poured money into developing sites and "content," convinced that there would be a return at some point in the future. And, at the very least, a lot of advertisers were willing to pay money for the dubious privilege of pasting banners and logos on sites that produced no revenues at all.

In 1996, my friend Gary, having launched one of the most publicized early commercial Web sites and become quite successful, decided that Web sites in general were a bad idea. "The Web is stupid," Gary would say. He was a sought-after expert by then. "Nobody knows how to use the Web."

But lots of people were convinced that there was a way to use the Web, a killer app so obvious and so right that it would define the way money could be made in cyberspace. Thus Amazon.com. Thus eBay. Each emerging next great idea about the Web had its own trajectory, and the synergistic effect was astonishing. From 1995 to 1998, the U.S. Internet economy grew at a rate of 175 percent. By 1998, when TechNet began talking with the Democrats about political Web sites, the Internet was already employing around 1.3 million people and generating $301 billion a year in revenues—slightly less than the entire American auto industry but more than the entire U.S. telecommunications industry.

Of course, bad ideas kept coming, as did lots of mediocre ones. Most commercial Web sites were hastily assembled because some hyperventilating marketing person insisted that the Web was the future.

By the time the 2000 campaign was in full swing, political sites—including for-profit sites stuffed with political news and campaign information—would proliferate. But now most professional politicians were notably slow to get it. Bob Squier, the veteran media consultant advising Al Gore, was among the few who understood the scope of the change that was taking place. "This isn't about the people who live online already," he said to me of the Web strategy he thought Gore should embrace. "This is about getting to swing voters." Squier, a trim man with a tan, showed no signs of the cancer that would take his life only a year later. He leaned back in his leather desk chair. A classical-music station was playing, softly, and his bookshelves were lined with Hemingway first editions. "The two technological changes that have had the biggest influence on politics so far were the automobile and television," he began. "Mass automobiles and mass TV dissolved old political structures. Automobiles, by the end of the Second World War, became so ubiquitous that they made suburbs possible for working-class people, and that changed the nature of ward politics. Television made it possible to reach individuals, and that changed how you do stumping."

Squier smiled. "The Internet is more than another medium. It's going to change politics," he said. "Everybody knows that. But is it going to change politics in this [2000] election? Is it even going to have the impact that television did, the way that television changed politics after the Kennedy-Nixon debates? Probably not." Squier gestured at the PC on his desk, a machine that I'd been told he was the last one in his office to adopt. "There's some baby steps," he said. "Nobody really understands how to use the Internet in politics yet. But we will."

And there were signs that the savvier Washington operators understood it, too. Over at Tony Podesta's lobby shop, the firm name had been changed to Podesta.com. I teased Podesta about it, but the lobbyist was unruffled. So what if "dot.com" was a done-to-death, trendy catchphrase? In Silicon Valley it might seem overworked, he said, but in Washington the dot.com identified Podesta as someone who understood the future. "In a year, everyone will be doing it," Podesta assured me. "You're gonna have to be there [on the Web]—it'll be like not having a phone number."

But Podesta, like Squier, was part of the avant-garde in Washington: most politicians still had an aide print out their e-mail for them. Even Al Gore, the leading early adopter and technophile in government, needed a little push when it came to setting up his own state-of-the-art Web site. Or at least that was how Wade Randlett saw it, and why he decided to introduce Gore to John Witchel.

" 'So fraught with rage, the Angry Clam plotted the destruction of the world,' " John Witchel quoted in a deep voice. He laughed, as if to make a joke of it, but his eyes flashed anyway.

John Witchel was by no means the most significant player in the network connecting Silicon Valley to Washington. He was a friend of Randlett's, and he gave money, and he had a willingness to help out that would make him useful on projects like Al Gore's campaign Web site. Witchel wasn't an established "industry leader," though; nor was he a symbol who could be marketed to D.C. like Kim Polese or Jerry Yang. What was interesting about Witchel was the way he represented, in his own idiosyncratic way, something about the political attitudes of Internet entrepreneurs—the way he spoke for the youngest, largely nontechnical, up-and-coming millionaires who were multiplying in the industry by 1999.

I wasn't always able to follow John Witchel's conversations—one morning, standing up, he summarized for me a chart describing the business relationships among hundreds of new companies, in astonishing detail and with biting asides about the character of each company's top executives—but the emotional content of his remarks tended to come through quite clearly. *The Angry Clam* turned out to be the title of Witchel's current favorite book, an ironic, late-nineties MBA version of *Jonathan Livingston Seagull* filled with self-conscious and somewhat bitter philosophizing. Witchel had been devouring all kinds of reading material lately, as if he were trying to make some sense of the life he'd found himself, at thirty, mastering.

The son of "classic old-school Upper West Side liberals," Witchel had been raised in New York's reform Democratic clubs, surrounded by good causes. "That kids' book *Free to Be You and Me*," he reminisced. "That was me. I grew up on Ruth Messinger and the ERA and the *Ms.* magazine song about Willie and his doll." Instead of feminism and liberal politics, though, Witchel plunged into a different world in 1986, moving across the country to swim on an athletic scholarship at Stanford. "It was the height of Reagan's popularity," he said. "And I quickly discovered that the Hoover Tower spoke louder than the English Department." Witchel complained about the "unpleasant conservatism" he found among his peers at Stanford, "a kind of insane new privilege," but he also grew to despise "useless PC whiners." As a rather rambunctious frat boy, he cheerfully terrorized several of the smaller and nerdier students, and remembers flushing Jerry Yang's head in the toilet more than once. "Made it a bit difficult later on when I had to go to Yahoo! and ask for favors," Witchel said ruefully. "I guess I should have figured Yang would be a billionaire before I was."

Witchel also found Jessica Wheeler in California. A tie-dye diaper baby originally named Raspberry Hummingbird Sundown, she had been reared on whole-grain bread at Wheeler Ranch, a famous Northern California commune, then fled for a marketing job at Oracle Software. She was nearly as tall as John, and athletic, with a sweet, messy grin. "We understand each other," Witchel said of his wife.

After college, the couple moved to San Francisco, where Witchel, by the time he was twenty-six, had set up a Web consulting business that was the first acquisition of USWeb. Witchel became a partner in USWeb, then the country's largest and fastest-growing Internet consulting firm, with more than twelve thousand employees. It integrated Web design, marketing, e-commerce, and back-office services for all kinds of businesses, both in and outside the Internet sector, and it set the standard for professional Web-site development.

By 1999 Witchel was also a member of the boards of seven companies, including the Rainmaker Capital Group, 1stUp.com, and I-Impact, and in the process had amassed more than $10 million. His business trajectory had resulted in a confusing set of political coordinates. Witchel hated Jimmy Carter, Pat Buchanan, baby boomers, and slackers equally. He believed in brains, good sportsmanship, supporting the arts, and hard work. He did not believe in unions. "I have no problem *at all* with crossing a picket line," he told me once. "Nothing would make me happier than busting a union." Witchel stood up and mimed hoeing. "You know who I think needs unions? Anyone who works bent over like this, and that's it. If you're not a farmworker, it's fucking ridiculous."

Contemptuous as he'd grown about the "political mush" of his upbringing, Witchel still wasn't entirely content with the high-tech ethos. One afternoon in his office, he mused about the meaning of it all. "The thing about Silicon Valley that's a problem for me is that it's just all, all about money," he said. "At the risk of being elitist, that's ultimately distasteful. These people make money, they start to smell like money, dress like money, fuck like money. It's spiritually bankrupt. It makes their whole culture ugly and hollow.

"The amount of money in this industry is obscene," Witchel went on. He closed his eyes for a moment, then gave a hostile half smile. "See, the problem is that nobody in Silicon Valley has died yet. Usually people get rich, they screw everyone, then at the end of their life they repent and do good things with their money. Carnegie, you know. Public libraries. The Rockefellers. I guess we'll have to wait about twenty years to see a real renaissance and flowering of the culture out here. Once everyone starts to die."

I'd been spending time with a lot of guys like Witchel lately: young, rich, loud, and aggressively self-confident. By some odd quirk of genetics, most of them were physically big as well. I felt ridiculously female and frail watching these giants bang around their offices, scowl at the screens of their tiny silver laptops, or stride through crowded financial-district bars clutching tankards in their paws and booming hello. Witchel liked to play with the persona of masculine excess, but it wasn't really his brawn that stood out. This was a very smart and deeply angry man.

Until 1999, the CEO of USWeb had been Joe Firmage, a young man so rich and determined that for years most people in Silicon Valley pretended to ignore his heartfelt proselytizing about UFOs. After Firmage began to talk publicly about his obsession—even buttonholing President Clinton at one point, and handing him a flyer about alien intelligence—he was eased out. Mark Kvamme, a son of venture capitalist Floyd Kvamme at Kleiner Perkins, took over, to the great relief of investors in the firm. Witchel, still a partner, remained tight-lipped about the change. "I was always taught that people's private beliefs were their own business," he said. "I guess the nineties proved that wasn't true for business as well as for politics."

Wade Randlett, though, was working hard to convince Witchel to get involved in politics. He wasn't one of Randlett's first targets, but by 1999 I'd started to notice Randlett referring to Witchel more, and would frequently see the two of them out for beers. It was in a noisy, alcohol-drenched San Francisco bar that I first heard Randlett introduce Witchel as "the guy who's doing the vice president's site," and realized that Witchel was more than just another rich donor.

The USWeb connection was important to Randlett because, he felt, the company was the acknowledged leader in its field. It wasn't a superstar company like Yahoo! or eBay, but in the Internet world it was respected. Randlett had a plan for creating a "strategic alliance" between USWeb and the Gore 2000 campaign: if Gore was going to have a Web site, he felt, it should be designed by the top-ranking Web-site design company. "We're gonna say, 'Welcome to the Web, this is our world,'" he said. Randlett wanted Witchel personally to design Gore's site. Witchel would make a more effective ambassador to Gore than either USWeb's previous or current CEO—the former with a belief in aliens, and the latter a scion of a Republican dynasty. And since, in Washington, there were far fewer seasoned Web professionals at work in political campaigns than there were print-ad specialists or television consultants, Witchel and Randlett would possess an air of authority and expertise.

Randlett also seemed to have an intuition about Witchel's longer-term political potential. "This is a guy who has something to say," he told me one day in the early spring of 1999. It was late morning, the sky shimmering on and off with rain, and Randlett was drinking a smoothie as he flipped through the papers on his desk. "John represents the new kids in the Valley. He understands where the New Economy's going in a way the older companies don't."

I left Randlett at his office and headed to the airport for a reporting trip to Seattle. I was wrapped in a blanket, headphones on, when the pilot interrupted a medley of Gershwin tunes. "Folks, for those of you who're interested, the Dow just broke ten thousand," he said.

Our plane was still glued to the runway by fog, its tons of metal stuck on the ground like a metaphor for the industrial age, but the khakied businessmen in front of me started cheering. Somewhere, in the city behind me, I knew John Witchel was laughing as hard as he could.

Late in March of 1999, Witchel—still waiting to hear whether he officially had a contract to design Gore's Web site—was asked to fly to Washington on a day's notice and meet with Gore's key campaign advisers. Stuffing an extra tie into his computer briefcase, Witchel took the red-eye East, and met for three hours with Craig Smith, Peter Knight, Karen Skelton, and Monica Dixon.

Witchel was determined to create a site for Al Gore that would demonstrate the candidate's "at-homeness" on the Web, while remaining accessible to nontechnical voters. He designed an unprepossessing blue-and-white, folksy, straightforward set of pages, written mostly in the first person, Witchel said, to "create the impression of sincerity."

But Witchel's design wasn't embraced wholeheartedly by the Gore campaign team. After a few frustrating phone calls, Witchel said that the staff in Washington was just too unfamiliar with the medium. Every Web professional knew that the most effective Web sites were understated. On-line cool depended on forswearing newbie fascination with animation and glitz; it was like having the confidence not to wear beads and sequins at the Oscars. "I *know* my approach is money, it's a hit," insisted Witchel. "But I'm not sure that, given the pressures du jour, the campaign is going to accept it. They may get seduced by more bells and whistles."

I called up Celia Fischer in Los Angeles. She was working on a screenplay, and kept insisting that she was retired from politics. But she'd been convinced, by Randlett, to sit in on some of the discussions about the Web site: she had a huge amount of experience in campaigns, and understood the issues Gore faced as he tried to integrate this new medium into his plans.

Fischer thought that any problems with Witchel stemmed not from technical or aesthetic differences but from the much more fundamental anxiety that insiders felt around innovation. In her view, the Web itself was probably threatening to Gore's campaign staff. "We had a fax machine in 1980, and it was like the coolest thing," she said, recalling her early work on Democratic campaigns. "Then there was express mail. Each four-year cycle brings wildly new challenges. New stuff bothers people who will never unlearn what they came in on. They attack it because it's new."

The Internet, Fischer added, was particularly threatening to Democratic Party regulars, because it destroyed the traditional basis for their own accumulation of power. "If you're a campaign organizer, an old hack like me, you were inculcated in a system of geography," she explained. "Voters live in a ward, a precinct, with an address. The Internet takes away your control of your ward."

Randlett thought that by designing the Web site, and providing John Witchel to be the point person for it, he would get credit and respect from Gore and his people. But the Web site was creating a few of its own problems. Not only did it highlight the campaign's lack of comfort with new technology but it raised questions about political control. I was sure that Gore's campaign staff hated the idea that the Web site might diminish their own power, or empower voters to act independently. Fischer agreed. "The party can straddle all of this for a while and not have to choose," she reflected. "But once you create a Web community you cannot control it. You will not be able to stay 'on message.' And that means there's going to be a power struggle."

CHAPTER twelve

It was impossible not to hear about the power struggle for Al Gore's soul. Fischer was wrong only in using the singular: from the very beginning of 1999, Gore's campaign had been steeply accelerating into power struggles on every conceivable level. They were not just about choosing a Web site but about picking a staff. The fights were not just about the staff but about the message, the schedule, the campaign headquarters, and the fund-raising. They were petty, and they were big. One week Bob Squier was the anointed media star, the next his former partner and archrival Carter Eskew had replaced him; then Tony Coelho, a former House whip and a consummate Hill insider, took over and hinted at hiring a whole new set of consultants. The whole thing was a mess.

Part of Gore's organizational problem was the familiar one, described to me by both Randlett and Fischer, of "too many cooks spoiling the broth." But part seemed to reflect the larger problem of Gore's political identity. Should he stick with the pro-business, pro-technology, New Democrat line that had served him and Bill Clinton so well in their first term, or should he reinvent himself in an effort to put distance between himself and the disgraced President? Should he hail the New Economy or pay tribute to the forces of the Old Democrats—the labor unions and ethnic constituencies—who had supported their party so loyally during the impeachment crisis?

Al Gore's first official campaign trip in February 1999—after years of planning and ten months of unofficial stumping, but before explicitly announcing his candidacy—was a less than decisive statement about his direction. The New Hampshire snow swirled photogenically enough, and Gore smiled and waved nobly. Accompanied by his erstwhile rival, the liberal Representative Dick Gephardt, he nodded to the Old Party; hailing the growing economy, he acknowledged the New Democrats. But the themes Gore cautiously tried out were far less sweeping than his usual proclamations about the future, the planet, and the New Economy. "Let's be sensitive to the problems that real families have," the vice president said, launching into a speech condemning traffic jams. "We're seeing the daily commutes get longer and longer."

Gore also addressed the problems of lost bags at airports and hard-to-read medicine-bottle labels before flying to Iowa for the next stop. "The person who deserves to be our next President is the one who understands how tired working parents are," he concluded.

The approach was being spun as Al Gore's populism, but it was also a frank copy of President Clinton's successful "mini-initiatives"—all of them poll-driven and tested by focus groups—which had infuriated official Washington with their lack of gravitas. How could the commander in chief, the leader of the free world, the captain of the Republic be reduced to babbling about trifles? But Clinton's hundred-dollar tax credits, his stumping for school uniforms, and his speeches demanding that insurance companies pay for an extra twelve hours of postpartum recovery had been wildly successful, according to Democratic pollsters. In a way, the approach was a vindication of the New Democrats and their rejection of a large role for the federal government. And it underscored the values of business and the Internet world, where commercial "narrowcasting" to people who defined themselves by their lifestyles replaced communication with communities in which people identified themselves as citizens of a republic. What Gore, like Clinton and the New Democrats, was recognizing was an increasingly suburban electorate concerned above all with the minutia of its own daily life, suspicious of "big government," and eager to have its own domestic preoccupations made the center of national attention.

As Al Gore stumped through the Northeast snow, Wade Randlett was planning how to work around these problems. "Message, money, and operations," he said. "These are what matter in a campaign. We want to be right in the middle of all of them."

Late one evening in March 1999, Randlett hustled me down a deserted street in San Francisco's Multimedia Gulch and into a dark club where jars of vodka infused with herbs and fruits gleamed like jewels over a long copper bar. The crowd was wealthy and hip, with clusters of new media designers and producers standing around and chatting self-consciously, trying to act like grownups. Randlett hesitated over the jalapeño and cucumber infusions, then ordered a vanilla-bean vodka. "Cheers," he said, settling onto a stool and clinking his glass against mine. "We got Gore to come for a TechNet event here April 6; it's confirmed. And I'm gonna brand the shit out of this one." Randlett took a sip of his drink, happily. "It's gonna be tech all the way," he said. "High tech and the New Economy. I'm gonna make it a big, fat symbol of everything that's good about Silicon Valley."

If Randlett wanted a message about the future, he couldn't have done much better than to land the CEO of E-Loan, Jeanna Pawolski, as his host for Al Gore's first official fund-raising event as a presidential candidate. Pawolski was the Internet success story of the moment, a straightforward young real-estate agent who, with her even younger colleague Chris Larsen, had decided to offer home mortgages over the Internet just a year ago and was now poised to take her company public with an initial offering valued at $55.2 million. Randlett had befriended the classically nerdy Larsen and become a member of the board; despite making only $6.8 million in revenues in 1998, and losing $11.34 million, E-Loan's value was widely expected to soar.

It hadn't taken much to convince Pawolski that a major media event at her home with the vice president would boost E-Loan's profile. Randlett argued that it was an equally irresistible opportunity for Gore, who could point to Pawolski—a single mother who'd made a fortune through hard work and new technology—as an example of his faith in the future. "Al Gore needs to *reek* of the twenty-first century," Randlett said, explaining the reasoning. "I want every word he speaks, every event he does to show that tomorrow is great."

In the same vein, Randlett thought the fund-raiser, billed as a "family-friendly" afternoon with Al and Tipper by the pool, should signal Gore's identification with the culture and values of the New Economy. Pawolski's home—a huge and fairly hideous mock Tudor up a winding driveway, in the horsey heart of old-money Woodside—had, until the Internet boom turned the Social Register upside down, served as the home and stronghold of Shirley Temple Black, the doyenne of California Republicans and a leading Reagan-era fund-raising hostess. Now Randlett was bringing the new guard into the same halls where Hoover Institute fellows had once mingled with Ed Meese. Beneath alarming chandeliers, whose stiff pink contours suggested an oversize drag queen in hoop skirts, he planned to have the upstart millionaires of high tech show that a different set of political powerbrokers was now in charge. Dress would be "casual," and kegs of beer would supplement the Chardonnay and sushi. Randlett was trying hard to get members of the Grateful Dead—who'd started scandalizing the decent citizens of Palo Alto thirty years ago and still maintained a following among the Valley's oddball entrepreneurs—to provide the music.

There was a bottom line to all this countercultural cool, however. It was the "money" part of Randlett's "message, money, and operations" strategy. If things went well, Pawolski's party for four hundred would haul in close to half a million dollars for Gore's presidential campaign. In addition to his regular and reliable stable of donors—solid Gore supporters like John Doerr and Sandy Robertson, who had no qualms about mining their extensive networks for money—Randlett was recruiting new members to serve on the event's finance committee. In Randlett's scheme, finance-committee members were "wholesalers" bringing in the bulk of the money through their personal contacts; Randlett himself intended to mop up the remaining "retail market," which he calculated at about $75,000. "Credit for this event is going to TechNet," he vowed. "Anyone else can come, but I'm making sure we own it. I'm gonna show that I control the spigot—and if I turn it off, it's off."

In an office basically the size of his chair, John Witchel listened intently to Randlett explain the rules for finance-committee members. "Nothing over the legal limit," Randlett reminded him. "The key is volume: a thousand a head, two thousand a couple, and they can bring their kids for free." Witchel nodded. "I'm signing 'em up," he said. "I tell clients, 'This is a trade show, not a political rally—all the important people in the business will be there.' I tell my [USWeb] partners, 'There's three reasons you have to come: networking, access, and your kids will think you're cool.' Basically, it's 'Be there or be square.' "

The reward for the day's top fund-raisers would be an intimate dinner with Gore that same evening, at John and Ann Doerr's home, but Witchel's eagerness to sell tickets was motivated by more than a desire to pass the salt to the vice president. Appearing in public as one of the Valley's serious political players was certainly appealing, as was the chance to network with Doerr and other finance-committee heavyweights. But Witchel was also still waiting on final approval of the Web site he'd designed a month ago for Gore, and growing frustrated with the lack of response from Washington. He had no idea where his relationship with Gore might ultimately lead, but he knew that he needed to get as close to the vice president's inner circle as early as possible if he wanted a role in the campaign. And he definitely wanted one— partly to do a favor for Randlett, whose political judgments and guidance he followed loyally, and partly, I thought, out of some idea he had about adult public service. "Every administration has business leaders, important voices, experts it turns to in a crisis," Witchel had said to me once, when I asked if he envisioned himself as part of a future "kitchen cabinet" for a President Gore. "I've done well in this economy, I believe I understand it, and I want to be in a position to be helpful if I can."

But Witchel had heard little from Gore's staff, whose responses to his overtures were opaque. Witchel, worried that Craig Smith and others in Washington mistrusted him, talked the situation over with Randlett. He decided that, as Randlett pointed out, "money never hurts," and that he should make his own loyalties and value to the campaign clear by welcoming Gore to California with $30,000 or $40,000. "The basic idea is to contribute, without strings attached, and to create the impression that I can be useful," Witchel said. "Without getting all crazy and coy about it, there's not a much better strategy."

Witchel's enthusiasm for raising money cheered Randlett, who continued to fight his undeclared war for territory in the campaign. "Mindshare," he called it, using marketing jargon. "We want 100 percent of their mindshare." Randlett had never trusted Gore's Washington-based staff to fully appreciate TechNet's importance, or to give him the prominence he believed his efforts warranted. Even after his remarkable fund-raising for Gore's Leadership '98 PAC, Randlett knew better than to relax.

In the paranoid, disorganized, and ruthlessly competitive atmosphere of a campaign, someone like Randlett could fall—or be pushed—from grace the minute his numbers wobbled. It was crucial that the April 6 event succeed. "I'm not gonna be bumped out," he promised. "I work, I work early, and I work effective. I'm not going to be ignored."

Randlett's last-minute work started several days before the sixth, with "walk-throughs" of the two sites—Pawolski's home and Doerr's—and resembled nothing so much as the business on movie sets. There were the same officious young men with clipboards, and women in sunglasses with cell phones; the same staggering, overwhelming, and ultimately irrelevant checklists, the same behind-the-scenes shoptalk as anxious staffers tried to convince each other that their jobs were important and glamorous. Walk-throughs were about the raw material of politics: camera angles, lighting on "his" face, extension cords, tape marks for where speakers would stand, microphones, booze.

For Gore's event manager, introduced to me only as "Chris," the job was simple, if incredibly aggravating in the execution. Chris was an extremely stylish, intelligent, charming, insincere black organizer dressed in an exquisite sage-green suit, whose thankless task it was to make all of the details align correctly. He mediated between the White House advance team and the florist; between the Secret Service and the grips in charge of the sound; he flattered the hostess's assistant and consulted with the hireling in charge of valet parking and went over the photographer's invoices with Randlett, trying to figure out how to fit the expenses into the strictures of campaign-finance law. Chris sighed a lot. He rolled his eyes. He put his hands together in supplication and wheedled, he talked on his cell phone; he said "I hear you" and turned on his heel. "My job," he told me bluntly, in the middle of a crisis—one of at least six that hour, this one sparked by the abrupt, huffy resignation of a caterer whose vinaigrette had been insulted—"my job is to make sure that everyone who gives money gets to touch *his* hand. That's what it's all about."

The grass at Pawolski's was still soaked from heavy rains the day before, and a large inflatable alligator floated belly-up in her pool. A crew of ponytailed roadies, on order from Chris, were sulkily taking down the stage they'd just assembled at a lesser authority's command. Pawolski's assistant, frantic about the destruction being unleashed on her employer's carefully tended grounds, waved helplessly at campaign staffers as they strolled away, unheeding, over the flower beds. "I'm not cut out for this," she kept saying, wringing her hands. "I'm really not. I can't handle this."

Wade Randlett was everywhere, supervising, though most of the real work was being handled for him by TechNet's Elizabeth Greer, unflappable as always.

Accompanying Greer was Jessica Wheeler, John Witchel's wife, who had helped TechNet the previous year with events during Gray Davis's gubernatorial campaign. Wheeler was lending a hand with logistics again, though this time, thanks to Witchel's fund-raising, she was supposed to be treated as a donor and not as staff. In any case, Wheeler usually did what she wanted to do; now, she came up behind Greer, who was listening politely to a self-important White House functionary, and poked her. "Come on," she said conspiratorially. "I got Wade in the car already."

Greer and I climbed into the back of Wheeler's new black BMW convertible, clutching our hair and shivering, as she raced over back roads, singing along to a rock station turned up loud. At the edge of Woodside, an electronic gate swung open, and we sped up a long driveway shaded by live oaks, winding past brooks and fields to the estate where John Doerr lived with his wife, Ann, and their two young daughters. The Doerrs had a white, solar-paneled compound, vaguely Southwestern in style, adorned with modern sculpture and hotel-like walkways connecting the rooms. The guest building had halogen lights and exquisite Oriental rugs; the kitchen, where we began the walkthrough, was immaculate, with the children's first-grade drawings arranged neatly on the Sub-Zero refrigerator.

Doerr's assistant Angela Valles, a brilliant and terrifying control freak wearing a pin-striped navy suit, was guiding about two dozen advance people through the main house. "There is no way we can fit a twelve-top table against this wall," a woman from Gore's White House office said desperately. "We agreed to seven tens, period, and I don't have the authority to change at this point." Valles ignored her. "The twelve-top will go here," she instructed the event planner. "Refer to the seating chart I faxed you. We'll do photos outside, then bring people in through these doors." Two Secret Service men knelt to examine the doors, then rose, brushing off imaginary dust, and looked around in a friendly way. "Nice thick walls," one of them commented. Valles swept into the kitchen, followed by Gore people whispering miserably into their cell phones.

"In a lot of ways the White House staff is working on a low standard," confided a woman who worked for the California Democratic Party, surveying the scene. "They've been able to do shitty events and get away with murder, because they're so used to Bill Clinton's megawatt charm making everything better. Now it's different—if they screw up, nobody's gonna forgive Gore because he smiled at them." She flipped through her copy of the guest list. "Oh well," she said. "It's just dinner, I guess."

Jessica Wheeler and I slipped away into the hallway, where we examined the Doerrs' library. There was no fiction, just shelves of glossy architecture books, biographies and business sagas, and numerous volumes about veterinary medicine. Wheeler fingered some magazines, bored. We talked about books for a while, until Wade Randlett reappeared. "I've got to go see Roger McNamee," he announced.

Roger McNamee, Randlett explained to me as he drove up Sand Hill Road, ran his own venture-capital firm, Integral Capital, which had been incubated at Kleiner Perkins in 1991 and was still associated with the firm. I'd met him once before. A thirty-something banking whiz, McNamee had a generic California-guy informality and a knack for backing heavily hyped companies like Inktomi, Healtheon, and Critical Path. He was also an over-the-top Deadhead, steeped in the music and mystique of the Grateful Dead. McNamee's band—the Flying Other Brothers, featuring his brother, his sister-in-law, and several childhood friends—covered Dead songs with reverent discipleship; on occasion, the band performed with two of McNamee's Dead idols, Mickey Hart and Bob Weir. On the Web site for the Flying Other Brothers, McNamee was listed as contributing "lead guitar and technology investment" to the band; his brother as providing "guitar, vocals, and investment banking." They described their music, without any apparent irony, as "an updated psychedelic sound of the sixties with a heavy dose of Internet mania."

"I didn't want to announce it publicly," Randlett said, gloating, "but Roger's pot-smoking hippie pals confirmed—Mickey Hart and Bob Weir are coming. Weir's giving Gore money. And the Dead are putting out a Gore 2000 poster of their own." He chuckled. "It's so excellent," he said. "I can't wait to see the photo of Al Gore drawing a beer from the keg and handling it to Mickey freakin' Hart."

Lunch had just been laid out in the reception area of Kleiner Perkins when we arrived, the usual opulent buffet. Randlett grabbed a prosciutto and mozzarella on focaccia, then headed for the kitchen, where he selected an Odwalla fruit shake from the refrigerator. McNamee bounded up to us. He had light-brown hair, a friendly smile, and a hearty handshake. "Got your page, Wade," he said. "What do I need to do?"

Randlett explained that he was worried about meeting his target, and was making one last push for donors who had not already maxed out on their contributions. McNamee began making a list on a scrap of paper. "I'll get you some new people who can contribute," he said. "What do you need — name, home address, Social Security?" He smiled at us, and moved over the table where half a dozen young investors and analysts were piling their plates with food. "Hey, pal," McNamee greeted one of them. "Listen, can you help me out?"

Randlett sighed, relieved. "That's what I call a professional," he said. "I knew Roger could take care of business." He waved at a woman coming out of the conference room, then excused himself. "I'm gonna go talk to someone for a minute," he said. "Have some lunch, I'll be right back."

I felt too shy to take a sandwich, but I stood in the reception area for a while eating jelly beans from a crystal dish and watching the light play on a grove of aspens outside.

Back at the TechNet office in Palo Alto there was a weird lull, an hour before the event began. Randlett opened the spreadsheet to see the latest figures on his work. He turned to Greer, who was rounding up the last volunteers to ferry them over to Pawolski's. "Good job, Lizzie," he said cheerfully. "It's not over," Greer said.

The event itself was anticlimactic. John Doerr rushed up to the podium with the energy of a miniature windmill and cheered for the New Economy; Governor Gray Davis lumbered to his feet and cracked some lugubrious jokes. Gore showed up late and got off to a bad start by announcing, inaccurately, that he knew everyone there was concerned about Kosovo. In fact, only Pawolski — whose Serbian ancestry had been diligently concealed from Gore by his briefers — appeared to recognize what the vice president was talking about. By the time his speech ended and the photo line began, most people were on their third drink.

The lawn was still sodden, and women in strappy sandals milled about, shivering and complaining about the cold. Inside, by the bar, David Ellington introduced me to the only other non-Caucasian visible in the room—a short, irritable Rainbow Coalition organizer named Butch Wing, who grumbled about the New Democrats. I took my Calistoga and wandered outside. Roger McNamee, now wearing a tie-dyed shirt over his Dockers and holding a guitar tightly, was launching the band into "Secret Agent Man." Some Grateful Dead tunes followed, and then Tipper Gore could be seen sitting behind Bob Weir with her mouth fixed in a professional smile, playing the congas. "Hey, she's a pretty good drummer," Al Gore remarked, to nobody in particular.

Over on the patio, Jessica Wheeler whooped and embraced her father as he wandered through the crowd with a mild, slightly spaced-out smile. "This is Bill Wheeler," she announced to a young investment banker, who didn't seem to recognize the man behind 1968's most famous commune. But now Wheeler was fifty-four, and baby Raspberry Hummingbird Sundown was Jessica. "Dad, don't you love this place?" she said. "Yeah," Bill Wheeler said. "Great party."

At the end, I couldn't find Chris to ask why Al Gore had failed to shake the hand of everyone who gave money, but it didn't seem to matter. As David Ellington drove me home to San Francisco, ranting excitedly about the possibility of a stock-market crash, I saw a few donors still standing in line by the pool to get Mickey Hart's autograph.

CHAPTER thirteen

The storefronts of East Palo Alto offered fried-fish take-out, hair braiding, and a variety of social service—the Ecumenical Hunger Program, the I Have a Dream Tutoring Program—before they yielded, without warning, to the broad, magnolia-lined avenues of Palo Alto. Suddenly, the black people disappeared. Bike lanes, bordered by immaculately trimmed public lawns, materialized.

Farther downtown, Palo Alto was divided into parking zones marked by coral, aqua, and purple placards that suggested the city planner was a demented interior decorator heavily influenced by *Sunset* magazine, circa 1965. Tall flowering trees shaded rows of mansions; the sidewalks were germ-free, adorned with tubs of cyclamen and other artificial-looking flowers. Despite the Stanford students studying at outdoor cafés, Palo Alto had none of the scruffiness associated with a college town: no irritating loud music, no funky food co-op, no used-clothing stores staffed by girls with pierced lips. It was an oasis of upscale, if archaic, taste amid the crass malls and highways of the Valley's booming sprawl.

In the coral zone, at a new Thai restaurant, Wade Randlett sipped his beer and teased the busy waitress. "It can't be too hot for me," he told her, ordering lunch. Randlett had just returned from Washington, and he'd been eager to fill me in on his trip. He began with news I'd already seen in the newspaper: the Federal Elections Commission had just released its first-quarter 1999 figures for individual contributions to presidential campaigns—figures that didn't even include the recent haul at Pawolski's—and Al Gore was still the top earner among Tech-Net's board members. Some executives had hedged their bets—Eric Schmidt of Novell gave $1,000 to George W. Bush and $1,000 to Al Gore; Dan Case of Hambrecht & Quist gave $1,000 each to Gore and Bill Bradley—but Randlett's years of work positioning the vice president appeared to be paying off.

But Republicans had always eventually pulled in more money from the business community than Democrats, and George W. Bush was widely regarded as what Randlett, with grudging admiration, called "a freakin' fund-raising *machine*." I knew that Randlett was realistic about Gore's ability to permanently out-raise Bush. There was something more than money that was making Randlett so chipper. Never a shy man, he was more confident than I'd seen him in a long while, and gloating over his own cleverness. "It's like that whole Foucauldian paradigm of power," he said, out of nowhere, as he dug into his curry. He took a big bite. "Power is everywhere."

Randlett's interpretation of Michel Foucault was idiosyncratic, at best—he apparently considered the subversive French philosopher to be a kind of Machiavelli for late capitalism, whose work could serve as a practical guide for political entrepreneurs—but his insight about the omnipresence of power in the context of campaigns was right on target. He had figured out yet another way to insert himself and his techies into the Gore campaign. "I'm not going to spend all my time trying to get the campaign bigshots to take my calls," Randlett announced. "I'm going to get deeper and deeper into the organization, until I'm everywhere. There is nobody too low on the totem pole for me to meet with."

I was seeing the end of what had passed, in Randlett, for patience. He had set up his chess pieces carefully: John Doerr's relationship with Gore had long been firmly established, and now Witchel, as Gore's Web-site designer, might become another TechNet operative with direct access to the vice president. Randlett's own fund-raising successes had won him the right to be taken seriously. But he wanted more.

By analyzing the infrastructure of the campaign and listening to the complaints of its low-level workers, Randlett had come up with an attack plan that relied less on courting powerful allies than on winning over staffers in the unglamorous but essential areas of advance, scheduling, and MIS. Monica Dixon, for example, a longtime Gore aide, had told Randlett that the advance team was working without laptops. "That's not how it should be," Randlett said. TechNet, he told Dixon, could help make the teams' jobs easier, could bring them into the modern world with gifts of high-tech equipment backed up by expert support. It was pathetic, he said, that campaigns were still using technologies that had been discarded by every small business five years ago. Why shouldn't advance have a dozen digital cameras, so decisions about event locations could be made quickly? Why shouldn't stressed-out scheduling staffers have access to the best time-management software? Why shouldn't Gore's MIS guy have an engineer from Oracle on call full-time, dedicated to answering his every question and helping him figure out the best way to run things?

I thought Randlett's idea was extremely smart: to the overworked, unappreciated campaign staffers used to Washington norms of inefficiency, he must have appeared as an angel from a better place, bearing a message of salvation. "Instead of me complaining to the campaign, asking them to pay attention to me, I'm calling the people who do the work and asking how I can help them," he said. Randlett signaled for another beer. "We make their jobs easier; we respond to what they need."

He paid for lunch, and we strolled along Palo Alto's main street, past Restoration Hardware and the most tastefully landscaped Burger King I'd ever seen. Right before the train station, we turned into a peach-colored stucco office building and went upstairs to TechNet.

Things had been changing at TechNet, president Reed Hastings having finally left. The Republican and Democratic political sides were even more like separate businesses thrown together by chance in the same office space, and, apart from the rabbity young receptionist, there was little sign of a larger shared purpose. I greeted Elizabeth Greer, who was going over a spreadsheet in the corner office she shared with Randlett, and asked what had happened with Hastings.

"Well," Greer began. "Remember Gary Fazzino?" TechNet's first president, Fazzino had lasted "about ten minutes," Greer said, before realizing that he was over his head and returning to his job at Hewlett-Packard. To replace him, John Doerr and the board decided they needed a young, mediagenic CEO who had both high-tech and political experience. "Reed Hastings had a pure software background, he had money, he had worked on charter schools — he was perfect," Green recounted. And when John Doerr—who, as Greer pointed out, "has the strongest personality in the world"—approached Hastings to take the position as TechNet's president, the young CEO agreed. "He said he was planning to start a new company but that he'd give us some time," Greer recalled.

Hastings, however, never quite caught on to managing the organization. Partly, I thought, it was because he didn't really understand politics. "Reed approached TechNet like it was Intel, with ten thousand employees," Green said. "He didn't understand how personal the power was here." The two teams—Greer and Randlett on the Democratic side, and their Republican counterparts, Lezlee Westine and Mike Englehardt—were busy making their own rules, raising their own money, pushing TechNet where they thought it should go. It was a joke around the office that TechNet had an invisible CEO.

Hastings's management style wasn't the only problem, though: Randlett's years of skillful media manipulation and organizing were paying off. To most outsiders, TechNet was now firmly identified with the Democrats, and Greer had been hearing about the fuss at board meetings. There were regular, angry phone calls from CEOs to Doerr about Randlett's appearances in the *San Jose Mercury News* or on C/NET, announcing a new TechNet-Gore initiative. "Some members are mad," Greer said. "They're asking why Wade's running around D.C. saying he's TechNet. Why is this guy the face of our organization?"

She broke off as Randlett walked in. Greer, it was clear, shared his opinion that a lot of the complaints were sour grapes from Republicans who had never been able to find a political director as successful at fund-raising and organizing as Randlett. Yet it wasn't obvious what would happen next, and whether the next president of TechNet would take a stronger line against Randlett's autonomy than Hastings had been able to do.

"So," said Randlett, settling into his chair and putting his legs up on the desk. "As I was saying, the thing about going inside the campaign in stealth mode—it works for us, it works for them. We're gonna make sure Gore gets the first really new-politics, wired-politics campaign. It's time."

As it turned out, this particular idea of Randlett's would fizzle. Nobody at the lower levels of the Gore campaign would stick around long enough to develop an allegiance to Randlett, and the people at the top were too busy jockeying for their own power to pay much attention to him. Randlett would make some friends, make some enemies, and see most of his efforts dissipate into the nobody-in-charge black hole of the Gore campaign.

But all through the spring and summer of 1999, Randlett kept fighting, as in June, when he brought John Doerr to a high-level meeting with key Gore aides to argue for the need for more attention to Silicon Valley. "The campaign just goes to John and me, and figures we'll go to everyone else," Randlett complained to the politicos. "They know how to call people in New Hampshire. They know how to call Iowa precinct heads. If they want Valley endorsements, they have to call directly."

At the meeting, Doerr had warned the campaign staff that he saw "a decent amount of frustration" on both sides of the relationship. Tony Coelho had responded with an uncommon admission: according to Randlett, the head of Gore's campaign had told Doerr, "Basically, we're married, no matter what you do. We're stuck with technology—the environment and technology define Gore for voters. It's what he's always gonna be viewed as, so we know we need you. It's a done deal."

Randlett was obviously impressed. "Campaigns are like government agencies," he said. "They never admit they need you." Emboldened, Randlett made a pitch. "Look," he said, "Republicans aren't brain-dead, they've looked at what we've done. It's like a piece of HTML—once you put it out there, your competitors can use it. So instead of catching up, they leapfrog."

Randlett drove his point home. "As of July 1, George W. is gonna have a lot of support, and come out to the Valley and talk about all our issues," he said. "What are we gonna do?" Randlett proposed more Gore-Tech meetings, or, "at the least," some phone calls from the vice president to key high-tech executives. And he asked for a direct liaison with the campaign to be appointed, "so Silicon Valley stays on the front burner."

Everyone seemed to agree, and Randlett and Doerr flew home. But nothing really changed. In private meetings in Washington among Gore's inner circle, the vice president's strategy was furiously being debated: Should he move the campaign headquarters to Nashville? Should he hire former Jesse Jackson adviser Donna Brazile? Should he distance himself even further from his boss, or run against the "vast right-wing conspiracy" that had entangled Clinton in the impeachment scandal? In any case, it would turn out, doing more with Silicon Valley wasn't Gore's most pressing issue.

Luckily for Randlett, though, he had almost completely adopted the Silicon Valley perspective on human events, which gave him an edge when it came to getting past humiliating defeats. It was hard to feel like a failure if your idea tanked in Silicon Valley, because the thing about Silicon Valley was that there was always another good idea. Good ideas, bad ideas, mediocre ideas, and radical, "paradigm-shifting" ideas came along so fast that everyone was constantly churning out and offering up their own new ones indiscriminately, almost completely unfazed by failure.

So Randlett started plugging his next, even better idea. By the time I saw him one Saturday morning in June at the TechNet offices, he was well into a proposal that he was about to pitch to Joe Andrew, the national chair of the DNC. With characteristic overconfidence, Randlett asserted that he'd discovered the killer political app for the Internet.

He wasn't talking, this time, about developing hokey red-white-and-blue Web sites for Gore, or putting the Democrats on-line with the kind of embarrassing graphics that old industrial companies used to demonstrate how hip they were. No, he said, this time he had an unbelievably good idea, one that would revolutionize politics. He wanted to create an e-Party.

I sat across from Randlett, reading through the pages of his proposal as he took them from the printer. "It's rough," he told me. "I don't have the wording right yet. But this will give you an idea."

I looked at the first page, which was studded with chipper, corporate memospeak. "Lead with vision," it said, "drill down to specific issues. What's the viral substance? The medium is the message, and the branding is key." Randlett saw my face, and motioned me to keep reading. The jargon, he said, was "all just framing" for the main idea of his proposed DNC Web site: a Web site that would be "a small-∂ democracy portal," highlighting issues of concern to voters, and presenting them in a nonpartisan way. Basically, all Randlett was talking about was a Web site that would do what many smart New Democrats were trying to do around the country. Instead of engaging diehard partisan voters, Randlett wanted to identify issues that targeted the concerns of swing voters, largely married Protestant women, "without left-right food fights." Instead of delivering pat speeches, he wanted to make the Web site a forum for interactive chat, and a place where voters could let their own opinions be heard. Randlett had some ideas about content—he thought gun safety, paying down the national debt, or education reform might work—but he felt that the Web site should focus on a new issue every three months. Whichever theme was chosen, he wanted it to be lifted from the Republican agenda, and thus have "a realignment quotient, something that makes Republican moderates scream."

"How do you make a party relevant in the Internet era?" Randlett asked rhetorically. He looked enormously pleased with himself. "The Internet makes parties irrelevant," he said. "You have to understand how parties work. The DNC's client isn't the activist at the other end of the modem—their client is the candidate. So why should we use the Internet to empower candidates if we can use it to disintermediate them?" Randlett caught my eye and blushed. "What?" he said defensively. I shook my head. It was bad enough, I chided, when he started citing Foucault, but *disintermediation* was over the top.

"OK," Randlett said, jutting out his chin. "I prefer *reinvent* anyway. The point is, we're going to reinvent parties by giving up the power of the machine, where you tell people what to do." He sketched out a pyramid on a scrap of paper and pushed it over to me. On the top, it read "DNC"; in the middle were "cells/wards"; at the bottom were voters. "Machine politics worked really well in 1936," he explained. "It made things work by dividing people into wards and controlling it all geographically, by dispensing manna, by telling people who to report to. It was very grassroots, and people loved it because politics were on the ground, where they lived. But now we want to flip it. The other theory is to do it upside down—I hate to invoke Foucault again, but his theory is you get power because the power is everywhere."

I must have looked baffled. "Here," Randlett said patiently. He showed me his sketch again, drawing arrows from bottom to top. "The problem for the DNC leadership, if they flip the pyramid, is they're at the bottom," he said. "The voters are supreme, and all the stuff in between is a great big market—random, chaotic, guided by an invisible hand. Now, in our model, the DNC is the sysadmin and not the boss. They don't get to choose the content; they're just the platform for the market to organize. It's not Barnes & Noble, it's Amazon.com. It's not Windows, it's Java. Why is it powerful? Because you give it away."

It was an impressive if somewhat dizzying assortment of metaphors. I wondered what the political professionals who had spent their entire careers in the Democratic Party would think about being called "sysadmins," mere technicians changed with administering a network, and whether their desire for the votes and money represented by Silicon

Valley and its New Economy would overcome first their confusion, then their concern about what this "new paradigm" signified for their personal power.

"Hey, there was a time when people put 'attorney at law' as their ballot designation because it helped them," Randlett said airily. "There was a time when the fat balding white guy who gave a lot of money could run everything." He gave a mean smile. "Too bad," he said. "Things change."

A week or so after our conversation, I saw the draft of a memo on "The e-Party Initiative," which Randlett was preparing for Joe Andrew at the DNC. The presentation had lost some of the inflammatory rhetoric that Randlett was prone to use when he practiced his spiels on me. Most of the digital-revolutionaries-storming-the-fortress-of-the-ancien-régime language had been replaced by boilerplate reminiscent of political direct mail: "America's citizens" were being "empowered." And Randlett's ideas had come down to earth a bit, with an analysis that appealed to the self-interest of Democratic Party officials even as it offered them the opportunity to cash in on the allure of the next big idea coming from Silicon Valley. He was pitching the e-Party initiative as a collaboration between high-tech executives and the DNC. As he explained to me, this memo would be delivered along with a promise to deliver $2 million in Valley money to implement the plan. "It's still a rough draft," he said, handing it to me. It read:

> The national Democratic Party is committed to reinventing what it means to be a party in the same way that Amazon.com reinvented what it means to be a bookstore. . . . Political parties over the last 50 years have been built around the dynamics and economics of broadcast radio and television. The key political unit has been the precinct, and the job of the party has been to segment these precincts in order to communicate to potential voters in cost-effective ways. The communication has been almost entirely one-way.
>
> Parties have had difficulty differentiating themselves ideologically because of the relatively broad spectrum of candidates within each Party. As a result, the Party's role has evolved from candidate selection to fundraising. Because the fundraising role tends to exclude (by both means and inclination) Party acti-

vism has become the province of an increasingly narrow, less-representative group of citizens.

. . . The Internet permits an entirely new communications paradigm. First, the Internet allows us to identify and organize communities of interest without regard to geography. Second, once organized, these groups can use the Internet to be much more politically effective.

So far, Randlett was simply echoing the conventional wisdom among political professionals. As Tony Podesta had predicted just a few months ago, everyone in the political world had been discovering that not being on the Web was "like not having a phone number," and hard-right Republican representatives from Oklahoma were competing with liberal Democrats from Massachusetts for the services of Web-site designers who could tell them how to catch up. It was also true that, just as Bob Squier had foretold, nobody really understood the medium — politicians were generally still treating Web sites as illustrated brochures, and few grasped how to use the interactive capacity of the Web to identify and target supporters. But behind the scenes both parties had figured out that the Web might be a powerful fund-raising tool, and DNC and RNC officials were lobbying the Federal Elections Commission to change its campaign-finance rules to permit on-line donations.

Washington was still in relative infancy when it came to using the Web, and Randlett was betting that guidance from Silicon Valley, and the suggestion that America's tech leaders could help bring politics into their bright, successful new world, would have a powerful appeal. His e-Party initiative leaned heavily on the sexiness of Silicon Valley, and the promise that the industry, as he wrote, would "not just add technology to the Old Party, but transform it radically. We believe that democracy was the first viral marketing scheme."

He talked about the potential for his e-Party to take over and improve the execution of standard party tasks; to be "a powerful enabler of citizens by providing useful data, substance, and community-building tools that will allow any citizen to organize for better schools, cleaner parks, a candidate for town council, or the next leader of the free world." Because of the Internet, Randlett argued, "an e-Party can—without imposing its self-interest—help citizens gather signatures, walk precincts, form virtual Democratic clubs, register voters, get people to the polls, all while debating the great issues of the day." He hinted at the "added value" that Internet chat, e-mail, and Web marketing techniques could bring to polling. And he suggested that "existing DNC work" like polling and campaign advertising could be brought under the e-Party umbrella.

Yet Randlett was too canny to believe that the DNC *wanted* to radically transform itself, or that its leaders were interested in being disintermediated out of their jobs. The deal offered between the lines of his proposal was a very familiar, Old Politics one. Give us a seat at the table, he was suggesting, and we'll bankroll the feast.

Randlett was proposing to create a new fund-raising entity much like Gore's Leadership '98 PAC, or the Republicans' Team 100. His group would gather together technology executives and give them a seat on the board of the DNC's e-Party initiative in return for contributions of $350,000, $100,000, or, for the youngsters, $25,000. Randlett presented it as a start-up, with "JA [DNC chair Joe Andrew] as entrepreneur, TWR [Randlett] as venture capitalist."

After handing the DNC some "seed money" to launch the e-Party initiative, Randlett, operating under the title of national chair, would then "network to raise the first round of venture money, as a capital, not annual investment." In return, his "investors" would become part of the e-Party "team," invited "not to every DNC event, but only to the team's events where the team's subject matter is discussed, whether with POTUS or senators." Shrewdly, to avoid poaching of his exclusive list by other DNC fund-raisers, Randlett also specified that the team would have its own events, and that competing fund-raisers would not be allowed to invite team members to "other Pay Per View events." In addition to their honorific titles on the board, team members would get to "manage the technology" directly for the e-Party initiative, overseeing the development of a Web site, a comprehensive voter database, and a chat/e-mail component.

It all sounded good. But I remembered that Gore's campaign, similarly pitched about the potential of the Internet to improve its political fortunes, had failed to turn over its Web site, its high-tech message, or its political agenda to Wade Randlett and his Silicon Valley executives. Gore had happily taken Randlett's money, warmly expressing his gratitude, but had not yielded the slightest bit of control over his campaign. It seemed unlikely to me that Randlett, disappointed in his efforts to work around the bugs in his relationship with the tech-friendly vice president, would fare much better with the DNC, where insularity, competitiveness, and a dislike of ambitious outsiders were even stronger. I resolved that, on my next trip to Washington, I would find out what the Democrats really thought about turning themselves into an e-Party.

CHAPTER fourteen

When I started asking around about the impact of all Randlett's big ideas, and about his Washington–Silicon Valley maneuvering, it turned out that the e-Party initiative had gone almost unnoticed. Instead, I kept hearing about Randlett's failure to work around one of the most persistent and unsolvable bugs in the network: personality. And I saw how a few New Democrats were beginning to focus on coming up with their own plans for addressing their problems with Randlett, and with the Valley in general.

The dining room of the Four Seasons Hotel in Georgetown was peachy and pink and green, with tables set close enough to allow elaborate greeting rituals yet far enough apart to ensure discretion. "I like to come here for breakfast because I always run into someone I know," said Holly Page, the chief political strategist of the DLC. Page was in her early thirties, with an air of energetic enthusiasm, and over toasted bagels she let me realize how hard various factions were going to fight to claim ownership of the high-tech sector.

Randlett and Doerr, with a few other executives, had made two recent visits to D.C., the first to meet privately with Gore's campaign managers and express their "concerns" about various aspects of the relationship, and the second to lobby on a bill limiting software companies' legal liability for damages arising from Y2K-related problems.

Page couldn't discuss those meetings, since she hadn't participated in them. But she was interested in setting the historical record straight. "In 1995," she reminded me, "the DLC introduced a new brand into the American political marketplace, called the New Democrats."

Delicately dropping the names of such Silicon Valley luminaries as Regis McKenna and Sandy Robertson, and steadily praising her boss, DLC chairman Al From, for his perspicacity in forging connections between moderate Democrats and business, Page poured out a narrative of the relationship between high tech and her brand that seemed long on political science and, I noted, a bit short on politics. I didn't doubt that she saw the value in having high tech endorse the aspirations of the DLC. But it was harder to see what the DLC, as Paul Lippe had been saying for years, was *doing* in Silicon Valley.

Well, said Page, the DLC was meant to be "a think tank, a source of ideas, a vehicle for developing leadership and policy," and not a machine. "We don't really do organizing," she said somewhat stiffly.

Nonetheless, Page insisted that the DLC should be credited for reaching out to organize high tech on behalf of Clinton and Gore during the 1996 elections. "Remember, we're the ones who first hired Wade Randlett to work Silicon Valley," she said. She had a direct and sweet smile. "Remember, in fact, Wade and I were drinking buddies, and I convinced the DLC to put him on salary, because Al and I could see how important it was to educate the [high-tech] executives about politics."

The elbowing for position among ostensible allies, of course, had begun quite a while earlier. I'd never heard DLC people dis the New Democrat Network, but the subtle digs back and forth between Tech-Net and the Washington-based NDN and DLC were familiar. "The New Democrat Network is just trying to soak up the money we've identified," Wade Randlett had sniffed in 1997. Simon Rosenberg, though less blustery and much more circumspect in his phrasing, had been commenting for years that TechNet "still has a lot to learn."

Page hadn't heard about Randlett's proposal to turn the Democrats into an e-Party, nor did she know that Randlett was trying to set up and direct a new Web site for the DNC. She hadn't heard about Randlett and Doerr's recent visits to Gore's top campaign managers, nor had she sat in on the Hill discussions about the Y2K legislation. I asked Page what she thought about TechNet's rapid growth overall, and whether she thought it had replaced the DLC as the link between Washington and the Valley.

Page stirred some NutraSweet into her coffee and looked at me thoughtfully. "So," she said, as if changing the subject. "Tell me something. What do you think about Wade?"

I left Page and went over to the DNC—not to the party headquarters but to the grubbier building across the street where the Democrats' media messages were produced, and where the DNC's television, radio, print, and on-line specialists worked on getting the word out. This was where, logically, Randlett's team should have been coming to discuss plans for the new Web site it wanted to set up.

An official involved with the DNC's Web site took me into a messy storage room, sat me down at a table piled high with old files and stacks of videotapes, and, as Page had, asked me a question about Wade Randlett. "Who the hell does he think he is?" he demanded.

The DNC official was a longtime political media insider, with little patience for the new hotshots from the Valley who'd been knocking on his boss's door. "Wade overplays his hand in everything, especially in this building," he said. "But I can tell you, he absolutely doesn't touch our real Web work. He and his donors have a very different vision than we do about what should be done."

Most of the people in the DNC's Web division, the official explained, never crossed paths with Randlett, John Witchel, or Randlett's "team" from the Valley when the Californians came to meet with DNC chairman Joe Andrew. "We purposely stay out of their way, so we can keep them happy," he said. "They want to believe they're reshaping the political landscape to be different than politics as usual. The reality is that it's *not* different. We have the same message, the same focus as ever."

Another DNC staffer joined us, moving some cardboard boxes out of the way and taking a folding chair. We huddled together in the dusty room. It was not a clandestine meeting, but it definitely felt unofficial— especially since nobody wanted to be quoted by name. The woman who'd just come in told me how, a few months earlier, she'd gone out to California for a meeting with Randlett and several executives. "I will never be able to work in Silicon Valley," she declared.

"We sat in this huge boardroom at Kleiner Perkins, in these big chairs," she went on, sounding incredulous. "I was expecting just casual conversation, but they started to lecture me on what the DNC should be doing. I was exhausted and wasn't yessing them enough, so people got upset. They think they know it all, that because they're tech experts they're brilliant at everything. They think because they made new businesses they can create new politics." She rolled her eyes. For someone who'd spent years defining, spinning, and delivering the Democratic Party's message in every conceivable medium, it must have been enormously frustrating to have her political expertise dismissed out of hand. And for someone who knew as much about the Web as anyone in Washington, it must have been grating to be treated like a newbie, and told condescendingly that the Internet made everything she knew irrelevant.

"People out West don't understand the choices we have to make every day," she said. She fiddled with a stack of papers in front of her and looked up. "Joe Andrew had visions of building an Internet center, but it's not gonna happen, OK, because that money can be better spent on other tactics," she burst out. "The Democrats are not going to give up TV. I mean—" She paused, trying to regain her composure. "I've been a political organizer," she went on more calmly. "I know how to define George Bush for swing voters. I know how to maintain and activate our base. I know how to read NCEC data, for God's sake: Randlett's people don't even know what the NCEC [the lobbying and polling group National Committee for an Effective Congress] *is*."

The DNC official was sounding annoyed again. "They're just incredibly naïve," she said. "Their attitude is, Why should they bother to come learn anything from us? I heard Wade tell his people that if something can't be done, he'd just talk to the President."

As for the specifics of Randlett's e-Party proposal, the DNC staffers made it clear that they were not getting involved. As far as they were concerned, the e-Party was about money, not ideas. It was fine as a device to get rich donors interested in contributing to the party, but it wasn't a real initiative. "Across the street," the DNC official said, waving his hand in the general direction of the DNC's main offices, "they're used to dealing with the care and feeding of donors. That's fine, but keep it separate from our work—we have a lot to do."

He sighed. "Look, whatever they want to do is fine. As long as it doesn't touch our shop."

Across town, the corridors of the Longworth House Office Building were cool with old marble, and the ladies' lounges still had dark leather-covered fainting couches in the anterooms. Congressman Cal Dooley, a Democrat from California's rural Central Valley, greeted me, his haggardly Lincolnesque features and old-fashioned, country-doctor bearing somehow very reassuring. Despite the copies of *Business Week* ("Internet Anxiety") and *Newsweek* ("America Goes Hollywood") on Dooley's shelves, not to mention the lumbering throngs of baseball-capped tourists outside his door, he and his office retained the air of a more serious era.

Dooley was a leader of the New Democrat Network and a fervent believer in the Valley's political potential; Simon Rosenberg had told me that Dooley's grasp of the importance of high tech was "stellar." Dooley thought that a message combining faith in technology with the promise of education could pull in new, wealthy supporters while at the same time calming the "real anxiety" of blue-collar Democratic workers afraid of being left behind. "Anyone looking into the next century sees the importance of technology," Dooley said, clasping his big, bony hands together and leaning forward. "The party that understands it, and can provide leadership as we transition into a new economy, is going to be the majority party of the future."

Dooley seemed a likely candidate for go-between, someone who could help TechNet and the New Democrats on the Hill work together, and help the resultant bloc sway traditional members of his party. "My primary objective is to build a coalition of Democrats who will move the party toward a pro-growth agenda," he said. "And the technology sector provides us with a constituency to help us achieve that."

The alliance among TechNet, Gore, and the New Democrats that Dooley described sounded schematically perfect, yet Dooley didn't want to talk about how it was playing out on the ground. It took me more meetings, a number of them with people who would speak only on background, to piece together the story of what had happened when the attempts to bring everyone together crashed on the issue of Y2K legislation.

After his visit to Gore's camp with Doerr, where he demanded more attention for TechNet and Silicon Valley, Randlett had returned to Washington with a larger and highly publicized delegation of Silicon Valley executives. The TechNet group intended to lobby Congress in favor of a bill that would protect companies against litigation related to Y2K failures—a bill the White House had already announced it would veto. As *Roll Call* had explained in an insightful analysis, "The bill, which was written for GOP leadership by two prominent business groups, may divide Democrats, infuriate the trial lawyers and open the door to a gold mine of campaign donations from business owners, insurance companies and lucrative high-technology companies. Leadership sources said the bill provoked a scramble among GOP leaders to champion the issue and to become the 'go-to guy' for the blossoming high-technology industry as this Congress proceeds."

Now, lined up against the bill were the Democratic leadership, trial lawyers, and consumer groups; behind it were big business and most of the Republicans in Congress. And underneath all the arguments about frivolous lawsuits and corporate responsibility and who should pay for Y2K programming glitches was partisan politics. The Valley and the trial lawyers hated each other. The Old Democrats sided reflexively with the trial lawyers. And the Republicans wanted to drive a wedge between the Democrats and the Valley.

When I arrived in Washington, Dooley and his colleagues had been working on a compromise version of the Y2K bill and forging ahead with plans to bring twenty-three members to California the next month for a TechNet–New Democrat summit. Rosenberg was busy spinning the Y2K fight as "not really important at all." There had been lots of handshakes at hotel breakfasts where everyone promised to stay in touch and work together. But it was still not at all clear which side Clinton and Gore would choose on the Y2K bill, or who would come out a winner.

I finally got Dooley to talk about it all with me, a few days after our initial meeting. "This is an example of the political immaturity of the technology sector," he said sorrowfully, reviewing the Y2K fight to date. "The legislation got off to a rocky start, then was hijacked by the Chamber of Commerce and Republicans who wanted to use it against the White House. When TechNet appeared in the conversation, they were in a situation where they had to side with a business position that, frankly, was engineered by pure partisan politics. The Republicans created this to be a wedge issue, and [Silicon Valley executives] allowed themselves to be used in some way." Dooley shook his head. "I hope every time they have an experience like this they'll learn a little more," he said.

I was unsure whether the Valley was learning how to handle the compromise and maneuvering and partisan politics of the Beltway. Despite all the efforts of New Democrats like Dooley and Simon Rosenberg to work around the cultural differences between themselves and high tech, it was pretty obvious how entrenched attitudes were, on both sides.

A few weeks later, the Valley's testy reaction to the Y2K fight convinced me that it was, in fact, premature to talk about "learning a little more" if "learning" was supposed to suggest real change. Right after I'd returned to California, Randlett had flown to Washington, bringing a group that included John Doerr, David Ellington of NetNoir, Paul Lippe of Synopsys, and the Critical Path CEO David Hayden, to meet with thirteen Democratic senators and lobby for the bill. I heard the gossip from Ellington, who found the politics of the entire trip amazing. Ellington was less triumphalist than many Valley executives, and shrewder about the realities of partisan politics. And though he was acutely aware of the problems that high tech's arrogance tended to create for the industry on the Hill, he couldn't resist gloating a bit about what he judged to be the Valley's victory on Y2K. According to Ellington, the trip marked a moment when "it became clear that TechNet could kick some butt."

Ellington told me the story of going to Capitol Hill with gusto. The group, herded along by Randlett, had trooped into a meeting room in the Senate Office Building. "The place was no bigger than my living room," Ellington recounted. "And in they came: Dianne Feinstein, Ted Kennedy, Jay Rockefeller, Lieberman, John Kerry, Bob Kerrey, Evan Bayh, Paul Wellstone—I mean this room was *packed* with senators."

It was also packed with ego. And even with so much competition, John Doerr's stood out, according to a Hill aide. The venture capitalist's approach to lobbying—less an attempt to persuade than a blunt presentation of nonnegotiable demands—astonished the senators, who were used to deference, indirection, and tact. Senator Jay Rockefeller, in particular, was taken aback. "John [Doerr] wanted everyone to know that if they blew this, they can't make up on a lot of little easy things to win us back," Ellington said. "Rockefeller, I mean his entire life is privilege, he's got so much power, and he's staring at John like, 'Who the hell are you?' And John looks right back like, 'I'm who the heck I am. Who are *you*?' It was intense. I was whispering to the guy next to me, I said, 'Get me a camera—this is a historic moment. That's old money versus new money right there.' "

Ellington laughed. "Rockefeller called John naïve: 'I don't know you, John,' he went in that condescending patrician voice. 'But you must be naïve to think you can come up here on Capitol Hill where I've been trying to do this for twelve years." John was hot, like, 'You guys are completely blowing it on Y2K, you're gonna drag down your party and the White House. We've spent the last three years building the Democrats' relationship with the Valley from zero—don't wreck it.' They got into it. A staffer tried to tell John that you can't talk to a senator like that."

Dianne Feinstein stepped in, trying to reduce the tension with some crosscultural translation. "Let me explain," she told Rockefeller. "Where these people come from, they see things differently. When they have a problem, they need it fixed right away. Either you fix it for them or you don't. It's not about building a relationship for twenty-five years."

John Kerry, who had called the meeting, was sitting next to Doerr at the head of the table. "Now hold on, John," he began, but Doerr interrupted. "I'm not having it," said the venture capitalist. "None of you have ever been sued, and I have. If we don't get a bill passed that limits liability, you're screwed."

Ellington paused. "You know," he said to me, "things are really changing. Even to this day, Rockefeller's grandfather is still the richest man who ever lived, more than Bill Gates, anyone. But now everyone wants to be down with the future. Old money isn't everything. Rockefeller saw all the senators weren't supporting him. He heard them saying, 'Hey, we're Democrats, we have a new relationship with high-tech business. This is the number-one guy in the Valley. Why are we messing with him?' What could he do?"

At the end of the negotiations a bill was sent to the White House with the support of virtually all of the New Democrat Network—sixty-one out of sixty-three NDN members. After some delay, President Clinton announced that his concerns about consumer protection had been addressed, and that he would sign it.

But people in Washington and in the Valley drew very different lessons from the fight over Y2K. According to Wade Randlett, it had only helped TechNet to establish a reputation for playing tough. "On the Hill, it spread like wildfire that it was OK to kick the crap out of the senators on Y2K," said Randlett, satisfied. "We reinforced that this is not a triangulation where you're trying to balance opposing interests. This is politics, and you have to choose."

I understood, then, that TechNet's obstinacy on Y2K had not simply been about Doerr's implacable hatred of trial lawyers. By signaling his refusal to participate in a kind of politics standard among traditional

Democrats, Randlett was trying to position TechNet as something new, as more than a traditional interest group. He knew how interest-group politics went: an interest group can yell but never defect; it makes allowances for political exigencies and in return gets favors at another time. When Republicans tried to wedge Clinton by making him sign a bill outlawing gay marriage, for example, national gay groups grumbled, but they understood; they stood by their man, and, three months later, got Clinton's endorsement of their employment nondiscrimination bill. Randlett thought they were suckers; more to the point, he believed that only the weakest players had to abide by those rules. TechNet, he argued, was not weak; it wasn't another pathetically loyal Democratic constituency waiting its turn for favors. The industry was powerful enough, Randlett felt, to set its own terms.

Simon Rosenberg saw the whole thing very differently. The Y2K bill Randlett claimed as a victory for high tech Rosenberg regarded as a victory for Republican partisans, who had forced a split between the President and his own supporters while putting Rosenberg's New Democrats under unnecessary political pressure. "The Republicans wanted to make the White House choose between high tech and trial lawyers," he said, fuming. "They won. This isn't high tech's bill at all, and they're kidding themselves if they think they were setting the agenda."

Rosenberg himself, I thought, was going to have to work even harder in the future to overcome the problems created by the Y2K fight. He agreed: a big role for the New Democrat Network was exactly what he had in mind. "We are the ones who are positioned to talk to all sides," he said. "We understand the mentality here, and we understand the importance and ethos of the New Economy." But Rosenberg also made a point I hadn't heard him make before—one that indicated that Randlett's fly-in-and-go-ballistic tactics might finally be spent. "I think the fight shows that TechNet, if it's going to be serious about politics, has a fundamental decision to make about representation here," Rosenberg said. He was letting me know that NDN members were digging in their heels about *their* town, *their* way of doing business, *their* control of the relationship with the Valley. "You have to have a presence in Washington if you're going to understand how Washington works."

In business terms, what I was seeing was a battle for brand. After the 1998 elections and the impeachment scandal in 1999, the DNC was preparing itself for the next round. And as the political calendar moved inexorably toward 2000, the Gore campaign was becoming the next battlefield in an ongoing, many-sided political war between Old and New Democrats, New and Old party partisans, East Coast and West Coast. As Silicon Valley stepped onto the stage of national politics, a struggle began over who controlled the message, who managed the money, who would get public credit and behind-the-scenes power.

At the simplest level, the struggles played out among individuals, as different people elbowed for position. One obvious example was Rosenberg, who had played an inside game for years, managing a high-strung stable of members while keeping his eye on the big prize. "We're about changing the Democratic Party," Rosenberg would repeat, when wranglings over legislation or money or personality threatened to pull his New Democrat Network apart. He was smart and plugged-in, but his devotion to the long-term goal of changing the party was constantly coming into conflict with concrete politics—which, like most of human affairs, took place in the short term. Now his interest in high tech—a business in which "short-term" meant a week and "long-term" meant six months—presented an even greater challenge. If Rosenberg were to enlist high-tech executives in the service of his long-term goals, he was going to have to find effective ways to attend to their immediate interests.

Another example was Randlett, whose trajectory had compressed into a few years what it had taken many political operators years to achieve. Randlett had the advantage of working fast, and the disadvantage of trying to do everything. He may originally have built TechNet as a power base, hoping to become, like Yasir Arafat for the Palestinian people, the "sole legitimate representative" to Washington in the eyes of Silicon Valley, and attempting, in turn, to represent the Silicon Valley brand to politicians. Not surprisingly, Randlett annoyed the hell out of people, like Rosenberg, who wanted to claim that they'd thought of it first—as well as all those who preferred to speak for themselves and make their own deals.

Randlett hadn't succeeded on every front with TechNet, but by 1999 he'd done enough so that nobody in Silicon Valley saw the point in creating an alternative organization. He had direct access to the White House—a point that rankled with the NDN, which had to endure the condescension of CEOs who thought House members were too unimportant to bother with. He had some direct access, by virtue of providing money and infrastructure help, to Gore's campaign. And from the outset he had identified himself with the heavyweights of Silicon Valley, beginning with John Doerr—the people whom, sooner or later, Gore, members of Congress, and politicians and fund-raisers of all stripes would have to go to.

There were, nonetheless, plenty of systemic problems that Randlett had been unable to work around. It was well known that he had incomplete coverage of the Valley, where plenty of Republican CEOs, especially the powerful Jim Barksdale of Netscape, resented him for TechNet's noticeable Democratic bias. Outside California, he'd never "grown the network" to the degree he'd hoped: a few scattered trips to Seattle or Virginia weren't enough to begin, let alone sustain, the kind of purposeful organizing that would transcend geography.

And even some of Randlett's friendly relationships posed problems for him, if he wanted to remain at the center of the Silicon Valley–Washington connection. Sandy Robertson, for example: the financier had his own independent relationships, predating Randlett and TechNet by years, with everyone from Al From to Al Gore. Robertson was supremely well connected in the financial community, and needed no introduction from anyone to get an audience in Washington. He was on the board of the DLC—the actual governing board, as well as the letterhead one—and he was a big Democratic donor, whose contributions were counted as his own, not TechNet's. Robertson was a prize, but how could Randlett claim credit for him?

Or there was Tim Newell, who had been overseeing the Gore-Tech meetings in 1997. Now he was working for Sandy Robertson in San Francisco, and rumor had it that he was going to head Robertson's new on-line investment-banking firm, E-Offering. Newell gave money to Democrats, and he kept his ties with Washington. He remained Randlett's friend, but there was a constant, low-level sense of competition between the two men. What did Newell think about Randlett's direct dealing with the White House? Who was he going to allow to represent Silicon Valley to his old friends on Gore's staff? Now that he was a Silicon Valley executive in his own right, did Newell want someone else to speak for him?

Or, at a greater remove, there was Tony Podesta, who, it was rumored, was in the running to be appointed as head of the Gore 2000 operation for California. If the lobbyist took the job, was he going to try to deliver Silicon Valley as part of the overall state package, without going entirely and solely through Randlett and TechNet? If Podesta didn't wind up doing the job, and another Washington figure did, the problem remained the same: Would the Gore person for California have his own independent relationships with Silicon Valley, and if so would Randlett be squeezed out? Or would Randlett's fund-raising for Gore be preemptive, and convince the campaign that it couldn't win in California without his help?

And through it all there was Rosenberg, whom I tended to see as Randlett's Washington counterpart, his Beltway twin. The two men still had a relationship in which closeness and competitiveness were hopelessly mixed up: they praised each other, did each other favors, and thought about stabbing each other in the back every week. Professionally cooperative and personally friendly for years—Rosenberg had even introduced Randlett to Tamsin Smith—they jostled ceaselessly for position and prestige. Each grudgingly gave the other credit for hard work, yet each also insisted that he was the real glue holding the Silicon Valley–Washington network together, and the best informed about both worlds. "I'd just like everyone to know," I'd once heard Rosenberg inform a group of high-tech executives, "that I was the one who first told Wade he should use e-mail."

And all these questions about individuals were just part of the problem. When it came to ideology, and the implications that Silicon Valley's entry into politics had for the direction of the Democrats, things got even more confusing. Ideology, of course, was still mediated by individuals and individual ambitions, but nothing in the big or small picture was simple. I thought I'd watch Randlett and Rosenberg, Tim Newell and Sandy Robertson, Cal Dooley and John Doerr thrash their differences out in person, as the New Democrats sat down with Silicon Valley's most politically engaged executives and tried to figure it all out.

CHAPTER fifteen

There's a peculiar mixture of giddy self-importance and tedium that makes most conferences hard to sit through. By midafternoon on the second day, once the bagels are gone and the fifth speaker's slogging through his PowerPoint presentation, you start to see people discreetly unpinning their badges and slipping out of the hotel lobby for a little fresh air.

At the New Democrat Network's 1999 California retreat—a three-day conference in July for members of the House New Democrat coalition, co-sponsored by TechNet—none of the twenty-three congressional attendees ever strayed. This was the largest event Simon Rosenberg and Wade Randlett had collaborated on, with close to a hundred participants holding dozens of meetings, and it made, on the surface, an impressive display of political purpose.

I planned to tag along for all three days. I wanted to see how much Silicon Valley really cared about this conference and, by extension, about the New Democrats of Washington and politics in general. Would Rosenberg be able to entice the Valley's top executives into his network? Or were they just being polite to the tourists?

In either case, the members were ready. All through panel discussions of broadband regulation, slide shows about education, and seminars on supercomputing—with breaks for weak coffee—they, at least, hung tough.

Perhaps they were mesmerized by the chance to mingle with Silicon Valley's biggest stars—including John Doerr, Brook Byers, and Sandy Robertson; legendary techies like Sun Microsystem's Bill Joy and Marc Andreessen; and executives from such Internet successes as eBay, C/NET, and Charles Schwab. Perhaps the members were eager to peek inside the labs of hot biotechnology companies like Geron and Genentech. Or maybe it was the promised Napa Valley winery tour and "sunset dinner" at Francis Ford Coppola's estate that turned a conference, finally, into an irresistible vacation, a chance to partake of Pinot Noir and grilled quail with the spouse in tow.

But a lobbyist for AT&T—a chatty, athletic woman, one of the twenty-odd lobbyists and company reps who'd paid $1,000 each to attend the retreat—gave me a different interpretation. As we cruised down 101 toward Silicon Valley the first day, she gestured at a congressman eagerly peering out the windows of the tour bus and pointing out high-tech landmarks to his seatmate. "You know why this is so big for them now, right?" I didn't have to answer. The lobbyist smiled. "Money," she said.

Money was certainly on everyone's mind. Most of the Washington delegation listened gamely during the conference to discussions of telomerase enzymes and Java Remote Method Invocation and fiber optics. Some of the geekier Hill staffers seemed thrilled to swap tech tidbits with their California counterparts, or simply to gaze in awe at Bill Joy in the flesh. But, mostly, what grabbed the crowd's attention was the giddy reports on the state of the booming New Economy.

It was impossible for anyone in America, by August 1999, to dismiss what Ariel Sharon, in a very different context, had liked to call "facts on the ground." One fact was that the information-technology industry, broadly speaking, had created about sixty thousand new jobs a year for the last five years; that is to say, gainfully employing tens of thousands of real individuals, albeit in frequently unprofitable businesses, in districts all over the country. Another was that cyberspace was making new millionaires at an amazing clip: about sixty-four each week in the Silicon Valley area alone. And even if the near-slapstick frenzy of would-be Internet investors seeking more and more ridiculous castles in the air to fund was just "essentially speculative activity," as traditional businessmen sniffed, the persuasive fact on the ground was that the investors, along with the fully 61 percent of other Americans who now played the rising stock market, were doing better than ever on the profits of irrationality.

Part of the mystery seemed to emanate directly from the nature of software and Internet companies that were, by definition, immaterial. In a sense, the Internet industry was like Clinton's politics, which produced ever-climbing approval ratings without any apparent "real" input. But the phenomenon had its practical and political effects. Jeff Bjornstad, the sharp, confident chief of staff for Seattle-area congressman Adam Smith, explained his logic straightforwardly. "Even the most marginal Democrat can get twenty or thirty grand from labor just for starters," he told me. "But once you start to be seen as pro-business, a New Democrat, it dries up. When we opposed trial lawyers, we lost ten grand, when we opposed the teachers we lost twenty." Bjornstad cleared his throat. "So how do you fund a campaign?" he asked. "I'm not saying that Adam's going to change his principles, but those votes cost us."

Bjornstad had urged Smith to ask the high-tech executives how the country could best help Silicon Valley continue its amazing growth. On cue, the executives responded with a checklist of issues, including the rules governing tax write-offs for corporate-research costs and the Federal Accounting Standards Advisory Board's accounting procedures for valuing employee stock options. Simon Rosenberg, sidling over to me, sighed. "We have to take it easy," he said. "I think this sounds too much like we're pandering."

The point had admittedly crossed my mind the day before, when a congresswoman perched on a sofa in Marc Andreessen's opulent living room insisted that, though her district had no high-tech businesses, she nonetheless had been voting "solidly in favor of high-tech issues for years." Her eyes overflowed with sincerity. "Really," she explained, taking a piece of salmon wrapped in grape leaves. "For me Silicon Valley's like the whole feeling of the pioneers, the risks people take, the explorers. . . ." Overcome, she put down her fork. "It's really a spiritual thing for me," she said.

The real draw for most of the participants, though, was nothing as literal as campaign contributions. Somehow, the very *idea* of money — Silicon Valley money, specifically — exercised an almost pornographic hold on the imagination of everyone who had come to the retreat. Money was different out here: big, wild, a little scary. It made $227 million appropriation bills seem tired and old-fashioned.

At Sandy Robertson's seminar on "The Revolution in Financial Markets," at Charles Schwab, or during the discussion of e-commerce at eBay, or when Dan Case and John Doerr presented their "Thoughts on Globalism and the New Economy," I watched New Democrats gawk like rubes at the numbers swirling around them. "Intel has nineteen thousand employees, and seven thousand of those are millionaires," an executive would begin, or, "I'm twenty-four, and this is the second company I've taken public," or, "There've been twelve hundred tech IPOs in the last eighteen years, with a current market value of $2 trillion." Dizzying recitations of impossibly inflated market values, compensation packages, and multimillion-dollar buyouts had the congressmen shaking their heads and gasping for air as they frantically took notes. At least three junior aides took me aside and asked me — "confidentially," they said — what I thought about the viability of the Internet start-up sector. "I just got offered a job," one breathy young woman told me. "And it's for more money than you would believe, just to write some business plans for them. Is this for real?"

Cal Dooley tried hard to keep his colleagues' enthusiasm at seemly levels, and sternly kept guiding the discussions onto higher ground. "I want to make sure that you understand we don't think of Silicon Valley as an ATM," he told a roomful of high-tech executives on the first day of the retreat.

Wade Randlett was also watching his speakers carefully. The wealth of Silicon Valley, an NDN staffer had complained, made its moguls "arrogant beyond belief," even as they remained ignorant of the way government worked. John Doerr had at least learned to engage in some preliminary flattery — "We admire your commitment to public service and your ability to handle a very, very difficult job" — before telling politicians what to do. But others didn't always waste time on subtlety.

Dan Case, the deadpan young investment banker from Hambrecht & Quist, a boutique firm specializing in technology, opened a seminar on new financial markets for the NDN members. The brother of AOL's chief executive, Steve Case, he had a clipped, insolent voice and was wearing a beautifully tailored dark suit. Standing at a podium in Charles Schwab's downtown offices, Case ticked off the tasks currently facing government, as he saw them.

"One, education," he said. "Can we fix that? It's broken. Two, FASAB. Can we leave that alone?" Case didn't wait for a reaction from his audience. "The R&D tax credit, can we keep doing that, please? And financial-services reform, let's finish up with that. It's been ten years, and it's not relevant anymore." Case gave a small nod and sat down. The congressmen applauded gamely.

John Doerr's opening remarks were friendlier, though delivered at his usual speed-freak pace. I saw Wade Randlett relax as Doerr launched into his presentation on the implications of the New Economy, a crowd-pleasing show no less effective for its familiarity. When Doerr preached, politicians—even those who didn't grasp the significance of his reach, or entirely understand how the Kleiner Perkins network provided an infrastructure for TechNet's political machine—got religion. His authority was unquestioned; his opinions had the weight of law. Other CEOs were courted for their donations and listened to politely, but for Washington John Doerr still *was* Silicon Valley.

Doerr raced through his standard futurist hyperbole, then offered policy recommendations. Hands off the Internet, he told the NDN members, don't regulate broadband, enact campaign-finance reform, privatize a portion of Social Security, trade with China, and keep Russia in Europe. He talked passionately about the need to improve K–12 education—"We just need the will to act"—and ended by forecasting an even bigger, faster, longer high-tech boom that would "transform the world economy." Congressman Silvestre Reyes, representing one of California's poorer border districts, rose to his feet. "I don't think that I've ever spent a better hour in a briefing," he said humbly.

Yet there were stirrings of discontent underneath the New Democrats' adulation. I was surprised, in fact, at how much classically Old Democrat hand-wringing about class and race surfaced—albeit obliquely, referred to with delicacy as "issues of access" or "inequality concerns."

Congresswoman Loretta Sanchez, the New Democrat from California's Orange County who had unseated the archconservative "B1 Bob" Dornan in 1996 by mobilizing Latino voters, was the first member to speak up and confront the bankers. "When a family lives ten people to a one-bedroom house," Sanchez said, "and the grownups are working two jobs each, and they have no phone . . ." She paused. Sanchez, eager to appear as if she were more than just another traditional bleeding-heart minority Old Democrat, had introduced herself that morning as a fervent capitalist from "a long line of investment bankers." But she sounded troubled now. "People like that in my district, they're just not gonna buy computer equipment," she said.

Dan Case didn't alter his expression. "It's a very Darwinian world we operate in," he said calmly. "It's not a fair world, there are a lot of losers." His fellow panelists nodded. "Of course," Case went on, "we all have to take some responsibility for social-class issues, but basically we're in the growing-the-pie business, and it's someone else's job to redistribute it." Given the "delightful uncontrollability" of financial markets, he suggested, business matters would require most of his attention in the near future. The seminar broke up with a promise to discuss education and related inequality issues later that afternoon.

I walked past Sanchez and another congresswoman, who were buttonholing Doerr and asking his advice about primary-school education. Over in a corner, Tim Newell was huddled with David Ellington, talking a little business. I couldn't understand the deal, but I heard the men laugh as they swapped numbers. "Three million," said Newell. Ellington stabbed the air with an unlit cigar. "Fuck no," he said. "He's in for twelve in the second round." Newell slapped him on the back. "Let's go to lunch," he said.

The whole problem of money—and of no money—was at the heart of what proponents of the New Economy grappled with as they tried to formulate solutions to "issues of inequality." In 1998, Democrats like *Business Week* editor Marvin Mandel, writing in the DLC's magazine, *Blueprints*, in the winter, had warned that "the New Economy is widening the income gap." In line with an approach long advocated by New Democrats, notably Al Gore, Mandel urged more attention to education, warning that "the U.S. cannot accept an economy divided between education haves and have-nots." A year later, the market's fantastic success had increased the pressure on politicians not to raise such issues at the risk of sounding grudging, Luddite, and negative. But the figures were clear: in every state where there had been growth in the high-tech sector, income inequality had increased; even in California, where the boom was most dramatic, child poverty had worsened. Most members of the House New Democrat Network, even as they bubbled over with optimism about the New Economy, still expressed their belief in finding ways to overcome inequality. "We cannot leave anyone behind," Cal Dooley firmly said, as he addressed a group of businessmen in early 1999.

But most of the Silicon Valley executives at this NDN conference, though they willingly expressed their support for education, were unlikely to think much about poverty as the country's most pressing problem. The rural poor of Cal Dooley's district, or the working-class parents with lousy schools represented by Congresswoman Loretta Sanchez, weren't easy to visualize for people who worked in companies where receptionists were college-educated twenty-four-year-olds with tens of thousands of dollars in stock options. Blue-collar workers in general weren't part of their world: most techies spent their lives at the office, surrounded by people very much like themselves. Perhaps they'd see the FedEx guy one day, or say hi to a mechanic when they dropped off their Porsche for a tune-up.

They wouldn't have to deal with the jostle of classes found in a large city, where all kinds of people are forced to share streets, subways, libraries, marketplaces. The suburbs of Silicon Valley, like suburbs elsewhere, drew very effective class boundaries. There was a growing number of working families in the Valley at risk of homelessness because of the insane run-up in real-estate values, but they didn't shop at the Stanford Mall. There were the archaic employees of the public sector who were rapidly being squeezed out of the Valley by the boom, but they didn't send their kids to Los Altos High School. In general, the working class and the poor in the Valley were invisible to the well-off: the suburbs performed their great separating function, even as the market eroded the last common spaces of civic life.

All of this made the issue of "inequality" more abstract, less immediate. And even if Silicon Valley's prosperous leaders did arrive at some visceral awareness of the gaps between their wealth and others' poverty, they were unlikely to believe that government could fix it.

What they did believe in was growth. It was an understandable faith, since many Valley businessmen and Internet executives were young enough never to have experienced an economic slowdown. The three-inch-thick briefing book that Simon Rosenberg handed out to conference attendees had page after page of testimonials to the power of the idea. There was the White House statement on the New Economy, with its bold headlines ("Deficit Eliminated . . . Fastest Economic Growth Since Kennedy . . . Jobs up 18.9 million since January 1993 . . . Unemployment Lowest in 20 Years . . . The World's Most Competitive Economy Again"). There was the *Business Week* story hailing "The Net Effect," ranking Microsoft as number one in its Global Top 1,000 companies. There was an entire section on e-commerce, and a report explaining why the U.S.-based Internet economy was, by itself, now one of the major economies in the world, having grown in just five years to a sector as big as the energy sector, or the automobile industry, or telecommunications. And there was Alan Greenspan's remarkable confession to the Senate in June 1999, which began, "Something special has happened to the American economy in recent years."

What remained hard to convey to outsiders, for those at the center of the digital revolution, was the world-turned-upside-down quality of the experience. Tim Newell tried to explain it. "I can't believe the speed," he told me, his face flushed as he described his start-up. E-Offering had been launched in January 1999, with the backing of Sandy Robertson and other Internet-savvy bankers; as the official investment bank of E-Trade, it took other Internet companies public, managing their IPOs and finding on-line investors. "It's the most intense thing I've ever done," Newell said. His voice was hoarse. "It's like a campaign, only permanent."

For entrepreneurs like Newell, Moore's Law, about the exponentially increasing computing power of chips, and Metcalfe's Law, about the exponentially increasing value of growing networks, were models for an entire business philosophy that had no room for caution. It was a truism to them that a rising tide would lift all boats, and almost incomprehensible that anyone could remain poor while the high-tech boom continued. Doubt was, simply, crazy.

"This thing is moving fast, faster than ever before," began David Pottruck, the president of Charles Schwab, during a seminar about on-line investing. We were gathered in a Schwab conference room in the heart of San Francisco's financial district, some of the members' staff scribbling notes earnestly as the captains of Silicon Valley talked. Tom Kalil from the National Economic Council had come out from the White House. Super-smart and unpretentious, he seemed like a bit of a closet nerd himself. Kalil sat next to Newell, who'd been working next to him in the White House less than two years ago, and now lived in a flat in a Pacific Heights mansion with a panoramic view of the bay.

Up on the dais, Pottruck coughed politely. He had just explained the phenomenal growth of the on-line trading sector—from 2 million to 6.3 million households in the last sixteen months—and was extolling the social and economic benefits of a fully "democratized" market. An old-fashioned Washington policy type raised his hand with a timid objection: wasn't the scale of Internet trading risky, and shouldn't there be more oversight of this new world?

Yes, Pottruck admitted, the entire process was not without risk. "There is some pain that comes with growth," he said. "Existing companies are struggling to reinvent themselves, there may be some downsizing and layoffs. . . ." He shrugged. "But there are new companies every day, and new investors." Sandy Robertson, sitting beside Pottruck, jumped in. "It's Schumpeter's creative destruction," Robertson commented. "But happening at Internet speed." Beside me, Kalil cracked a smile.

A former Treasury Department adviser stood up. "I hate to be the skunk at the garden party," he said, clearing his throat, "but while it may be possible in your New Economy that stocks will only go up forever, uh, what if it's also possible that the business cycle will return?" Pottruck's face went cold. The New Democrats looked at him in confusion. "And what happens," asked the skunk, "with all this democratization of financial markets when the market goes back to normal?"

Robertson, the senior optimist, again took the question. "I, too, am worried about excessive valuations," he said soothingly. "The Internet is a great thing that's happened to our economy, but given that, many Internet stock prices are unreasonable." He nodded reassuringly. "Even with a correction, there will still be new issues," he said. "There's always a risk, but underlying all of this the fundamentals are great." His fellow panelists looked relieved, and chimed in to agree that the fundamentals were great.

Not everyone at the seminars that day shared the financiers' conviction that "making every American an investor" would solve all social problems. I was a bit chilled, myself, at the way the people of the nation had gone, in one generation, from being considered citizens to "consumers," and then, with incredible speed, from being consumers to "investors." Given such enormous shifts in identity—many more Americans now owned stock than voted—I wondered which of the responsibilities and rights of citizenship would still obtain in another twenty years.

But my old-fashioned worrying was beside the point. Other Silicon Valley optimists put their faith not, like the bankers, in financial markets but in technology itself. Not only had technology launched the longest boom in the nation's economic history, they said, but it was poised to address social problems that had heretofore remained intractable. According to an executive from Intel, who spoke in an afternoon session at the Hyatt, the problem of inequality, for example, was "solving itself, because the equipment and connections are becoming cheaper and more accessible, so inequality will solve itself over a decade or so." Challenged, mildly, by a reporter from the on-line news service C/NET, who asked how technology would eradicate slums, he corrected himself smoothly. "I said that the problem of hardware and access will be solved," he said. "Of course, there's still a huge educational divide you have to consider."

I took notes, for a while, making occasional entries on a page in my notebook that I'd entitled "New Economy Speech Crimes." The list included new horrors like "to incent" and "to content," along with the simultaneously inspirational and grasping cliché "to empower." It struck me that most of the worst New Economy verbs had been recycled from old-economy businessbabble, in the same way that many of the core business concepts trumpeted by prophets of the New Economy owed a lot to the managementspeak of corporate America: "teamwork," "leadership," "enabled decision-making." And it was the same with the political rhetoric that I found most objectionable. Corporate America had long pronounced itself in favor of education and children; in their day, Carnegie and Rockefeller were probably as smarmily interested in helping the less fortunate and as voraciously ambitious about creating their own wealth as the new Internet millionaires were now. The historian Lawrence Goodwyn, in his *Democratic Promise: The Populist Movement in America*, wrote about the similar national ethos of Gilded Age America, which, he noted, "contained a number of contradictions: it was visionary, complacent, energetic, and romantic. . . . It was a time when great fortunes were being amassed by a few, admired enviously by the many, and exalted as a testament both to individual worth and to the merit of the Republic."

There was, of course, a modern tenor to those parts of the language that had to do with the technologies themselves. Bill Joy, the chief engineer at Sun, had come to this retreat to talk about the impact of technology on society. Though he had been introduced by Randlett as "the man John Doerr believes is the smartest man in Silicon Valley," Joy, dressed in old corduroys and a ratty handwoven sweater, made little attempt to discuss his astonishing scientific insights with the members. A year later, he would make headlines by eschewing the universal optimism of his peers, and warning, in a twenty-thousand-word essay published in *Wired*, against the uncontrolled development of "dangerous" new technologies without regard to ethical standards. Even his mild statement that all technologies needed to be carefully evaluated for their impact on society would be seen as a betrayal of the forward-looking mind-set of the industry.

But for now, Joy was content to deliver a standard-issue futurist rant that revealed little more than the confused libertarian roots of what used to pass, in the pre-TechNet era, for political thought in the Valley. "Heisenberg for the House," one aide whispered to me as Joy spouted about "nonlinear" and "quantum" and "chaos" and "paradigms." But the connection between Joy's scientific and economic thinking grew even murkier as he evoked, in succession, Thomas Jefferson, George Gilder, and former Grateful Dead lyricist John Perry Barlow to describe the "post-scarcity" digital utopia that was on its way. Joy grabbed the room's attention when he detoured to attack Microsoft as the source of all evil in the high-tech world—"bad software poorly designed by a monopoly to perpetuate a monoculture of systems"—and put a plug in for antitrust enforcement. Then he took a few questions from politicians who were clearly awed. "How is government going to change?" one asked him. Joy didn't blink. "There's a whole new paradigm . . ." he began.

Men like Joy were sincere. They drove me crazy. It was possible to stand at the rear of the Grand Hyatt's Continental Ballroom with the Mexican waiters, watching fifty white men and five white women from the richest valley on earth discuss the democratizing influence of the Internet, and register the irony. But I was also aware of how unexceptional and mild, in the context of American history, these particular rich people's selfishness was. If one of TechNet's young millionaires sounded heartless when he trashed unions, it wasn't because he was an industrial-age capitalist trying to wring more wealth out of his downtrodden employees. If a venture capitalist called for welfare reform, he might honestly believe the government had failed, for decades, to lift enough people out of poverty. It was probably their idealism that grated on me the most, and I resolved to try to ignore it.

There was less idealism, and a lot more political savvy, at the next day's session, in which the members of the New Democrat Network discussed, among themselves, their prospects. A few Silicon Valley figures had remained for the meeting, but the group was mostly Washington insiders. Simon Rosenberg ran the discussion; he had an unshakable enthusiasm for New Democrat politics, and a level of energy high enough to stand out even when surrounded by entrepreneurs. He led off a pointed analysis of the movement's strategy, with an unlikely salute to Republican activists. "They are a group of people who, for forty years, worked to change the nature and direction of their party," he began. "From the time when they launched the *National Review*, to the election of Reagan, to putting Gingrich in as Speaker, you see how they very deliberately went about building an infrastructure to achieve their goals." He looked sternly at his members.

"The challenge for us is, Are we going to be friends of change, or are we going to be trying to push it back?" Rosenberg said. "We are on the right side of history here, but we need to build an infrastructure and an organization that can make change happen."

Rosenberg clearly believed that high tech was an essential part of the "infrastructure" that New Democrats needed. Silicon Valley, he went on, could provide not only money but crucial "intellectual property" for New Democrats who saw the country's information revolution and New Economy as demanding a new set of political attitudes. The congressional and presidential elections of 2000, Rosenberg concluded, signified "a generational battle to determine which party will be the party of the New Economy."

Rosenberg turned the microphone over to Chris Gabrieli, a Boston venture capitalist who had spent years in New Democrat politics. Gabrieli was the chairman of the NDN, a formidable fund-raiser, and a politically shrewd organizer. Friendly and casual, he agreed with Rosenberg that a "partnership" with high tech could give New Democrats a powerful political boost. But then he confronted the high-tech industry with surprising bluntness, characterizing most of its executives as "not involved, unbelievably unsophisticated, free riders." Gabrieli grinned disarmingly. "But if you tell them they are, they won't get up off a dime. How do we harness them into a movement that has the passion of the civil rights or the antiwar movement? How do we get them to care?"

Adam Smith, the young and combative member from Washington who had assumed a leadership role in the NDN, picked up from Gabrieli. High tech, he argued, was ready to hear the message of New Democrats, just as voters in general were. "For three consecutive cycles, the Democrats have been running as liberals against right-wing extremists, and now the parties are at a draw," he said. Smith, who had won in a blue-collar district south of Seattle with a pro-business message, had a near-evangelical conviction. "The average swing voter hates this," he insisted. "It's the same old crap over and over again, and they're deathly sick of it."

Smith dismissed liberals who charged that New Democrats were simply morphing into Republicans. "Worse than not being able to distinguish yourself from Republicans," he said acerbically, "is distinguishing yourself by having a horrible position." The New Democrats, he went on, would do better by distancing themselves from tradition. "We should say, 'Hey, the Republicans were right about a few things.' We should stand up and say we can be fiscally responsible, not that we should build more government programs. People hate traditional politicians—they want a change. We have to get a little Jesse Ventura in us."

There was applause, and then Wade Randlett, the last speaker on the panel, picked up Smith's argument smoothly, intending to wrap up. "The tech community isn't interested in business-as-usual politics either," he said. "There's a real fight for their loyalty now." Randlett evoked the example of yesterday's star speakers. "John Doerr and Dan Case have no business being in the Democratic Party, if we're talking about the party of eight or ten years ago," he said. "We got them because the Republicans did everything wrong. If the Republicans *stop* doing everything wrong, then we'll lose people like that." Talking more slowly than usual, but emphatically, Randlett repeated his mantra: "We need to beat the Republicans by eliminating tension between social and business issues, get to the center on business issues first and fast, and then let the Republicans fail."

But Smith, his voice betraying an edge of anger, jumped in to attack Old Democrats in the House, who, he charged, stayed in power by expanding government programs and thus their own ability to distribute patronage and political favors. I saw again just how passionate this crusade "to change the heart and soul of our party" was for New Democrats, and how well it meshed with Randlett's own crusade to make government smaller and more like the businesses of the New Economy.

"There's a viewpoint that we have to spend money," Smith said. "We have a lot of constituencies we have to reach, and people say we can't unless we spread money around. That's a political strategy—but it's not passing out checks that's the key to winning.

"To win, we have to show we're different from traditional interest groups. Nothing secures my future more in my district than going against traditional interest groups."

Not all of Smith's colleagues seemed convinced; many, based in districts heavy with older blue-collar voters or farmworkers, preferred not to alienate anyone. Computers in classrooms were fine with voters, they felt, but so was Medicare; successful members needed to practice a more nuanced fence-straddling when it came to proclaiming their "New"-ness.

But Simon Rosenberg, who had raised funds for the NDN precisely by attacking his own party's orthodoxy, concurred with Smith. As he saw it, ordinary voters were already swinging to the center, and responded well to the pro-business, pro-tech New Democrat message. "In areas where the New Economy is strong, we're doing well," he pointed out. "In the western corridor from Washington State to San Diego, there's only one Republican seat, and that's [Silicon Valley moderate] Tom Campbell. If we stay true on the economic stuff, we'll win."

The NDN's challenge, Rosenberg told his group, was weaning Democrats away from the money provided by traditional interest groups. "Our problem as a party," Rosenberg declared, appropriating the language that had dominated the California retreat, "is that the biggest source of our venture capital now comes from labor, which is a group that's becoming less and less important, and representing less and less of a percentage of American voters." Rosenberg looked around the room at the handful of CEOs and bankers who were still left. They were all nodding in agreement. "We have to replace labor's investment in the party with investment from another source, and hopefully from a source that's growing," he said. "Let's catch up to this new world we're in."

It was over a hundred degrees in Napa Valley the next day, and our group had tasted half a dozen wines before reaching the wisteria-covered pergolas in the courtyard of the Niebaum-Coppola winery. I sat on a stone wall, worn out, watching the NDN's Silicon Valley conference wind down.

A pale Hill staffer with a divinity degree from Georgetown joined me, and confided that he'd been offered a job at C/NET. "What do you think I should do?" he asked, in agony. He clearly had believed, even a week ago, in the idea of public service. Tim Newell, ruddy with Pinot Noir, stopped to talk and clapped him on the back. "It's great out here," he told the staffer heartily. "When I interview people from the East, they want to know what the salary is. When I talk to guys who've been working in the Valley, all they want to know is what the options are. This is a whole new world."

Newell moved on. I waved at Roberta Achtenberg, a pro-labor lesbian firebrand who had run, unsuccessfully, as the left-wing alternative to Willie Brown for mayor of San Francisco before morphing inexplicably into a lobbyist for the city's Chamber of Commerce. She smiled professionally and kept talking to the high-tech lobbyist at her side. "I don't know what you should do," I said to the divinity student. "What do you think about everything you've heard at the conference?"

Tom Kalil joined us. He was dressed for the heat, in shorts and a T-shirt with a picture of Intel's founder and the legend "Bob Noyce, Teen Hero." I turned to Kalil with relief. "Tell him where all this is going," I said, and stood up, looking for a water fountain. "You're the economist."

Across the lawn, a few smaller, older Washingtonians were steering their wives toward Coppola's main dining room. Tim Newell and David Ellington were under a tree, still booming at each other about deals. They had a proprietary air about them as they stood overlooking the winery's great hall, where tiny lights were flickering on in the summery dusk. Not only are we smarter and richer than you are, their body language said to the congressmen trudging past them, but we live in a prettier place. The scent of roses and hay filled the evening, and we went in to dinner.

On the bus home, Simon Rosenberg sat with his arm around his wife, happy about the success of the NDN–Silicon Valley Conference. Some of the members' aides had smuggled a few extra bottles of Cabernet on board, and were lifting paper cups and using their cell phones to call over to the people on the next bus. Randlett and Ellington seemed to be trying to have a serious business conversation, but the laughter drowned them out. A staffer started singing "California Girls," and another held up her cell phone. The people on the other bus, equally tipsy, were trying to lead us in a chant. "What do we want?" came a hoarse shout from the phone, and the group shouted back, "Broadband!" Then, "When do we want it?" "Now!" There were cheers, and another toast, and I heard Ellington explode with laughter as a techie burst into "Do You Know the Way to San Jose." The New Democrat bus rolled on through the warm night.

PART FOUR
system crash

CHAPTER sixteen

As usual, Wade Randlett was on the phone when I got to his house. It was the last week of August, a slow time, and he'd told me to stop by around four. His dogs were used to me by now, so after they'd sniffed hello and wandered away I amused myself by making a catalog of objects in the little room where Randlett worked. I saw a T-shirt crumpled up on the desk, along with a moldy container of salsa and a bag of blue tortilla chips; four phones; three calculators; some haphazard piles of papers, a stapler and some pens. A pair of work boots had been kicked off on the floor, next to a gym bag and some grimy dog toys.

"I always try to see what's changed in the decor since the first time I came here," I said to Randlett as he hung up. He chuckled. "Not much." His arm shot out, gesturing at the mess. "Uh, I guess I have a new printer." I stood and looked at the walls, while Randlett started whipping through his e-mail. "It'll just be a minute," he promised. The pictures of Randlett with President Clinton hadn't been there in 1996: they all dated from later fund-raising events. One, in a nice wooden frame, featured the menu from Randlett's first Silicon Valley dinner for the President, side by side with a snapshot of Clinton giving Randlett a thumbs-up.

Out in his backyard we settled into patio chairs, and Randlett, sipping from a glass of water, broke the news. "So," he said, studiously casual. "I guess the big thing is that I'm leaving TechNet." He coughed. "I know it kind of messes up your narrative," he said, "but hey, think of it as just a little plot twist."

I'd seen Randlett in barge-ahead mode plenty of times, when he was so convinced of the rightness of his ideas that he could barely pause for air or stop himself from making profane little outbursts of delight at the acuity of his own analysis. The slowness of his speech now made me wonder how much he understood about the story he was trying to put together. And what did he want me to understand?

I'd heard in June that John Witchel, after announcing his "retirement" from USWeb, was working on a new start-up, something to do with Internet-based services for independent contractors. This company, Randlett told me now, was called Red Gorilla, and it was "hot," and Randlett was going to work for it as a vice president of business development. "I talk to people on the phone, get them to write checks, set up meetings, build strategic partnerships," he said with a grin and a shrug. "It's a pretty good use of my existing skill set." I wanted to hear more about Red Gorilla, and where Witchel and Randlett were planning to take the company, but I wasn't ready to change the subject. Why, I asked, given his success doing politics, would Randlett pick this moment to leave TechNet?

Carefully, Randlett explained his dissatisfaction with Roberta Katz, the Netscape general counsel who had become TechNet's new president at the beginning of the summer. "She's a disaster for TechNet," he pronounced. "Bad politics, bad judgment."

As I'd suspected, once Reed Hastings left TechNet in the spring, the board began to think about a candidate who could rein Randlett in. On hand was Roberta Katz, a confidante of Jim Barksdale's, the Republican co-chair of TechNet. She was also trusted by John Doerr, who appreciated her sharp legal mind and wanted to reward her work against Microsoft—work that had rebounded effectively to the benefit of his Kleiner Perkins companies.

Katz got the job in June 1999, and began a reorganization of TechNet. In a decision that baffled most of the TechNet staff, she removed the responsibility for fund-raising from the Democratic and Republican political directors and their staffs, and put it all in the hands of a "bipartisan" fund-raiser, Eric Sklar.

Randlett understood immediately that the move was an attack on his power. He'd originally been enthusiastic about Katz's hire, probably because he saw her as a ceremonial director who would insulate him from Republican criticism. Certainly, he had never intended to give up his role of guiding TechNet. "I wanted to make it double in size, raise more money, and be more effective than any other PAC," he told me. "And to do that the status quo isn't acceptable. Roberta says she wants to slow down, expand what TechNet does. She doesn't want to just raise money for candidates.

"She wants to do member service now," he said cuttingly. "Whatever that means. I thought winning on 211, winning on charter schools, winning on federal-securities litigation, and winning on Y2K and winning on the R&D tax credit—I thought that was serving the members pretty well."

I kept listening, but my mind was racing as I scrambled for explanations. On the one hand, it shouldn't have been at all surprising that Randlett, surrounded daily by such ludicrous amounts of wealth so magically and instantaneously obtained, should have succumbed. People in California talked about it all the time. Even my friend Francisco, a psychiatrist who'd spent his entire professional career deliberately throwing away the privileges his training had given him—going to work in county hospitals and poor people's clinics, treating homeless drug abusers and immigrant schizophrenics—even he had caught the bug. "I feel like I'm stupid," he said morosely one night over dinner. "Everyone else is making a killing in stocks, they're day-trading, they have brokers. I think, You idiot, this can't last forever. Are you gonna be the last one to get in on the boom?" Francisco had poked at his potatoes. "I can't imagine going to work for an Internet start-up or anything," he'd said. "But I'm starting to feel shame that I'm not rich yet."

More to the point for someone like Randlett, there were people like Tim Newell, who'd left the White House for an investment-banking job with Sandy Robertson. Randlett had been disdainful when Newell subsequently left Robertson Stephens for his own start-up venture. "Look, Tim wants to have an apartment in Pacific Heights," he had said loftily. "That's fine, but then that's what he does. He can't pretend he's doing real politics anymore." And there were people like Witchel, whose extraordinary energy and entrepreneurial drive were almost irresistible: Red Gorilla would be his third company, and I had no doubt Witchel would make it a huge success and use it to start his fourth.

Maybe, I thought, Randlett was just tired. Not tired of being poor—he certainly lived like a rich person, with his Jaguar, his handmade suits, and his trips to Paris with his fiancée. And even if it was all juggled wealth, and he was worried about living beyond his means, hadn't he successfully landed a seat on E-Loan's board, and couldn't he apply himself to finding other similar slots where real cash was bound to follow? No, I thought, Randlett was probably just tired of being the gofer, the technician, the staffer, the hired hand. He was tired of placing his own phone calls, and submitting his expenses, and traveling on frequent-flyer miles to political events where he was expected to hover in the background. "I'm thirty-three," he said. "Then I'm gonna be thirty-five, then forty. Is it worth my life energy to fix TechNet? It's a twenty-year effort to build a political organization that's as good as AIPAC [the American Israel Public Affairs Committee]. This way, I get to go hang out with a bunch of young entrepreneurs and get 500,000 shares of stock, and pick up my girlfriend after work and sit outside having margaritas at Zuni Café. Why should I stay?"

The fact was that the balance of gravity had shifted, and political power was not, anymore, the kind of power young men like Randlett aspired to. He knew, up close, how much it really mattered to be the staffer with the vice president's ear—or even to be the commerce secretary. He knew that things had changed: government was basically over, and with it the political magic that had fueled Randlett's desire for ten years. What counted now was business; business was the real measure of a man, the standard that overrode all others, the place to be. "I don't want to fart around with a political job," he said. "I want to go be an entrepreneur."

There had to be more to it than that, though. In the weeks that followed, I asked around, wondering if Randlett's departure was entirely voluntary. "There are a lot of people in D.C. who are surprised Wade wasn't dealt with earlier," one lobbyist told me. According to some Washington insiders, his cockiness and lack of tact had prompted constant complaints to TechNet's board. "I'm amazed he survived as long as he did," Simon Rosenberg said. "Wade made his job rougher than it needed to be, because he had sharp elbows. A lot of people were gunning for his head." But Rosenberg sounded worried, as well. "As rough as his style was, Wade got things done," he said. "You had to respect him. His relationships here were deep and broad. It's very hard for me to see another person at Wade's level who could pull the same things off."

I had to agree: despite his "elbows," Randlett was going to be very difficult to replace. It made me intensely curious about John Doerr's role in bringing this chapter of Silicon Valley's relationship with the Democrats to an end. I found it inconceivable that Randlett had left against Doerr's wishes. But had Doerr decided to dump him?

Randlett emphatically did not want anyone to think that his relationship with John Doerr had soured, and he tried to convince me that things were still fine. Back when TechNet began, he reminded me, and Tom Proulx of Intuit had threatened to pull out his money if Randlett was hired, Doerr hadn't hesitated to dump Proulx. For two years, Doerr had given Randlett implicit and explicit authority over the organization; even the hiring of Roberta Katz had been done with his approval. So why, I asked, wouldn't Doerr step in now to reinforce Randlett's position in the fight with Katz? Randlett waved the question away. "John called this morning," he said, "and sounded kind of panicked that I was leaving, and said we had to talk every day for the next month." But in that case why would Doerr let him go? I looked at Randlett, who was uncharacteristically quiet. "I'm not going to ask John to decide between me and Roberta, because I don't want to stay," he said finally. "I don't think John really understands what TechNet is turning into, but it's not going to be the kind of organization I want to run."

I heard a very different story from an entrepreneur who offered— "on deep, total background"—his own interpretation of Doerr's motivation. "He is a beady-eyed, vicious, money-grubbing motherfucker," the entrepreneur said. "John Doerr cares about one thing, and that's money. His partners [at Kleiner Perkins] probably got tired of having him put so much time into politics, with so little return, and so they had him yank the plug." He laughed bitterly. "Wade?" he said. "What would Doerr care about Wade? When it helped the firm to have a lot of press and establish itself in Washington as *the* VCs to go to, that was fine. But it's old news now, and it doesn't make money. There's no principle at stake here. If Doerr's starting to get shit about Wade and TechNet from CEOs he needs, then goodbye Wade."

It did seem likely that Randlett's departure had as much to do with changes in TechNet—and the industry overall—as it did with his admittedly abrasive personality. It also seemed likely that Randlett's ability to raise money and garner press for Democrats had finally been too much for Valley Republicans. Randlett had been telling me for months how Roberta Katz couldn't "get" the connection with the vice president. "She hates it that we do so much for Gore," he said.

And Randlett had been unable to fix or work around the bugs that surfaced as the industry grew more fragmented. The established companies wanted to set their own agendas; newer businesses were looking for full-time help to deal with specific problems with government regulatory agencies or legislation. "As companies mature and their government-relations offices get professional, they'll need TechNet less," a Washington-based Democrat had told me a year earlier.

Increasingly, the range of different and often conflicting interests that had been emerging had made it impossible for Randlett to unite everyone under a rubric as broad as "technology." Biotech companies didn't always want to spend time on e-commerce regulations; chip manufacturers didn't necessarily share the same concerns as software start-ups; venture capitalists in North Carolina resented the dominance of California firms. And while general themes like education remained part of the overall philosophy of TechNet, there were few issues that could galvanize the entire industry as Proposition 211 had done.

Randlett's departure, according to the Washington Democrat who spun it for me, was really about the end of an early, experimental era — a moment in which callow start-ups and radical venture capitalists had tried to take politics by storm. "This is the big companies winning," he said wearily. "They want more control. They want things slower, they want to do things the H-P or Intel way. The more cautious actors are exerting their control over the process, and Silicon Valley is going to look a lot more like every other industry now."

I got Randlett on his cell phone, as he was loading some files into the back seat of his convertible, and he agreed. "Yeah," he said bitterly. "It's the revenge of the megasaurs."

"This is the last big lift," Randlett said. He was still at work on the DNC Web site he'd been raising money for — the same project, now in its final and most watered-down iteration, that had been fought over earlier by DNC officials who resisted his input and his e-Party hype. Simultaneously, he was working on the last Silicon Valley fund-raising dinner he had planned for President Clinton. A working version of the Web site was due by the first of October; it had to be up and running when the President announced it at the dinner on September 17, by which time Randlett was supposed to have delivered half a million more dollars to the DNC. He groaned. "I feel like I'm almost done, and then I've got to toss a goddamn sofa over the fence."

It wasn't simply the size of the tasks he faced that worried Randlett, or the insanely tight deadline. The DNC, he said in outrage, was intent on screwing up his last and best project. "It sometimes feels like the DNC will do whatever it can to ruin things, just on general principle," he said glumly. "I don't get it. They don't think the President should announce the launch of the DNC Web site, because it might conflict with his message of the day. I asked what message that was; they said they didn't know yet. It's like"—Randlett paused, and pointed his finger at his head like a gun—"What? They don't think the President, who's the biggest single asset the DNC has, should call attention to the fact that John Doerr is handing the Democrats a million dollars and the best Web site the Valley can build? Like this is a favor *we* want from *them*?" It was the kind of righteous, blustery, hard-ass rant I was used to hearing from Randlett, but it had a weird kind of poignancy now: I knew that Randlett's enemies in Washington were ignoring all his tough talk, just counting the hours until he'd stop pestering them for good.

"I'm watching out for a sentimental moment," I said to Randlett as he drove me down to Palo Alto for his last day at TechNet. It was warm, and clear; perfect weather for Randlett's final event as Democratic political director. Tonight, Eric Schmidt, the CEO of Novell, would be hosting a DNC fund-raising dinner with President Clinton at his Atherton home. Schmidt, an outspoken foe of Microsoft, had been palling around with Clinton lately, seemingly doing his best to get close to the administration as the Justice Department's case against his competitor continued; he was a committed donor by now. So far, Randlett had pulled in $585,000 from the thirty-five other invited guests.

"Sentimental? Hope you don't mind a long wait," Randlett said dryly. He picked up his cell phone. "Hey," he said to Kim Polese. The young Marimba CEO was calling in search of guidance about what she should say to the President that night; Randlett listened, then fired off his advice. "I think a quick pat on the back about crypto," he said. "Then how to fit the R&D tax credit into the tax bill—ask for a separate vehicle to get it permanent."

Randlett was in no hurry to get to work. He parked, and we ambled for a while through Palo Alto, stopping at an extremely upscale bathroom-fixture store. "Do you need any more proof that people here have more money than they possibly know what to do with?" he asked. We examined the French brushed-nickel showers, the cast-iron and porcelain claw-footed bathtubs, the copper sconces and marble cabinets. Randlett asked me to guess how much one bathtub cost—I hit it on the nose, at $3,500—and politely brushed off a saleswoman bent on helping him acquire some "top-of-the-line European divertor-regulator" fixtures. When he tired of the store, Randlett walked up University toward the TechNet office. "I'm still waiting for sentiment," I said, trotting along beside him. "Any moment," he said, pushing the door to his office open for the last time.

At around three Randlett seemed to fall into a kind of vague lassitude, which he said was "standard—I just get this midday slump these days." He cursed at his spreadsheets for a while, and methodically put forwarding messages on his TechNet numbers. "Remember when we went out with Jeanette after the Eshoo event and you drank three margaritas?" his associate Elizabeth Greer asked, trying to tease him into responsiveness. Randlett nodded without expression, and Greer scooped up her files and told him she'd meet him at the Schmidts'.

When we walked out, Randlett didn't say goodbye to anyone. We strolled through town—"I'll be so fucking glad not to see Palo Alto anymore," he said—and stopped at a newsstand to buy some cigars.

"How you doing?" asked the owner, an ancient, shriveled man in a cardigan. Randlett greeted him and picked out two eleven-dollar Cohibas. "Got another promotion?" the owner asked. "Yeah," Randlett said shyly. "Got a new job. Different company."

We drove over to Eric and Wendy Schmidt's house, with Randlett occasionally answering his cell phone. "Yeah, it's warm here," he told his fiancée. "But wear whatever—you'll look perfect." We crossed the border into Atherton, and Randlett told me to keep my eyes open for a bar—"and I mean a *dive*," he clarified—where he and his friends could go for a nightcap once the dinner with Clinton was over. John Witchel, who remained unquestioningly loyal to Randlett, was coming to the dinner with his wife and bringing Tamsin Smith along. The couples were planning to celebrate Randlett's last official presidential event together—and then to ditch the political hacks and, as Smith had told me, "drink a toast to the future." Randlett seemed most taken with the Dutch Goose, an unadorned cinderblock building sporting a wire-reinforced door. "Not bad for Atherton," he said admiringly. "Can't believe they let this one past the zoning board."

By the time we got to the gated driveway, Randlett's mood had improved, and he greeted the cops and state troopers and Secret Service officers cheerfully.

Wendy Schmidt, a poised, thin blonde, was waiting inside, trying to calm her two newly groomed Pekingese, who were agitated by the arrival of the bomb-sniffing dog, a stern German Shepherd. She scolded the bitch, who was sporting a lavender bow, then took us down to check out a huge tent that had been constructed over the swimming pool for the President's visit.

Randlett's cell phone rang, and he looked at the display. "It's the White House," he said. His jaw was set. Then he caught my eye and laughed lightly. "End of an era," he said.

CHAPTER seventeen

After Wade Randlett's departure, the disconnect between TechNet and Washington seemed enormous. The changes in TechNet had been greeted, largely, by yawns, and nobody rushed in to fill the power vacuum left by Randlett. I tried in vain to find executives who would talk to me about their pressing political concerns; people would mumble politely about "education," but their minds were elsewhere—most likely on the skyrocketing Nasdaq index. For the moment, anyway, Silicon Valley thought it had much less at stake in the world of politics than it had previously believed.

But some key players in Washington, by contrast, were becoming more focused on high tech, and even more interested in wooing the Valley. With Randlett gone, Simon Rosenberg was a likely candidate to take over a good deal of the role of go-between. It was true that he had a very different style of masculinity from Randlett. Rosenberg was small and intellectual, with a sharp wit. He liked irony more than overstatement; suits more than shorts; he spoke quietly, in an intense, almost conspiratorial rasp. But Rosenberg, like his California counterparts, was completely absorbed in understanding power. And he wanted it, now more than ever. "The whole entrepreneurial idea, the idea of innovation," he said. "This is the moment our party has to embrace those ideas."

I saw the changes in Rosenberg as emblematic of broader changes taking place as the values of New Economy businesses seeped into the culture in general. Rosenberg had grown up in a Democratic Party tradition that, though it had moved steadily rightward from the days of his socialist grandfather, was nonetheless built on an allegiance to political institutions and a belief in good government. He understood how businessmen did business, but he didn't idolize the rich. Now, with a perfectly respectable Washington salary, Rosenberg himself was beginning to feel the lure of the boom. "My wife and I talk about it all the time," he acknowledged once in an e-mail to me. "Are we crazy not to move to California?" I warned him that Californians put sun-dried tomatoes on their bagels. "I kind of like sun-dried tomatoes," he wrote back.

Rosenberg saw the way that Internet businesses had changed the rules of the road for traditional businesses as a metaphor for the impact the NDN could have politically. "In giving our members knowledge and intellectual property, we're Amazoning the Democratic Party," he said to me over a rushed coffee during one of his frequent trips to San Francisco. "Our members have an operational knowledge of the global economy that's unmatched, even though we're not on the right committees, even though we're not in the leadership. These issues are going to be what we have to deal with—like figuring out Cold War policy was a generation ago. Whoever commands them commands the party."

One issue that Rosenberg had decided to make a centerpiece of the New Democrats' expertise was trade. In early 1999, I'd watched him unsuccessfully try to interest a roomful of high-tech executives in Clinton's efforts to bring China into the World Trade Organization. The President had just announced, over the objections of liberal human-rights activists and protectionist Old Democrat unions, that integrating China into the global economy would "revolutionize" Chinese society; New Democrats saw Clinton's initiative as a way to achieve their free-trade and foreign-policy goals, which were aggressively supportive of American business and of globalization.

But a lot of Silicon Valley hadn't been willing to make trade in general, or trade with China in particular, a big part of its lobbying agenda. Over breakfast in a Netscape conference room, I'd watched Rosenberg and Representative Anna Eshoo, with earnest support from Marc Andreessen, keep explaining that the Chinese market was a huge potential gold mine for American high-tech companies. Yet while the big, established companies with large foreign sales — Hewlett-Packard, Microsoft, and Intel among others — didn't need convincing, Rosenberg's pitch left a lot of the younger executives unmoved. For some reason, trade issues — crucial as they were politically to the Clinton administration; important as they seemed to congressmen and lobbyists — were too abstract, or not immediate enough, to grab the attention of most Valley hotshots. "I don't know," said Rosenberg, frustrated, after the breakfast. "We shouldn't have to spell it out for them — this is about *their* growth."

But now, in December 1999, Rosenberg was ready to try again. Trade, because of the World Trade Organization talks in Seattle, was at the center of public attention, and it seemed to him that high tech and the New Democrats had a role there.

Seattle had seemed the perfect place for the WTO to hold its end-of-the-century round of ministerial negotiations on global trade. Seattle was supposed to be a shining example of the wonders of the New Economy. America's most unionized city had been transformed by the boom into the proud home of the world's grandest software empire, Microsoft, and the world's most famous e-commerce site, Amazon.com. A Boeing company town had survived the downsizing of the American defense industry to become the world's largest exporter of aircraft. A blue-collar port that relied on manual labor had become a haven for high-tech start-ups and information workers. Its international, Pacific Rim identity spoke to the benefits of the global free market; its sixty thousand new millionaires spoke to the rewards of unfettered entrepreneurship. Seattle was hip yet ambitious, informal yet plugged in: a place that was supposed to symbolize all the WTO's hopes for the future.

At stake in the WTO negotiations were issues of every conceivable size and complexity, from establishing levels for specific agricultural subsidies to defining the impact of human rights on global trade. But if the interests of the 135 different WTO member nations were in conflict, with smaller and poorer countries charging that the talks were just a way for the United States to dominate the global economy and "rig the system," as one Japanese diplomat told the press, the domestic political interests in play were equally heterogeneous.

For the Clinton administration, the trade talks were a highly visible opportunity to push the free-trade agenda it had promoted so aggressively, against the wishes of Old Democrat allies like environmentalists and organized labor. New Democrats in the White House and Congress saw the WTO not just as a symbolic place to make a stand but as a way to concretely advance pro-business, pro-growth, globally-minded policies that, they believed, would yield greater economic returns for American business and thus greater political support for themselves. Rosenberg was arranging to bring some of the NDN's most articulate members to Seattle to lobby in support of President Clinton, arguing that New Democrats had a responsibility to bring some of the more "isolationist" sectors of the party into the light.

For the business community, the talks were a way to ensure that international regulations would favor American businesses in the next millennium. For the big high-tech companies that followed the WTO negotiations, they also presented an opportunity to keep the Internet as unregulated as possible. As Microsoft's Bill Gates, the co-chairman of Seattle's host committee for the WTO talks, put it, "There is incredible potential for the growth of on-line commerce worldwide. But we won't realize the full potential of that growth unless there are new trade agreements that eliminate the prospect of tariffs on electronic transfers and guarantee free market access for e-commerce providers."

The problem was that for nearly all of the smaller, Internet-based companies, the WTO was a very minor part of their pressing day-to-day business. Most of the high-tech executives I knew at smaller companies seemed oblivious to the importance of the WTO to their "globalized, world economy" futures; they didn't even know what the WTO was. Those who did were likely to be environmentalists who had heard about the WTO merely through Sierra Club mailings about its evils. Few, if any, out-of-state high-tech companies were planning to attend the meetings and conferences that would take place around the closed-door negotiations. President Clinton, Bill Gates, and the New Democrats were left alone to carry the banner of the New Economy to Seattle.

As it turned out, the Internet was visible in Seattle largely because of its function as an organizing tool for the tens of thousands of protesters and hundreds of nongovernmental organizations that, in an impressive display of "coordinated chaos," used e-mail and the Web to rally an unexpectedly huge and diverse constituency against the entire idea of the WTO.

The AFL-CIO, which wanted to see the WTO enforce stricter standards on child labor, the right to unionize, and working conditions, had planned a showdown with the Clinton administration, and had brought more than twenty thousand workers to Seattle for a massive protest march. Environmentalists, who feared the weakening of pollution standards worldwide, had built regional and international coalitions against global business. American, European Union, and Third World farmers had joined together for a sophisticated fight against the reduction of farm subsidies, the use of biotechnology to genetically modify seeds, and the domination of global agribusiness.

Their slogans covered just about every aspect of the New Economy that anybody could possibly object to, as I saw when I arrived in Seattle on a chilly, rainy morning in December for the second of five days of talks. A major demonstration had been planned for the afternoon, and I'd already heard reports of scattered rioting, looting, and police attacks.

I set off, skirting the blocked-off area surrounding the conference center where the trade ministers were supposed to be meeting, and made my way past a sudden eruption of signs. The unions were waving mass-produced banners in red, white, and blue, demanding protection for "working families"; environmentalists tended toward hand-lettered sentiments such as "For Trees and Jobs, No WTO." General dislike of globalization was expressed by the simple slogan "WTO: Blood Sucking Parasites," but my favorite poster, carried by French farmers, read "Hormone Beef No, Roquefort Cheese Oui."

I bought an umbrella and an espresso from a sidewalk vendor and strolled on. Brooks Brothers was closed. Fox's Gem Shop was closed. Niketown and Starbucks and The Gap were closed up tight, with sheets of plywood tacked across their facades. Downtown, a few employees barricaded themselves inside darkened department stores, watching the scene anxiously. Some lost environmentalists, dressed as sea turtles, wandered around in search of their affinity groups. College students with cell phones chatted on the sidewalk. A team of steelworkers, in orange caps, tried to direct pedestrians past the broken windows of Radio Shack.

There were strings of tiny Christmas lights everywhere, twinkling, and garlands festooning the lampposts. Policemen in black body armor, carrying rifles, stood blocking key intersections. Protesters, bareheaded, chained their arms together and sat down, blocking others. From time to time, a handful of kids in ski masks would suddenly appear and surge toward new targets, ululating, then retreat.

There was no traffic. Entire streets seemed empty, except for discarded leaflets and a few overturned Dumpsters. Contingents of protesters passed through, chanting, on their way to join the tens of thousands massing at the labor rally on the other side of town. Some bicyclists paused to cheer at the blockades; a few stragglers drank coffee at a kiosk. A helicopter hung low and loud overhead. The cops' radios crackled. There was yelling, far away, and I could see puffs of gas rising prettily from over by the convention center.

At one corner, surrounded by a knot of policemen wearing gas masks, an old man in a yellow rain slicker slumped on the ground, crying quietly. "Look what you did to him," a protester with a wispy goatee kept shouting, hoarsely, at the policemen. "Look what you did to him, look at him. Look." The gassed man wept. The protester shouted his accusations over and over. The cops, behind their visors, stared straight ahead through the rain.

Inside a drafty room at the old Town Hall building, where the most organized sector of the anti-WTO coalition had set up its headquarters, I nibbled on some Roquefort. The huge wheel of cheese had been personally smuggled into the United States by the French activist José Bové, in defiance of trade relations. A good-humored, mustachioed dairy farmer, Bové had become a hero to opponents of globalization when he vandalized a McDonald's to defend the honor of French cuisine. Now he was handing out snacks and chatting with a group of steelworkers while they waited for an audience with Congresswoman Maxine Waters.

Over in a corner, Mark Ritchie and Dale Wiehoff, old friends of mine and leaders of the Institute for Agricultural and Trade Policy in Minneapolis, were watching videos that a farmer from North Dakota had just shot for them on the streets outside. They had set up a bank of televisions, three tuned to local stations and one to CNN; a young IATP volunteer was monitoring radio reports.

"Holy smoke!" yelped Wiehoff, pointing to an armored vehicle lurching toward a line of protesters. "Look at the size of that sucker!" Wiehoff, a big man in a gray suit and glasses, was enjoying himself immensely; he and Ritchie, who had advised the European Union delegation during the GATT talks years ago, were used to negotiating "inside" the complicated discussions on global trade, and seldom had the chance to be entertained by street theater.

Ritchie and his allies from other nongovernmental organizations had spent most of the previous year meeting privately with each other and with trade officials, businessmen, and representatives of the various member nations' delegations. By the time they got to Seattle, they had a nuanced and insightful analysis of all the weak points where the global talks might break down. Meanwhile, Wiehoff had been organizing opposition to the Seattle talks on the Internet, linking up a wide range of groups from around the world and sharing information on protest strategies. IATP's WTO Watch Web site provided comprehensive and up-to-date coverage of the ministers' attempts at negotiations; it also served as a forum for discussion among foes of globalization. And now IATP's media operation in Seattle, run by Wiehoff, was turning out to be a main source of news and quotes for journalists who found it impossible to get past police lines or the official WTO press handlers.

Ritchie chuckled. He was a wiry man, with an intense, curious gaze, and he segued into an articulate, detailed analysis of the events that lasted for half an hour. "We're seeing the possibility of far-reaching change in the WTO, in the broader Bretton Woods economic system, and in global governance," he said. "Inside the WTO, the old process where the U.S. and the E.U. cut a deal and then imposed it on everyone else is a thing of the past." It was certainly clear that the United States had already lost control of this meeting: from a radio behind Wiehoff, I heard a reporter shouting excitedly about "riots" and "disaster."

I asked Ritchie what he thought about the immediate political consequences for Clinton, and for his New Democrat, high-tech business allies. He took a piece of cheese. "Well," he said, trying not to grin. "I wouldn't like to be trying to explain how popular the Third Way is with the people of the world right now."

Down the block, in the lobby of the Four Seasons Olympia Hotel, a group of well-dressed tourists perched on couches and swapped stories, seemingly oblivious to the stony-faced Secret Service agents posted by an escalator. I found the ladies' room and started drying my face with a linen towel. A woman in her sixties was standing by the sink, shaking with anger. "This is the first time I've taken a bus in fifty years," she told me. Her chin quivered. "I had to leave the car at home. Can you believe this?"

I couldn't believe it. Upstairs, in the New Democrats' suite, Simon Rosenberg had positioned himself in a window alcove and was talking excitedly on his cell phone as a television blared live coverage. The screen showed clouds of tear gas, people running, black-clad cops firing rubber pellets. The announcer was trying to explain something about the WTO negotiations. I heard the phrase "intellectual property rights" as the images wobbled, then went red, as a protester spray-painted the television camera lens.

Rosenberg hung up. "Labor is *fucked*," he announced. "This is going to be terrible for their image." His voice, always hoarse, was nearly gone by now. His colleague Sue Brodsky, who was conferring with security on her own phone, looked at her watch. "We have to decide what to do," she said.

"Do you really think it's safe to take our guys out on the street?" Rosenberg asked.

Brodsky looked worried. "It's only a few blocks," she calculated. "There's the AT&T event, then the grocers. Maybe we can skip something, but at six the reception's one of our major majors. I don't know how we can just not show."

Rosenberg jumped to his feet and started pacing. "Guys in suits, congressmen, they could be a target," he said. "I don't know, it's nuts out there."

All afternoon, Rosenberg and Brodsky steered their delegation of New Democrats through the chaos, ducking in and out of locked-down hotels, around barricades, and past banks of television cameras. By the time they arrived, late, at the Business Roundtable's evening reception at the home of the Seattle Symphony—"A Taste of America," the event was called—they were wet and chilled, and Rosenberg looked around for a drink.

Tuxedoed waiters circulated with platters of salmon and roast beef, and a tenor and a pianist performed at the base of a grand staircase. Under the chandeliers, several hundred lobbyists and businessmen mingled, clinking their glasses and laughing. There were gigantic urns of flowers, and gift bags full of Washington State products. An elegant woman in a tailored red jacket, a vice president of some kind at Boeing, pointed to a dozen burly men with radios who stood between the guests and the plate-glass windows that overlooked the harbor. "Boeing security," she said proudly. "They're all former FBI or Secret Service—best in the world. We lent fifteen of them to the event tonight."

Rosenberg took a glass of Merlot from a waitress. He looked drained. "Hey, we made it," said Cal Dooley, grinning. Dooley, a farmer himself, was the New Democrat most willing to concede that the WTO's positions on agriculture were problematic for a lot of people. All day he'd been meeting with the media, trying to send out the message that New Democrats believed that "environmental and human-rights concerns are real." It had been clear to Dooley since President Clinton's remarks at noon that the administration had already started to back down. Clinton, while arguing forcefully for the benefits of free trade, had conceded the "justice" of protesters' concerns about the WTO's secretive process, and was privately reassuring labor leaders that workers' rights would remain on the U.S. agenda, "at the core of our trade concerns." Rosenberg, however, was still combative. "What the hell is the point here?" he demanded. "I mean, globalization is a *fact*; it's not going to go away no matter how much anyone screams. Let's *deal* with it."

I glanced past Rosenberg, out to the rainy night. Directly in front of our building, a line of riot policemen in body armor, rifles up, was pushing an angry group of stone-throwing protesters up the street. There was a loud report, of a concussion grenade, and then a burst of smoke. I darted to the window, as people began to run and shots rang out. A Boeing security guard blocked me. "I'm sorry," he said. He had a police dog on a tight leash. "Nobody is going to be able to go out there for a while."

A week later the streets were clear. More than six hundred people had been arrested in Seattle, and the city had reported damages of nearly $13 million. The WTO talks had been completely derailed, "delivering," said *The New York Times* in a front-page story, "a stinging blow to Clinton." The administration's trade policy was in shambles, its relationships with allies were strained if not ruptured, and the continued existence of the WTO as an effective international body had been thrown into doubt. The entire week in Seattle, a White House official told me, was "a fiasco." Begging for anonymity, he bemoaned the "utter collapse" of negotiations. "We were in big, big trouble from the first day," he said.

And still Adam Smith, the feisty congressman from SeaTac, half an hour south of the center of the storm, was determined to put a positive spin on events. "It was a really successful week for New Democrats," he said firmly.

Smith, who had won his first election at age twenty-five, never wasted time hedging his opinions; he had a blunt, forward-driving intelligence more redolent of Silicon Valley than of Capitol Hill. "Labor needs to stop its apocalyptic rhetoric about how the global economy will drive us all into the ground," Smith snorted angrily. "I'm sorry, but that kind of talk contributes to the violence," he said. "I understand most of the protesters were peaceful, but when you have labor out there saying that the WTO will destroy everyone's job, technology is the enemy of working people—all totally unsupported by the facts—it makes people unwilling to compromise."

Smith caught his breath and started again, more calmly. "I argued with a guy this morning," he told me. "A supporter of mine, who said the New Economy's not good for working people, that all the new jobs are service-sector jobs. I said, 'What, answering phones for a software company for forty thousand a year is worse than busting your ass in a textile factory?'" Smith was heating up again. "I take this personally," he said. "My father was your classic blue-collar worker; he loaded bags at United Airlines for thirty years until he died of a stroke. That's the type of economy we want to go back to? That's what we want to mythologize?"

Smith sighed. "Labor's message has more sway than we like," he said. "Fear is a lot easier to pitch than saying, 'Hey, stop whining and start working and fix your situation. It's not about powerful forces beyond your control ruining your life.'"

I told Smith that those powerful forces, if their presence in Seattle during the WTO was any indication, seemed to include more grocers and paper mills than Internet companies. He laughed. "Yeah," he said. "Boeing, Weyerhaeuser, even the ag community was much more plugged in at the WTO than tech. Tech—well, they're just not very political. They're pro-trade but they don't get involved. And these type-A personalities in the tech community, they're always right." He paused. "I mean, not everybody lives the same life you live. When you're trying to push something, you have to understand what the people opposed to you care about. Tech shows up and just says, 'You're a bunch of morons if you don't agree with me.' They could get further by listening."

Then Smith got serious. "I think, ultimately, the tech community will come out over the China deal. They're willing to make less than perfect arrangements, like on intellectual property, because they understand the importance of opening trade. Globalization was supposedly inevitable at the turn of the last century. Then we found out it was optional, that instead of dropping barriers the world launched trade wars, which led to military wars, which . . ."

Smith let the image of the bloody twentieth century hang in the silence between us. "We can go down that road again," he said finally. "But I don't think we can afford, this time, to say that we're not gonna engage."

Simon Rosenberg, when I caught up with him by phone, didn't want, any more than Smith had, to discuss the failure of high tech to weigh in during "the battle of Seattle." Rosenberg was looking ahead—to the May 2000 congressional battle over approving China's membership in the WTO.

I knew that, rhetorically, most high-tech entrepreneurs recognized technology as a driving force for globalization; the small world made possible by the Internet was already a staple of business punditry. But in practical political terms high-tech firms lagged far behind older, mainstream businesses in agitating for free trade. "They just don't seem to get it," a frustrated Rosenberg had complained to me back in 1998. "If we don't get it right on trade, the New Economy isn't going anywhere."

The high-tech companies didn't seem to *care* that they didn't get it, either. "Simon has a bee in his bonnet about China," Wade Randlett had told me, dismissively, in the spring of 1999. "The fact is, only five people in the world care about trade with China as much as Si does." Randlett rolled his eyes. "Sure, John Doerr reads Thomas Friedman and thinks he's great; sure, he's on board intellectually with Si's ideas about globalization. But it doesn't make a tiny bit of difference to the way he runs his business every day."

I missed Randlett's cynicism now that, post-Seattle, Rosenberg was still claiming that there had been a "maturation" in the industry's attitude toward trade. "First of all, there's a big distinction between what happened in Seattle and what's gonna happen next year," he argued. "Sea turtles are not gonna be part of the conversation about China."

Then, he went on, AOL, just a month before the announcement of its proposed merger with Time Warner, had hired Lisa Barry, the chief foreign-trade lobbyist for Boeing, to work on the issue. TechNet, under Roberta Katz, had also announced its intention to lobby hard on China.

And Rosenberg insisted that labor's biggest priority for 2000 was winning back the House of Representatives for the Democrats. "Labor knows that pro-trade [Democratic] guys in swing districts are getting elected," Rosenberg said. "They know these guys need to be pro-trade, and so, despite its huffing and puffing, labor's being pragmatic. They're not gonna spend political capital on China instead of focusing on getting the House back."

It was a somewhat convincing argument, given that previous fights over trade with the Clinton-Gore administration had finally done nothing to slow the flow of labor-union funds into the Democrats' coffers. But trade was still an issue that I thought could expose the splits inside the high-tech industry, as well as the splits inside the Democratic Party—and it could crash the entire network.

CHAPTER eighteen

By the end of 1999, the fiction of "Silicon Valley" as shorthand for a political identity was completely inadequate to handle the reality of the new high-tech landscape. There had been major shifts in the high-tech industry as a whole, with a growing separation between the old companies—the very ones that had, in Randlett's view, taken over TechNet—and the newer Internet start-ups.

The "Big Iron" companies, like Hewlett-Packard, AOL, and Intel, were well versed in the language of Washington; they had professional government-affairs representatives on staff, and stables of Beltway lobbyists on call. These companies understood Hill politics, and their interests tended to merge with the interests of big business in general. To Washington, these companies were "high-tech": some glamour still clung to them, and they were seen as part of a forward-looking industry. But to the New Economy whizzes out West, who were busy founding Internet companies at breakneck speed, the information technology giants were already the past.

Even Rosenberg admitted the problem. The New Democrat Network could hardly afford to abandon its hard-won alliances with the largest, most financially generous, and most politically savvy high-tech companies, but neither could it afford to be seen by the young Internet sector as irrelevant, a tool of the very "megasaurs" that Randlett had ridiculed. Rosenberg sighed. "I'm beginning to understand," he said, "that this generational divide is the same in business as in politics. One thing you have to say about the New Economy—it's moving really, really fast."

People like John Witchel tried to explain to me how fast things really were moving. Witchel was only five or six months into Red Gorilla, which had a catchy name, a cool staff of about twenty people, and a business plan that called for providing Web-based accounting services to independent consultants. With help from Wade Randlett, Witchel had already stitched together an impressive network of partnerships with other Web-based businesses, cell-phone companies, and Internet service providers. He had generated a lot of interest from potential investors, and hired a number of smart young executives. The Red Gorilla Web site was about to go live, and it was assumed, though not yet announced, that the company itself would go public soon.

"Nobody who started in business thirty years ago can understand it," Witchel said to me in January 2000. We were in his office, a brick-walled loft on a "transitional" San Francisco block south of Market, and Witchel, as usual, was pacing.

"My first company, for example—we were the first company acquired by USWeb," Witchel said, launching into his story with relish. He strode around the room. "I was twenty-six, and I drove down to sign the papers in a van with some friends. We were on our way to the beach for a weekend bachelor party, and we had some kegs and a couple of dogs. We stopped at the [USWeb] office and signed the acquisition papers, then walked outside to the parking lot, turned on the stereo in the van, and opened the kegs." Witchel paused, and looked at me to see if I was truly understanding the import of his words. I must have looked blank, because he took another tack.

"Or, look," he said. "It's like when a politician comes to see us, because we're the new generation of Internet whatevers, and the question he's trying to answer is Do you get it?" Witchel smirked. "That's a sucker punch," he informed me, "because the only right answer is 'Fuck you.' If they say no, they don't get it. If they say yes, duh, sure I get it, then you know they definitely don't." He laughed triumphantly.

Witchel was passionate on the subject of "getting it," which was shorthand for an entirely new set of attitudes. The shifts in the high-tech industry in the last few years had left him more convinced than ever that the Old Economy, in which he seemed to include the chip manufacturers, software giants, and ostensibly Internet-based companies like AOL, was over. The future, in which Witchel was investing his own time and money, giving seed capital and advice to half a dozen younger entrepreneurs, was here. "Even five years ago Hewlett-Packard mattered," Witchel informed me, as if stating the obvious. "H-P does not matter today. H-P is a setting star. Red Gorilla is a rising star. The CEOs who ruled Silicon Valley five years ago are middle-aged and corporate. Kim Polese, Charles Katz, Nick Grouf—*these* are the future." He paused. "Nick Grouf, PeoplePC," Witchel elaborated. "He's in his twenties. He still answers his own phone. He has the fastest-growing company *in American history*. This is a generation that's rich in a way nobody understands." He spoke with a fervor that made Simon Rosenberg's polite reference to "a generational divide" seem euphemistic: what Witchel was calling for was generational warfare.

I left impressed, as usual, by Witchel's astonishing self-confidence and his sales skills. But I had to think hard about the political implications of his diatribe. If Witchel was right about the changes in the high-tech industry, then the political model that Wade Randlett, Simon Rosenberg, and others had so carefully developed to link Silicon Valley with Washington couldn't help but crash now. And I had to conclude that, in fact, too much had changed, in just a few years, for version 1.0 of their network to survive.

Wade Randlett, for instance, had expended huge amounts of energy bullying recalcitrant politicians and coaxing stubborn Valley executives to come together, in return for establishing himself at the center of it all. It had worked for a while: as long as the industry was still young enough to run on the personal relationships among a handful of powerful men. But Randlett's network, ultimately, couldn't expand quickly enough to hold everyone who wanted to be a part of it. And with Randlett gone it was clear that the job was too big for any individual to manage.

Nor could the myth that Randlett had encouraged about the New Economy sustain itself. In conversations in Silicon Valley, the phrase "New Economy" had become, by 1999, as ubiquitous and shallow as the billboards urging consumers to "Think Different." The phrase John Doerr had used in 1996 to describe the basic principles of an emerging Internet economy was still applied indiscriminately to all kinds of companies by the media. But business and technological changes had been steadily modifying Doerr's original ideas, and executives knew they needed business plans more than general hype.

"New Economy" had worked as a slogan for New Democrats as well. But now, as New Democrats had to grapple with more and more specific issues that affected various high-tech interests differently, actually defining *whose* New Economy was serious business.

For New Democrats, the New Economy was an environment in which all kinds of liberal, Old Democrat ideas—about education, taxes, regulation, consumers and unions and trade—were going to be challenged, head-on. This meant regulations and laws on everything from esoteric standards to general guidelines for taxation; many of the issues had begun to be hashed out during Clinton's second term, in battles over legislation affecting encryption, digital signatures, Y2K litigation, copyright protection, and broadband access. It was all political maneuvering of a very familiar kind: specific companies or coalitions, with their lobbyists, would descend upon Capitol Hill and government offices, pushing for laws and regulations favorable to them and disadvantageous to their competitors. Though in 1997 Tony Podesta had bemoaned the Valley's lack of sophistication about lobbying, it turned out that, once they were faced with pending legislation, most companies had by now figured out how to start the ball rolling.

But passing specific legislation on the kinds of regulatory issues familiar to lobbyists was only part of the use that Rosenberg and the New Democrats had wanted to make of Silicon Valley. When it came to the big issues that would define the soul of the Democratic Party, the Valley's support was crucial: having Silicon Valley on your side—whether against the Republicans or against the Old Democrat way of running the party—was like having Michael Jordan on your team. Now, however, it seemed less simple: things had become far too complicated for New Democrats to present themselves, grandly but vaguely, as "the party of the New Economy." There were enough issues on the table, and enough different kinds of New Economy business with a stake in the outcomes, for someone in Silicon Valley to always be angry about something.

And then there was the other, huge problem that people like Simon Rosenberg were trying hard, if unsuccessfully, to forget: Al Gore. Far from being the leader who embodied the happy marriage between New Democrats and techies, Gore—despite his ubiquitous Palm Pilot—had been campaigning much more on appeals to "working families" than on promoting the wonders of the New Economy. And when he did praise Silicon Valley he didn't seem capable of following through with executives the way he had in 1997 and 1998.

For a while after Wade Randlett's departure, I kept expecting the Gore relationship with Silicon Valley to pick up. Randlett had butted his head so energetically, for so long, against so many people inside the DNC and the Gore campaign that I had partly believed the line promoted by his enemies—that his pushiness was to blame for Gore's falling away from the Valley.

But in fact the Gore campaign had been lurching aimlessly in general since it launched, righting itself just long enough to trounce Bill Bradley in the primaries, then sinking back into confusion. If Gore was ignoring Silicon Valley—and the general complaint from CEOs was that Gore, like a sullen teenager, "only calls when he wants money"—he was ignoring other constituencies as well, who found it just as hard to penetrate the swirl of competing interests and sub-sub-fiefdoms in charge of the campaign. "A year ago, people were saying Gore's outfit would take a while to jell," a Washington consultant close to the campaign told me. "It's still jelling."

TechNet wasn't doing much to help. The group was larger than ever, in terms of staff, but I thought very little sense of political purpose had survived Randlett's departure. Once a group that proudly declared it was the voice of "New Politics for a New Economy," TechNet had twisted arms, raising money in a forthrightly partisan way for both Democrats and Republicans. Now it was sliding into a generalized, think-tanky, trade-association kind of mush. On its new letterhead, TechNet's slogan read "New *Policies* for a New Economy."

In the spring of 2000, I called on Jeff Modisett, the former Indiana attorney general who had replaced Randlett, and asked him about it. Tall, lean, and Midwestern to the point of parody, Modisett was, I'd been told by everyone I talked to, "a really nice guy." The new Democratic political director, however, was quick to admit his lack of familiarity with Silicon Valley; he'd held a lot of meetings but still had no in-depth relationships with the TechNet executives. As far as politics went, Modisett had a long association with Evan Bayh of Indiana and was serving as general counsel and deputy chair for the upcoming Democratic convention in Los Angeles. Still, he was as far from a cutthroat backroom pol as anyone could be.

Modisett, charming and amiable, couldn't tell me much about how the Democrats in TechNet were relating to Al Gore. I asked whom he would talk to in the Gore campaign about organizing the Valley: who was Gore's current liaison with high tech? Modisett paused. "Well," he said finally, "I'm sure Tony Coelho would be interested." I pushed him:

the embattled campaign chairman was certainly not taking a hands-on approach to winning high-tech supporters; according to press accounts, Coelho was busy fighting with campaign manager Donna Brazile and looking for a vice-presidential candidate. Sky Gallegos, the woman in charge of California for Gore, was based in Los Angeles and had not visited the Valley for months. Was anyone else in charge? "At an operational level," Modisett admitted. "I don't really know who's seeing to us. Gore needs to spend time on relationships outside of fund-raising. Just a couple of hours a month to call and chat, the way Bush is doing so effectively—" Modisett paused. "Gore has a harder time selling himself these days in the Valley, I think."

The fact was that by the spring of 2000, Gore was being badly outmaneuvered in the Valley by his Republican rival. As anyone not fatally awash in hubris could have predicted, some Republicans had decided to eschew the right-wing extremism of their party in favor of a centrist, moderate, pro-business appeal. They understood quite well that the New Economy was a politically useful concept, and that New Economy millionaires were politically useful supporters, and they were working hard to win the Valley.

For over a year, I'd been getting e-mail from House Republicans, notably Oklahoma representative J. C. Watts, touting the GOP's special friendship with high tech and its sensitivity to New Economy business concerns. I'd seen various Republican members of Congress come out to San Jose in search of chat and checks; TechNet's Republican side, weak as it was, had never given up, and was still gamely organizing soirées. During the fights over Y2K legislation, House Republicans had unveiled what they called their "E-Contract with High Tech," accusing Democrats of stifling the economic growth of high tech through taxes, regulation, and antitrust suits. In the following months, I received regular diatribes from them against the Justice Department and Al Gore, and got updates on their support of that champion of American free enterprise Bill Gates. In early 2000, J. C. Watts even sent out an e-mail that tore into congressional Democrats "for claiming to support the New Economy yet failing to regularly update their Web sites." None of this was especially surprising; in the wake of the impeachment fiasco, it made sense for Republicans to regroup, look for ways to solidify their traditional business base, reach out to the businesses of the future, and distance themselves as quickly as possible from the social conservatives who had led them into such defeat. In January 2000, the Republican National Committee, calling Silicon Valley "the Main Street of the world," held its convention in the Bay Area. "The prominence of high tech as a transformative agent of American society has become so obvious as to make any politician foolish for not at least learning how to talk the talk, if not walk the walk," said Jim Pinkerton, a prominent Republican strategist and political adviser.

And now Texas governor George W. Bush was reaping the rewards. Even before he announced his candidacy for President, Bush had been romping through the Valley, fund-raising at an astonishing rate: between January 1, 2000, and the election in November, campaign-finance experts had estimated that he and Gore would each need to raise $2,893 an hour in order to run their campaigns. Cheered on by the manic, baseball-capped Greg Slayton of MySoftware and Peter Harter of EMusic.com, along with older and more predictable Republicans, like Jim Barksdale of Netscape, Bush raked in the money.

During the first few months of 2000, the Democrats tried to compete—at least when it came to fund-raising. President Clinton would show up in San Jose or San Francisco for fund-raisers; Gore would speak at a high-tech executive's house; the DNC would make another stab at big-bucks events. And yet the basic impenetrability of Gore's campaign remained the same. "It's Gore-world," I heard Simon Rosenberg sigh once, trying to explain some inexplicable decision of the campaign to Wade Randlett, whom he'd contacted for information on high-tech supporters. "Gore-world," Randlett agreed, nodding. "That's it."

If Rosenberg—one of the most plugged-in New Democrats in Washington—and Randlett—who had been perhaps the best connected political operative in Silicon Valley—were equally in the dark about the Gore campaign's plan for high tech, and TechNet's political directors were out of the loop, how was the vice president going to recruit high-tech supporters? Gore was constantly trying to raise money from the Valley—and, in April, had secured an astonishing $250,000 contribution to the DNC from Marc Andreessen—but he had otherwise disappeared from view.

And so had many of the formerly politically active figures in the Valley. "I think they just don't care that much," a Democratic organizer told me in April, frustrated. "They don't see that much difference between Bush and Gore on the issues that matter to them; they see Bush vacuuming up all that money, and they don't want to waste time backing someone they think might lose."

I remembered how "Gore and Doerr in 2004" had been the running joke among Valley New Democrats, back in the first blush of the love affair between the vice president and high tech. Even later, as the crisis in the White House grew, Doerr had stayed close to Gore and remained a loyal supporter of Clinton. But now things were different.

I heard from a TechNet member that Doerr had shown up at the TechNet offices, one day in May, to announce that he wanted the organization to focus its political efforts on supporting a November ballot initiative about California school funding. He did want to be involved with politics, he said, and he had written huge checks to the DNC to prove it. But he was personally going to put his energies into education. "I don't really care who's President," Doerr had reportedly said. "Either [Bush or Gore] would be fine. Winning on the initiative is my priority."

Doerr was chronically "too busy" to talk to me about politics, so I couldn't find out if it was true that his relationship with Gore had really deteriorated so badly. I called Kleiner Perkins one more time anyway, was rebuffed politely one more time, then hung up. I wandered over to my couch and, frustrated by months of stonewalling, flung myself down moodily. The June issue of *Martha Stewart Living* was open to a feature that praised lemonade stands as "a uniquely American kind of entrepreneurship." I flipped through the pages of the magazine, which looked glossier than ever after a recent and very successful IPO. In "Martha's Calendar," alongside admonitions to "clean outdoor grills" and "prepare tart shells for berry tarts," there was an entry. "June 29," Martha Stewart noted for her readers, "John Doerr's birthday."

Where was there any room for politics left, now that business had filled up every available space, every moment of time, every flicker of the public's attention? I remembered what Simon Rosenberg had said to me when he was trying to convince me that trade was an issue that could reconstruct the entire Silicon Valley–New Democrat coalition, and bring everyone together as Proposition 211 had in 1996. "We're not stuck with the old divisions," he'd said hopefully. "We're not living in 1994 anymore."

He was right, I thought. But neither were we in 1996, when the sparks of romance between Silicon Valley and Washington were flying; nor were we in 1997, when Al Gore's courtship of the Valley elite created such high hopes for a lasting partnership. Now, as high tech and political pundits alike were constantly reminding everyone, we had crossed the turn of the century, and were poised at the turn of the millennium, looking forward to a new dawn, and so forth. The rhetoric was exhausting, repetitive, banal. The reality was hard. And the system had crashed.

CHAPTER nineteen

The world doesn't come to an end because a particular network or system crashes: politicians and neo-Darwinian capitalists alike know that there's always the next hot idea, the next charismatic leader-of-the-moment, the next big thing, and they don't spend much time looking back.

John Doerr was off making lemonade. TechNet was making "policies." The specific network that Wade Randlett and Simon Rosenberg—each in his own way, and sometimes in collaboration—had been trying to build since 1996 was over. Now it was time to see when a new attempt at tech politics—what I thought of as version 3.0, the first version of any software that engineers took seriously—would emerge.

But when 3.0 was first released, in the early spring of 2000, I missed it. I didn't understand what I was seeing, because I thought I was watching a much older and more predictable political show. Rather than seeing a new attempt by some of the same operators, most notably the indefatigable Wade Randlett, to forge an alliance between New Democrats and New Economy entrepreneurs, I saw an attempt to resurrect the values and rhetoric of Old Democrats.

It began with a message from President Clinton. His State of the Union speech, in February 2000, was marked by a very different tone with respect to high-tech themes. Of course, much of the language about progress, economic growth, and America's children was so rhetorically vague that it could have been resurrected from virtually any speech by the President in the last seven years. And the cheerleading for high tech's role in creating "amazing prosperity" and "unparalleled economic growth" was certainly familiar. But, side by side with boosterish optimism, the concept of a "digital divide" had emerged as a centerpiece of Clinton and Gore's tech agenda in 2000. "Opportunity for all requires something else today—having access to a computer and knowing how to use it," the President declared. "That means we must close the digital divide between those who've got the tools and those who don't." Clinton's remarks—fleshed out in his budget, which was delivered the following week—signaled some new political circumstances.

One had to do with overall changes in public attitudes in the middle of the 107th consecutive month of economic growth: Clinton was betting that most Americans, given the country's enormous budget surplus, were willing to be more generous. In the midst of an unprecedented boom, it seemed easier for the White House to propose new social programs targeted at incorporating the "deserving" poor into the country's general prosperity. But I also thought that Clinton's own emphasis, post-impeachment, had shifted slightly; perhaps because he had so thoroughly proved his New Democrat credentials by courting business and ending "welfare as we know it," he no longer felt the need to reject anything that smacked of bleeding-heart liberalism. On the other hand, maybe he was simply thanking his liberal supporters, especially those in the Congressional Black Caucus, for their support.

In any case, President Clinton's identification of a "digital divide" in the State of the Union address, and the ambitious plans his budget spelled out to overcome it, had taken center stage in his discourse on technology. What I found interesting was how the very idea of a digital divide had changed over the last few years, and how its re-emergence now demonstrated the fact that much larger political changes than Clinton's were under way.

In 1995, the term "digital divide" appeared in a *New York Times* story on the "haves and have-nots" of cyberspace. The piece cited David Ellington, whose NetNoir had become the media's prime example of a successful African-American Internet business. Then, in 1998, the term gained general currency again, with a different connotation, follow-

PART FIVE

tech politics 3.0

ing a series of reports in the *San Francisco Chronicle* exploring racial imbalances in the high-tech industry.

In this new context, "digital divide" referred to employment discrimination. Examining U.S. Department of Labor documents submitted by government contractors, the *Chronicle* reporters had looked at racial-makeup reports and affirmative-action plans from fifty-four of the largest high-tech government contractors in Silicon Valley. (All but two of the companies protested the release of their affirmative-action plans—perhaps understandably, as thirteen of them had already been cited for failure to comply with affirmative-action regulations, and, in several cases, forced to pay back wages to black and Latino applicants and workers who had been discriminated against.) The newspaper report discovered what should have been completely obvious to anyone working in Silicon Valley: most high-tech companies were overwhelmingly white, with a significant Asian minority, and had almost no black or Latino workers. On average, the staffs of Bay Area high-tech firms were about 4 percent black, 7 percent Latino, 28 percent Asian, and 61 percent white. Furthermore, blacks and Latinos working in Silicon Valley tended to be clustered in factory or support-staff positions, not in professional, engineering, or managerial jobs. "Prosperity isn't being shared," Amy Dean, director of the AFL-CIO's South Bay Labor Council, told the *Chronicle*. "Silicon Valley is very much a tale of two cities—and the community of color is being left behind." And Manuel Pastor, a professor at the University of California at Santa Cruz, said that, according to his research, "It's pretty clear that there's an ethnic and occupational segregation going on in Silicon Valley." The newspaper report included predictable denials by high-tech CEOs, who insisted that their industry was a color-blind meritocracy. The archconservative CEO of Cypress Semiconductor, T. J. Rodgers, refused to admit that there was any problem with discrimination. "We hire the best people for the job regardless of race, color or creed," he told the newspaper.

The *Chronicle* report on the dismal state of equality in the high-tech sector provoked reader response that largely echoed Rodgers's view. "More affirmative action hucksterism," a typical letter to the editor called the story. In Silicon Valley, where the very idea of a digital divide was frequently seen as insulting, I heard similar dismissals of the series. "They always find something to complain about," one executive told me angrily. But many companies nonetheless scrambled to find ways to improve their image, a process that had led to the kind of tokenism that a black employee I knew at an Internet firm was always complaining about. "Watch," she said to me bitterly. "They're not going to invest in black-owned companies, not going to recognize black executives as equals, but now they're going to start talking about how much they *care*."

And over the next year, as she predicted, the meaning of workplace discrimination that had originally attached to the term "digital divide" began to fade, and the phrase morphed into a kind of shorthand suggesting that poor (read: black and Latino) children were without computers, that Silicon Valley wanted to remedy this and thus improve their education, and that Silicon Valley's professions of concern about education were related to its sincere desire for racial justice. The racial subtext of the digital-divide issue was still obvious, but its focus had shifted away from questions of hiring and promotion, or investment in minority-owned businesses. What came to the forefront was the less immediately divisive theme of primary education, with a corollary suggesting that a computer in every school could overcome the effects of racist inequality.

This approach was not entirely cynical, or without merit. Almost all the educators I talked to were convinced that without racial equality in access to technical education, black and Latino kids would fall behind first in school and then in employment opportunities. But there was something more to the puffery around Silicon Valley's campaigns to "overcome the digital divide." The language used by high-tech executives had a lot in common with the general approach of white America to such questions. It was a kind of Race Consciousness Lite, which suggested that persons and forces unknown had left some "communities" in an unfortunate state of lack, and that well-meaning benefactors, through donations and professions of "concern," could fix the problem, helping unfortunate children, along with a few deserving adults, to better themselves and join "the twenty-first-century workforce."

This digital-divide sleight of hand—defining the problem away from one of active discrimination and wrongdoing by white businessmen and toward a generalized problem characteristic of the poor—resonated with familiar New Democrat themes. Old Democrats talked about "discrimination," and even, occasionally, "racism"; if high-tech government contractors had failed to hire and promote qualified minority candidates in specific instances, for example, then they saw a role for government in demanding reparations and enforcing fairness. In contrast, New Democrats and their friends in Silicon Valley denied that there were systemic problems that the market would not solve on its own. They removed agency and responsibility from any institution, individual, or business, and made general societal conditions a kind of ether in which lamentable problems floated, removed from cause and effect.

"Digital divide's easy, the way these guys frame it," David Ellington had told me in one of his angrier moments. "It's all about education for the poor kids. But education is a twenty-year issue—what are they going to do *now* about the digital divide?" Ellington gave a sharp laugh. "Let me tell you, education isn't the only thing that gets you into the middle class," he said. *"Money* gets you into the middle class. Jobs with stock options. Capital."

According to Ellington, most white people in the Valley were unable to see how investing directly in black companies would "create jobs, create black wealth, grow the space in the economy where minorities can participate." Instead, he said in disgust, they talked about Headstart. "I sit at these meetings and it's really disappointing," he said. "They don't see money, they see K–12. I know black businessmen, *excellent* black businessmen, who can't get private equity investment to grow their enterprises, who can't get to the next stage. We don't need paternalism. We don't need self-esteem programs. We need money."

As Ellington never tired of pointing out, a government role in making capital available to minority high-tech businesses was necessary, because there were no white venture capitalists dedicating themselves to creating venture funds directed at black start-ups. "They'd rather do philanthropy, and feel superior, than invest," he said. "Equity is a profound statement. It means it ain't about charity, it's about believing in business. You rarely see white VCs sticking millions of their own money into majority black-owned companies, taking a seat on the boards, taking equity."

I knew that it had taken forever for Ellington—who ran what everyone agreed was the leading black-oriented Web site in the universe—to get white investors over and above the 20 percent share that AOL had bought of his company, NetNoir. By early 2000, there would be a spate of white investment in black-owned Internet companies (mostly those based in New York), but the process was slow. "If you're black and you start looking for investors, all of a sudden these white VCs get apoplexy," Ellington said. "When they see the skin color they freeze. They stop doing analysis of the business opportunity. There's some bullshit Internet companies out there getting tens of millions thrown at them—companies run by some twenty-four-year-old white kid. But I cannot get my calls returned." Ellington heaved an exasperated sigh. "I did due diligence for eight months, I got AOL as a strategic partner, I'm at the top of an Internet space that's making money and has a proved consumer base the size of Canada's—what more do you need?" Ellington turned his palms up. "They all say, 'David, you're great,' " he told me. "But they won't invest."

Ellington decided to put his own money and energy into "jobs and wealth creation" for minorities. In 1997, with entrepreneur Dan Geiger, he founded OpNet, a nonprofit organization that trained poor teenagers for careers in multimedia and Web-based businesses. "I saw all these black and Filipino kids being displaced from their homes [in San Francisco's] South of Market [district] by dot.com businesses moving in," he said. "At the time, people were into all this heavy symbolic shit about access—what poor folks need is a computer in every home. But I saw kids who needed *jobs*." Ellington was choosing his words carefully, but he was steaming. "I don't need symbolism," he said. "It's not like people are suddenly going to get rich because they have access to a PC. What they need is to find work in the industry, get promoted, get stock options, make some real money."

OpNet took its students, aged eighteen through twenty-five, through a six-week training course, then placed them in local San Francisco Web, game, and multimedia businesses. "We're saying, 'Invest in these workers,' " Ellington said. "Don't tell me it's so hard to find qualified workers that you have to go abroad and bring in Indian engineers on visas. You want to talk about the digital divide, don't talk about access—just hire someone."

Others had taken different approaches. John Templeton, a black activist and author who founded the Coalition for Fair Employment in Silicon Valley, had conducted his own surveys of the hiring practices of hundreds of technology firms. He pressured the Labor Department to investigate Silicon Valley firms that contracted with the government but had no affirmative-action plans in place; he lobbied the Congressional Black Caucus to look into charges of employment discrimination, and he acted as a liaison with Jesse Jackson, urging the civil-rights leader to raise the issue of racism in the Valley.

Jackson had come to Silicon Valley in February 1999 for a meeting with high-tech executives, coordinated by Templeton, with help, in part, from Wade Randlett and TechNet. After talking with Silicon Valley leaders, the Rainbow/PUSH Coalition decided to launch what it called "a West Coast outpost," with a focus on high-tech and Internet businesses. Using the general strategy that Jackson had used with Wall

Street — highly publicized meetings with top executives who promised to do more about hiring minorities — Jackson's Rainbow/PUSH Coalition hired Butch Wing to needle the industry on all matters related to race. And although T. J. Rodgers of Cypress Semiconductor weighed in with his opinion again, calling Jackson "the seagull that flies in, craps on everything, and flies out," most other CEOs paid at least lip service to the idea of diversity.

By 2000, Wing had become a familiar, tolerated presence at Democratic Party events and fund-raisers in the Valley, and, judging from the frequency with which politicians made visits to PUSH headquarters, I thought he must have been twisting some arms behind the scenes as well. I couldn't quite imagine how he was making headway with the industry, though; most high-tech executives continued to insist, against all factual evidence, that their companies were pure meritocracies, and that the high percentage of Asians working in Silicon Valley made it, as one manager told me, "a place where you see the most diverse workforces in the country." More defensively, and with some validity, newer and smaller Internet companies argued that the pressure of hiring as they raced toward their IPOs made it impossible for them to do aggressive minority outreach — thus their monochrome workforces.

In any case, Wing must have been cheered by a story in *The Industry Standard* in February 2000 that reported "ongoing investigations" of affirmative-action and minority hiring programs in the high-tech industry by the Equal Employment Opportunity Commission. "Sometimes I think it's important to send a message to an industry that race discrimination is not something we'll tolerate," the EEOC's vice-chair, Paul Igasaki, told the *Standard*. "Frankly, when I hear this claim in high tech that they don't discriminate, that makes me deeply suspicious."

The bitter feuds between Jesse Jackson and the New Democrats had faded somewhat by 1999, though a certain sour spirit lingered. Jackson himself had been moving, over the years, away from populist and insurgent rhetoric, into a conflicted but aggressive pursuit of business. Along with his chants about justice, he now offered paeans to economic growth as the engine that would eradicate poverty. Furthermore, in the post-impeachment environment, Old Democrats in general and Jackson in particular had been rehabilitated as the backbone of the President's support. The new climate, plus the standard anti-Republican pressures of an election year, had been forcing New Democrats to publicly embrace the concept of "unity" and to refrain from attacking their party's left wing.

Still, there were profound differences that no amount of election-year rhetoric could gloss over. Most revolved around a basic split between those who saw government as the most important force for ensuring the nation's well-being, and those who believed in the market and deregulation. Jackson and the Old Democrats, particularly the African-Americans among them, retained a bedrock faith in using government as an instrument of redress, while New Democrats were unlikely to see offices like the EEOC as anything more than instruments of what one disgustedly termed "old-fashioned, Neanderthal, socialist statism." The latter attitude, not surprisingly, was the one that prevailed in Silicon Valley. "Who are *they* to tell us who to hire?" a white executive at a Web-design firm asked me once angrily. "They don't even know what a programmer *does*."

In March 2000, with the specifics from the State of the Union spelled out in Clinton's budget, the concept of a digital divide had resurfaced once again. Clinton proposed spending more than $2 billion to overcome the digital divide, most of it in tax breaks for high-tech companies that donated computer gear and sponsored "community technology centers." His budget also proposed a total of $380 million in new initiative to expand broadband, Internet access, and Internet teacher-training programs. Highlighted was a request for $50 million to fund a partnership with the private sector to provide computers and Internet access to poor families. This last was the point of a press conference, to be held at John Witchel's company, Red Gorilla, which would introduce a high-tech initiative entitled ClickStart—a project aimed squarely at addressing the digital divide. ClickStart, it seemed, was not only a way to offer high-tech support for Clinton as he unveiled his budget proposal but a strategy for shoring up Al Gore as he approached the March presidential primaries in California.

I hadn't been terribly surprised to get the call from Randlett inviting me to the event. For the last few months, whenever I'd talked with Randlett, he'd protested that he was "out of politics." I didn't believe it for a moment. I knew he was still in touch with Gore's campaign, the DNC, and Simon Rosenberg. I knew he was still at least "helping out" with various Democratic fund-raising endeavors. And I suspected that he and Witchel and Tim Newell were up to something; I'd heard him mention, in an offhand way, that "the younger guys" in the world of San Francisco start-ups were considering how to have their own presence in politics, unencumbered by "the Old Guard." But I wasn't prepared to see Randlett choose the digital divide as the issue he would use to showcase his return to the political stage.

Randlett's ability to make connections and build political networks was undiminished. He had arranged to have Tom Kalil from the National Economic Council provide official administration commentary by phone during the event. He had urged Gore to release a statement deploring the digital divide, and the vice president had obliged, commending "those in the private sector who have already stepped forward," and announcing that "we take new steps today to turn America's digital divide to digital opportunity." Randlett had also made sure that the executives he'd selected to be a part of ClickStart were Democrats and Gore supporters, although, as usual, he'd insisted to reporters that the program was "completely bipartisan—of course we're confident that Republicans will want to be a part of the effort."

Looking at it with an open mind, ClickStart seemed to be just that: only a start, but at least an attempt to overcome some of the glaring inequities in access to technology that persisted in Silicon Valley. Looking at it more cynically, ClickStart could be seen as a backhanded way of admitting that, to date, the Internet had done exceedingly well by white people as compared to black; as an easy political score, since expressing concern about children and families in an election year didn't take much imagination; and as an attempt to build the image of Silicon Valley executives as community-minded citizens instead of cold, selfish robots. And, looking at it politically, ClickStart was Randlett's slap at TechNet, which could no longer claim an exclusive franchise on political events linked to the administration. ClickStart was Randlett's baby, and it featured an entirely new set of young entrepreneurs.

Here was the debut—or, better, the comeback—of someone who had spent four years building a network, watching as bugs emerged, trying valiantly to work around them, and then seeing the whole thing crash. ClickStart, I realized, was a relaunch, version 3.0 of Randlett's dream. It was a chance for Randlett to put Gore and the Clinton administration back in the spotlight as the advocates of digital progress and democracy, while putting himself back at center stage as the crucial go-between who understood both the Valley and the Democrats.

The press conference was held in the trendy but definitely start-up-size San Francisco offices of Red Gorilla. Randlett introduced his fellow panelists, a group of young, white CEOs from start-ups that had just gone public or were just about to. John Witchel was fidgeting beside him; Garrett Gruener, a venture capitalist and the founder of the Internet search service Ask Jeeves, was next, then Nick Grouf of PeoplePC, Charles Katz of 1stUp.com, and Julie Henderson from the Marcus Foster Institute in Oakland, which offered adult education and training. Eric Schmidt of Novell, and Neil Weintraut, a partner with 21st Century Venture Partners, sat in the front row. Randlett kept his glasses on, perhaps in an attempt to lend verisimilitude to his new identity as an Internet nerd and his opening remarks on behalf of "a bunch of geeks."

Randlett offered a brief overview of ClickStart: the U.S. Department of Commerce, he explained, would issue monthly $10 vouchers to households poor enough to qualify for food stamps; the households would add $5 of their own; the total of $15 would be paid to a company providing a stripped-down computer and basic Internet access. He gazed around the room. "We all know what an incredible driver the Internet has been for the economy," he said. "Now let's hear from the people who are making it work."

Gruener was clearly the lead manager on the project. A stern-looking man with a close-cropped beard, he spoke in the rushed, slightly aggressive tone favored by high-tech businessmen trying to indicate their seriousness. "We did the ClickStart program locally on Internet time," he said. "Now we're proposing it nationally. We got started without government sponsorship; now we want to be the private partner with the government, and enable a whole new set of customers." He directed a tight-lipped smile at Henderson, who was poised next to him, her hands clasped on the table. "It was an amazing thing to go out to Oakland and see these people with computers," he said. "Access to the Internet opens the doors to the wonder world."

Henderson, a thirty-something black woman, wore a professional smile and pearls. "Parents *want* technology," she began, explaining how Gruener and Grouf had come to Oakland the previous week to launch the ClickStart program at her nonprofit institute by giving away twenty-one computers. Her clients, Henderson said, related to the chance to explore the Internet "like kids in a candy store."

Then it was time for Tom Kalil, participating in the press conference via speakerphone from his White House office, to fill in the details. Methodically, Kalil went through the budget; his gruff, disembodied voice read off the numbers: $50 million proposed for a business-government partnership like ClickStart's, reaching 300,000 households; an eventual nine million households benefiting from access to the Internet.

Randlett wrapped it all up. "The most important way to close the digital divide is to give poor people access to the Internet in their living rooms," he said. "We're making it happen now."

As the event broke up, reporters milled around the display set up on a desk in the back of Red Gorilla, where the computer firm Be had a model of its "Internet appliance," a stripped-down computer capable of connecting to the Internet. Gruener, a member of Be's board, said that the company had designed a computer specifically for the poor people–government subsidy market, and could develop the capacity, over time, to fill every one of the nine million potential orders.

A few days later, Todd Oppenheimer, a contributor to the on-line magazine *Salon*, delivered a piece called "Greedy Clicks," attacking the entrepreneurs associated with ClickStart. "This has the feel of one of those well-meaning partnerships with industry in which government gives away the store," he wrote acidly.

According to Oppenheimer's calculations, ClickStart companies would receive, over three years, $540 in government subsidies and vouchers for every computer they "donated" to a poor family. Oppenheimer quoted Eric Schmidt as saying, "You can argue that this is self-serving, but our feeling is that while this is good for us, it's also good for the world."

As the *Salon* writer pointed out, during the five years envisioned for the initiative, the price of computers was predicted to drop significantly, which would mean a hefty profit for Be or other ClickStart businesses that deducted the current value from their taxes. Meanwhile, nonprofit community groups, unreimbursed by the government or business, were expected to provide all the technical and training support for poor families receiving the computers. Oppenheimer argued that high-tech companies, if they wanted to be genuinely philanthropic, would donate the hardware and Internet-access plans outright—and let the government's money be used to provide training. Why not "start now and show support for what's supposedly today's preferred approach to social problems: less work by government, more from the private sector?" he asked.

It was a question that Randlett refused to answer. "The lefties just like to complain," he said loftily. "We're *doing* something here."

CHAPTER twenty

The ClickStart press conference was the first fully public appearance of what Simon Rosenberg jokingly referred to as "Wade and the puppies"—a high-tech political operation, fully owned by its young operators, conceived as an alternative to the "disaster" that TechNet had become and the "irrelevance" of the Democratic Party's organizing efforts.

I knew that Randlett and Witchel had hosted a small dinner recently for Simon Rosenberg, with Beth Inadomi and Tim Newell, and were trying to get the New Democrat Network on board with their 3.0 schemes. And I'd been let in on another of Randlett's schemes—his plan to organize PAC.com, the first group of entrepreneurs that would make donations to candidates in the form of stock in pre-IPO and newly public companies. Randlett was keeping it very tightly under wraps, but I'd heard him describe the idea to some well-placed political consultants in a conference call. "It's cutting-edge," he'd argued. "Young Democratic businessmen using a new currency to support Democratic candidates? It's the New Economy in a nutshell; the Republicans will go apeshit." Then there had been quieter and more serious discussions about how to manage such stock contributions vis-à-vis the Federal Election Commission. Randlett was working with Hale

Boggs and Ron Turovsky, lawyers in Manatt, Phelps & Phillips in Los Angeles who specialized in election and campaign-finance law. They came up with a plan: PAC.com's twenty members would each contribute $1,000 a month to a different politician who met with them for dinner and conversation. That was the traditional part: what was new in Randlett's scheme was the idea that members should also give stock to PAC.com to put into a kitty and disburse over time. "We can cash it out and give it to a politician," explained Randlett, "and say here's five grand, or we can say here's five thousand dollars' worth of shares, you hang on to it and see where it goes."

But the idea of courting candidates with the market-driven, gold-rush allure of Silicon Valley unsettled some campaign finance reformers. "A sweetheart deal in pre-IPO stock has a backroom stench to it, even if it's legal," charged E. Joshua Rosenkranz, president of the Brennan Center for Justice at the New York University School of Law. "If you believe contribution limits mean anything, then making a contribution that explodes in value within a few days is a blatant subversion of them." Rosenkranz added gloomily, "Candidates are already treated as commodities to be invested in; we might as well slap logos on them. Contributing stock is the perfect completion of the circle."

But Randlett was undaunted. The FEC, in late July, would rule that donations of stock could be accepted, and PAC.com would go into business, pulling politics even further into the orbit of the stock market. Its young members—among them Randlett, Witchel, Tim Newell, David Ellington, Chris Larsen of E-Loan, and Joe Kraus of Excite@Home—would tell me proudly that, as Newell put it, they were going to "transform the business of politics and the politics of business."

Politics, Newell said, was the same as investment banking: "You have a product, you have to go out and raise money." He chuckled. "In a way, what PAC.com's about is just old-fashioned grassroots politics. It's grassroots organizing of millionaires."

Meanwhile, Randlett was working hard on other fronts to play up his sponsorship of a new group of young high-tech executives with a political agenda. Once again, he was talking to local reporters, hustling congressional staffers, raising money, setting up meetings.

The idea of a new group doing tech politics was largely testament to Randlett's drive, and to John Witchel's fervent belief in Randlett and the limitless power of his generation. But it also, I thought, said a lot about the nature of this particular moment in the high-tech industry, when the myth of omnipotent new business outshone even the myth of political power. "Sooner or later, on its usual lag, Washington will reflect us," John Witchel had told me. "Because all the power is here."

I'd never lived through a time when moneymaking was embraced with such unreserved gusto, such exuberant machismo: the excesses of Wall Street in the 1980s, or even of the first wave of the Valley boom in 1996, paled in comparison. The measured decision-making of a fifty-year-old venture capitalist like John Doerr looked slightly fusty, now that there was more capital around than anyone quite knew what to do with. The science itself, especially in biotech and nanotechnology, was still steaming ahead, but even technical expertise was less important to setting up a company these days than pure energy and the willingness to take a dare. Even after the Nasdaq downturn, true believers in the Valley kept going. "Greed is good," proclaimed the E-Trade billboard I drove past every day on my way to the grocery store. Another message, on the corner where homeless beggars with cardboard signs still waited for motorists to hand them quarters, was from the magazine *Forbes ASAP*, which covered Internet business. "Capitalism on steroids," it bragged.

It reminded me of something I'd just read from the days of the California gold rush. "It is not enough to tell me that you worked hard to get your gold. So does the Devil work hard," Henry David Thoreau wrote of the men who struck it rich in 1849.

San Francisco was changing fast. Real-estate prices had become the collective obsession of the entire city, one of the few subjects that could unite rich and poor alike and get them swapping horror stories. Rents were soaring, with one-bedroom apartments in unglamorous neighborhoods going for close to $2,000 a month. The median price for a single-family house in San Francisco hovered somewhere around $400,000, and most houses sold for well over the asking price. On my own block in the Mission, four houses had just been sold and a graffiti-covered apartment building was being torn down to make way for live-work condominiums; up the street, Radio Unica and the Tenants Rights Project were losing their offices to a software company.

And real estate was only part of it. I felt as if I were watching an entire generation of entrepreneurs, clutching one-page business plans, skateboarding at top speed down the hills of commerce, whooping, with day-traders racing after them and the rest of us knocked aside. It was all over-the-top, too much, even corny. A friend told me how, late one night in front of a Folsom Street nightclub, he'd watched a very drunk and angry boy scream at a bouncer. "You three-dollar-an-hour asshole," the boy had shouted, pointing both of his hands at his own crotch. "Look at me, I went IPO two years ago!" "It's like a cartoon," my friend said.

Even Simon Rosenberg noticed it. On one of his visits from Washington, I took him to a café at the edge of the Mission, where multimedia start-ups were replacing auto-repair shops, and brushed-chrome lamps illuminated new loft spaces. It felt oddly empty to me on the street outside: no more ladies lugging their sheets to the laundry, no guys kicking soccer balls around, no little kids waiting for the bus with their grandmas. Rosenberg looked around at the fashionable young people standing in line for lattes and blinked. "Wow, this part of town has really changed," he said. "It's becoming a real neighborhood."

John Witchel was delighted with the changes. A week after the Click-Start event, I stood in a big, nearly empty, newly painted room with him and several dozen overcaffeinated people in their twenties. There was a long table with beer on it, and some chips, and a platter of fancy sandwiches that looked like an afterthought. Outside, in the Mission Street twilight, the winos who inhabited the last ungentrified real estate in San Francisco were swearing at one another.

"Don't you dare call this an incubator," Witchel warned me, clapping a hand on my shoulder and offering me a beer. "I hate that word." His wife, Jessica Wheeler, stood next to him; eight months pregnant, her face had an aura of grownup weariness that made everything else in the room look shallow. "It's an overflow space," Witchel said proudly, gesturing around the street-level offices. "I'm renting space out to four pre-IPO companies in here. I'm on their boards. They're all bros from Stanford, these are gonna be my guys." He beamed at the young men around him, most of whom were a good foot shorter than he was. I almost expected Witchel to grab them by the head and mock-wrestle them to the ground. "Fratboy.com," he said with satisfaction. "Hey, hey, Charlie. Come over here."

Witchel's avuncular interest in entrepreneurs even younger than he wasn't new: he sat on the board of seven different companies that I knew of, was a regular lecturer at the Haas School of Business at UC Berkeley, and constantly combed Stanford for up-and-coming business whizzes. It was clear that he had already leveraged a significant amount of influence from his advice-giving, office-renting, investor-introducing ways, and this non-incubator was just one more step in making his virtual network real. "Look, if half of these dudes hit it big, I'm sitting pretty," he'd told me once.

But Witchel's passionate commitment to betting on new companies had always had an ideological dimensions as well. "The Internet economy right now, it's like a rave," he'd explained. "If you go to a rave it looks like chaos from the balcony. But on the floor it's clear what's happening, and what appears to be chaos is structured. The old companies are going, 'This is messy, this is overvalued, it doesn't make sense.' Well, yeah. From the *balcony* it doesn't make sense."

What Witchel wanted was to marry his Generation Equity business philosophy with a political agenda. "I've been thinking," he said. "Right now, priced today, politics is the bargain of the century. For $10 million you could do anything."

I remembered what Marc Andreessen had told me about his donation of a quarter of a million dollars to the DNC. It was, he admitted, "a lot" by the standards of politics. "But in my world," he said, "if I invested just $250,000 in a new company, they might think I wasn't all that serious." Andreessen had laughed, and referred to what he termed the "arbitrage" between business and politics in the current economy. "If you think there's a lot of money in politics now," he said, "you haven't seen anything yet."

As boys in T-shirts and flushed, tipsy girls swirled around us, Witchel outlined his thinking.

"Say you have ten new CEOs," Witchel began, "who share common components, and share an ideology and a basic view of the marketplace. You put together an old boys' club that commits to giving $100K each. Every month you hold a closed-door fund-raiser, you pick ten senators who matter, and develop relationships with them. Tell me you won't get listened to." Witchel took a swallow of his beer. "Not to be cynical, but this is pretty simple," he said. "It's not about a perfect world, it's about winning. The guys who look to me for guidance in how to get their businesses from A to B—they will come to understand how useful an investment this is."

I wondered aloud if Witchel was fantasizing himself as a next-generation John Doerr. His face darkened, and he scowled. "Venture capitalists are about making money. Period," he said in a slow, hostile voice. "That's it. Entrepreneurs are about accumulating power around themselves." He glared at me. "I am *not* a VC," John Witchel said. "I am an entrepreneur."

Simon Rosenberg was definitely intrigued by Witchel's plans; by the spring of 2000, he was coming out to the Bay Area every month, and made a point of checking in with Witchel and Randlett each time. He announced that NDN had entered into a "strategic marketing agreement" with PAC.com, calling it a "win-win deal."

"Simon's done a smart thing," Randlett told me, approvingly, of Rosenberg's stepped-up attention to younger entrepreneurs. "Unlike some in Washington, he listens to the constituency and asks for new ideas. He takes inputs from our community, puts them in his shop— spin spin, rinse rinse—executes them in the House, and comes back and says, 'Let's do politics together.' "

But Rosenberg also seemed to have his doubts. Part of it, I thought, was the anxiety of the short, brainy kid with glasses around rich, popular frat boys. He didn't really fit in with Witchel's confident, testosterone-fueled gang; he didn't drink as much or spend as much money; he wasn't a jock. Even though Randlett respected Rosenberg's political skills, Witchel admired his network, and both men declared that they wanted to work with him, Rosenberg, on some level, remained an outsider.

Substantively, I could tell that Rosenberg was torn between hitching himself to the Old New Economy or the New New one that was springing up. Witchel—and, to a lesser degree, Randlett—was openly contemptuous of old-line megasaur companies like Hewlett-Packard or Intel; but Rosenberg knew that those were the companies that had budgets for lobbying, reps in Washington, that understood the political system. The "puppies" in Witchel's posse of start-ups were far more glamorous, but also scarier. At any moment, they could become bored by politics and simply check out—or their fledgling start-ups could go down in flames.

I met Rosenberg early one morning in May for breakfast at W, a sleek, arty new hotel next to the San Francisco Museum of Modern Art. He was in town to set up the annual NDN Silicon Valley retreat, and was paying calls on everyone from old-timers like Sandy Robertson to Jeff Modisett at TechNet to Witchel, Randlett, and their protégés. He had nearly thirty members of Congress signed up to come out again and hear the high-tech gospel; they badly wanted to be where the action was, and Rosenberg was trying to figure out just how much anyone in the Valley cared to receive them.

We ordered, and I complimented Rosenberg on his pearl-gray suit. "Is it too much, you think?" he said anxiously. "I hate to look like such an East Coast guy." I reassured him: Rosenberg, with his excitable grin, couldn't look stodgy if he tried. "It's cool, Simon," I said. I meant it. After all, he was from a grownup world, and I admired him for not dressing like a slacker.

Rosenberg summed up the state of his network for me. In Washington, he told me, things looked pretty good for the New Democrats. "I think we've had a demonstrable effect," he said. "If you look at someone like Dick Gephardt, the most hard-core Old Dem labor guy on the planet, and listen to that speech he gave to the high-tech executives — well, it took until 2000 for those ideas to come out, but I think you can say we're doing our job."

Rosenberg was more circumspect about Al Gore. Like the seasoned campaign operative he was, Rosenberg could rattle off the figures for different states, analyze the national message, compare the current Gore strategy with what Lee Atwater had done for George Bush or Clinton had pulled off in 1996. He made a point of sounding cautiously optimistic about the vice president's trajectory, but he worried aloud about Gore's chances in the Valley. "He talked last week about the stock market, calling it 'roulette,' " Rosenberg said in disgust. "If you want to call America's markets a roulette game, I mean, does that show that you have a vision about the New Economy?" Rosenberg frowned at me. Since I in fact thought of stock markets precisely as gambling operations, I kept quiet. "We *want* to help him," Rosenberg said. "Is there a way to empower Wade and John and Tim and me to do for Gore what we want to? I hope so. I hope Gore's ready to listen."

Then we talked about trade for a while. Rosenberg knew that I thought trade with China was low on the Valley's must-do list; he went through the motions of convincing me, anyway, how much it mattered. The vote was a few weeks away, and it looked dicey: it still wasn't clear that the New Democrats would overcome the old, labor-oriented conviction that open trade with China was a formula for screwing their members. In the meantime, even though I'd seen Motorola's ads in favor of trade with China, and read reams about AOL's devotion to the cause, what stuck with me was a young Internet CEO's comment when I had asked him about the bill. "I don't fucking give a shit about two billion fucking Chinese," he said impatiently. "The Internet's American." I knew Rosenberg would argue, but it did seem that what *The New York Times* had concluded a week before the vote was right: high-tech companies—the bigger ones, anyway—had made a huge step forward in their political profile by lobbying for China trade, but they were only part of a much bigger business coalition, and unlikely to be decisive on their own.

All of Rosenberg's work, as he reviewed it for me, sounded solid. But it all added up to less than a shining new 3.0 launch. The New Democrat Network had a lot of weight in Congress, and had actually established a reputation as a source of ideas on high tech and the New Economy in Washington. It had a good set of relationships in the Valley, with a broader range of contacts than during the period Rosenberg referred to as "the days of one-stop shopping with TechNet." He hadn't been able to translate those relationships into an exclusively New Democratic base of support, though, or to use them as leverage for helping Gore. And, he admitted, he was still struggling to find his way in "a wildly diverse, internally competitive community" whose interest in politics remained sporadic and inconsistent. "We're doing better than ever," he said. He invited me to his NDN conference the following week. "But it takes constant work."

From David Ellington's point of view, "constant work" was just not as much fun as it used to be. Simon Rosenberg's annual New Democrat–Silicon Valley conference was under way, and I'd hopped on a tour bus -with Ellington—once again, we were heading to the wine country of Napa. Ellington was holding court in the back of the bus, in a Hugh Hefneresque circular seating area immediately labeled "our groovy conversation pit." He waved me over, and we opened our box lunches. Ellington looked older than he had on this same tour a year ago, and he began explaining why.

"When TechNet came along, it was . . . it was hot," he said, sounding nostalgic. "Everything was on Internet time. I'd be sitting in my office and I'd get a call from Wade. He'd say, 'Dave, I need you in D.C. tomorrow. Kim [Polese] will be there, Jerry [Yang]'ll be there, Joe Kraus is coming, get a plane.' We'd blow into town like we were revolutionaries. It was like NASA was in the sixties, when everyone wanted to hang around with astronauts. The Internet guys were like, 'Hold on, we're going to *space*.'"

Ellington smiled. "Wade pissed so many people off because he jumped protocol," he said. "But that's why we loved it. We were hacking the system."

Now, said Ellington, he was glad to work with TechNet, or with NDN, and he was perfectly willing to talk with Randlett or Witchel about their new group. "But it's not the same deal," he said ruefully. "You have dinner with the President for $50,000, there's the handshake, the photo—it's a formula, it has no relevance. It's over. The machine won. We're back to being regular businessmen."

It was just days before Jessica Wheeler was due to have their baby, and John Witchel—on the off-chance, I figured, that fatherhood might soften him and make him sentimental and a loser—was packing as much entrepreneurship as he could into these remaining days. We were sitting in his office, and Witchel, as usual, was wearing a beautiful blue shirt and a pair of khakis.

"You want a job?" he asked me.

"No, thank you," I said. I was smiling as politely as I could.

"Come on," he said gruffly. "I mean it. I'm not just being nice. You want to work here?"

"No," I said.

"You don't want a job? Come on, you want a job."

"Fuck you, John," I explained. He grinned at me happily. It was the right answer. "Fuck you," as he'd taught me, was always the right answer.

"OK," Witchel said, picking up the conversation where we'd left it. I'd been asking about Version 3.0 of tech politics: what was in it for Witchel—and, more to the point, for the young entrepreneurs he and Wade Randlett were cultivating? What did power mean to them? What were their political desires? What, in 2000, could Randlett and Witchel hope to accomplish by trying, one more time, to resurrect an alliance between New Democrats and high-tech millionaires?

"Why do we do it?" Witchel asked. He looked at me coolly. "Well, partly it's a game, a very intricate, high-stakes game, and since we *can* play, we want to." I didn't respond. He shrugged, and I could tell he was going to crack his facade and say something sincere.

"Here's the pitch I give," Witchel said. He stood up and addressed me as if I were one of his young Internet up-and-comers. "You're not gonna do this for the rest of your life, right?" he began. He was sweating a bit, and spoke with a barely controlled ferocity. He answered his own question. "No. Then you should get involved in politics. Why? Because it's your job. Because you can make a big difference. Because you have responsibility. OK, it was the revenge of the nerds, now the revolution's over. We drive every significant sector of the economy: the keys to the kingdom are squarely in the hands of twenty-three-year-olds. So what do you want to do?"

Witchel imitated his dazed mark: "Uh, what's the return on my investment?" He responded, "An increased participation at the higher levels of society. Like you get to sit down and have dinner with a senator and a couple of other CEOs, and hear the non-soundbite version of current events. It's really interesting, and not that expensive. I spend $125–250,000 a year, and if you spend anything near that you can be a player, too." He smiled. "They love that part of the pitch. It's like adventure travel with a social conscience."

He turned reflective. "But then I tell them, because we have to grow up. The real long-term goal for me is to be a trusted member of the business community, who can be counted on in a difficult time." It was the most humble, in an odd way, that I'd ever seen Witchel. He spoke slowly. "I tell these guys I don't believe that government is over. Silicon Valley will someday look like the rust belt, and government will survive. The time will come when there will be a national crisis, when it really matters to the country and to hundreds of millions of people what decisions get made, and it will all boil down to the opinions of a few trusted people. If I am needed, I want to be there. I want to be able to contribute. *That's* why we have to be involved now."

Growing up, the long view—it was a conversation I'd been having as well with Wade Randlett, who was looking remarkably happy these days. Randlett had bought a new house, and a gold Jaguar, and was getting married in a month to Tamsin Smith. Still, in and around his work for Red Gorilla, he was finding time to fly to Washington and work on politics.

I felt as if I were back in 1996, driving down to the Valley with Randlett, and listening to him spin his vision of a rich, powerful, plugged-in industry that would capture the Democratic Party for its mouthpiece and revolutionize the entire political system in the process. Just as in the old days, he was telling me about his successes in raising money, and getting inside Gore's campaign, and working with Simon Rosenberg to hustle the New Democrats; he praised his youngest recruits and trashed Republicans and bragged about the various political "incompetents" he'd terrorized on his last D.C. trip. It exhausted me, in the way that advertisements did: the upbeat glossiness and the refusal to look sideways, or backward, made my soul ache. But I couldn't help smiling as Randlett, oblivious, ran through his plans. The world was doing well by him, and he wanted to return the favor. He had a missionary glow, as if he could fling his own triumphalist narrative one more time at the disrepair, the mess, the worn-out, sad story of American politics, and create a whole new crop of winners, as energetic and self-confident and ahistorical as he was. "There's always a next generation in politics, just like in business," Randlett explained to me brightly. "You have to look at it like an entrepreneur." At the future? I asked. Where the market was going, what was coming next? Exactly, Randlett said, and pointed his finger at the ceiling. "It's not about what you've achieved," he told me. "It's only about how high you aspire."

acknowledgments

For their generosity, openness, and patience in teaching me about their worlds; for letting me endlessly tag along; and for allowing themselves to become characters, when they had only previously aspired to lives as real people, many thanks to Wade Randlett, Simon Rosenberg, Paul Lippe, Tim Newell, David Ellington, Beth Inadomi, Tony Podesta, John Witchel, and the other figures portrayed in this book.

For help in accessing and understanding information, in both Silicon Valley and Washington, my appreciation to more people than I can name, among them Rob Atkinson, Karen Branan, Sue Brodsky, Representative Cal Dooley, Celia Fischer, Elizabeth Greer, David Hart, David Hayden, Tom Kalil, Chris Larsen, Gilman Louie, Regis McKenna, Joyce Neustadt, Tina Nova, Lisa Quigley, Mark Ritchie, Jay Rouse, Greg Simon, Linda Sinoway, Representative Adam Smith, Jeff Smith, Larry Stone, Dale Wiehoff, and Morley Winograd. I wish I could thank the late Bob Squier in person for his gracious assistance.

I've been lucky to have support from the beginning from Sydelle Kramer, my indefatigable agent. My deep appreciation to Elisabeth Kallick Dyssegaard, my gifted and incisive editor, and to Lisa Kennedy, dear friend and brilliant reader.

ACKNOWLEDGMENTS

I've been guided throughout this project by the memory of my father, Matthew B. Miles, whose work as a researcher and writer was marked by integrity, insight, and passionate curiosity. For their careful reading, copy editing, and all-around loving support, I am indebted to my family: Betty Miles, Ellen Miles, David Miles, and Deb Dwyer; and especially to Katie Miles, whose inquisitive mind and joyful presence helped me at every stage, and to Martha Baer, who has made both the book and my life better in innumerable ways with her love and intelligence.